AUERBACH ON
ALPHANUMERIC
DISPLAYS

AUERBACH ON

ALPHANUMERIC DISPLAYS

AUERBACH®
publishers

princeton
philadelphia
new york
london

CONTENTS

PREFACE

This volume is one of a series of books covering significant developments in the information science industry. *AUERBACH ON Alphanumeric Displays* analyzes the segment that produces alphanumeric display devices used as input/output units for immediate access to computer processing and data files.

Alphanumeric display devices are contenders for the multibillion dollar computer data terminal market, which is currently dominated by teletypewriters and teleprinters. Display devices improve interaction between a computer and its users by a more effective matching of the data transfer processes. Display terminals are used on line at a computer center or at remote sites.

Up to now, almost half of the displays installed have been for stock quotation and airline reservation applications. About two years ago, the display industry entered a period of expanded growth based on the broadening capabilities of displays for a wide range of applications across virtually all segments of industry.

The alphanumeric display industry is approximately 10 years old. Alphanumeric displays are used today in four major market segments, the largest being the information services industry with approximately 45 percent of the units installed at present (including stock quotation and airline reservations). Existing system users buy displays to replace other terminal devices or to displace future needs for other terminals when expanding present systems. The displacement/replacement market accounts for approximately one-third of the installed base. New system sales and OEM sales comprise the balance of the installed displays.

The majority of the computer systems that can support alphanumeric displays are being installed for manufacturing. Their use should grow as more manufacturing firms expand their computing systems to include communications access to remote locations. The most widespread potential application for displays in manufacturing is expected to be inventory control. Inventory checking plus immediate inventory change recording and invoice preparation can be handled quickly and easily with display as a part of the system. Alphanumeric displays can be used in both office and plant.

The primary features of alphanumeric displays that often dictate their selection for computer applications are speed, noiseless operation, flexibility, and error reduction. Displays can provide more data at one time than electromechanical computer terminal devices and in formats that can be quickly and easily changed. Moreover, because the data is not permanently stored on the screen, it can be changed easily, thus simplifying editing and improving the operator's ability to detect and correct errors. The noiseless operation of displays makes them acceptable in many commercial locations such as hospitals and law offices. All of the features of alphanumeric displays tend to promote smoother interaction between the operator and the computer, as well as making them the kind of equipment ideally suited to today's modern office environment.

AUERBACH ON Alphanumeric Displays is an expansion of material derived from *AUERBACH Communications Reports*. This publication is a major unit in the *AUERBACH Computer Technology Reports*, a looseleaf reference service recognized as the standard guide to EDP throughout the world. It is prepared and edited by the publisher's staff of professional EDP specialists.

The material in this volume was prepared by the staff of AUERBACH Publishers Inc. and has been updated prior to publication. Due to the rapid changes occurring in the field, however, the currentness and completeness of the contents cannot be guaranteed. Information can be obtained from AUERBACH Publishers Inc., 121 North Broad Street, Philadelphia, Pa. 19107.

AUERBACH ON
ALPHANUMERIC
DISPLAYS

1. INTRODUCTION TO ALPHANUMERIC DISPLAY EQUIPMENT

The electronic digital computer was originally developed to provide a lightning-fast facility for performing arithmetical calculations. Today, analysts and designers are pointing out that rapid calculations are not really an end but a means for attaining even more useful and remarkable capabilities. A particularly important example of the computer acting as a tool, namely, as a component within a larger system, is the cathode-ray digital display system. Such systems can be designed for the display of alphanumeric characters, line plots of varying detail called graphic displays, or both.

Alphanumeric display systems enable data to be transmitted to a remote location and read in an extremely short time. Graphic display systems generate extremely complex graphs, line drawings, vector plots, and images that can be magnified, reduced, or varied in perspective. These systems can be either passive (closed to human communication during operation) or interactive (responsive to communication introduced by such different methods as key punching, switch tripping, light-pen operation, and teletypewriter messages). For passive, or noninteractive systems, the display is simply an output device, and the information presented on the screen is intended strictly for viewing by the user. In interactive systems the display operator becomes a part or component of the system. He may call for the display of particular data, activate a different program, ask for status information of the system, request changes in the size or content of the display, and even change the stored data by changing the image.

The alphanumeric display is an obvious threat to the ponderous type-

1

writer and teletypewriter. Similarly, the graphic display system is even now affecting the methodology of the engineer. If either the commercial user or the engineer is to benefit fully from these expanding technologies, he must understand clearly what they can accomplish. To understand these capabilities, he must understand the fundamentals of operation.

Display devices are used in many different data input and output situations. The unique features of the device often dictate its selection in a particular situation. Its speed, noiseless operation, flexibility, appearance, and ability to substantially reduce human errors are significant factors in the use of a display. However, since a display is only part of a total system, it is usually evaluated along with other terminal devices in relationship to the total system environment.

While the basic alphanumeric display device remains essentially the same, its uses may vary widely. Display devices can be connected directly to a computer for on-line operations or to some form of independent storage unit for off-line operations. As previously mentioned, they may be local to a computer or they may be remote. The display device may be self-contained in a single unit, or it may share a control unit with several other units.

The price of a display device is based on the type of application to be implemented. The price also depends on computer interaction capability, whether it is self-contained or shared, and its ability to allow a user to edit and format data as well as enter data. These features vary in display devices, resulting in a price range from less than $1,500 to more than $15,000.

Alphanumeric displays are available from computer manufacturers, systems and equipment manufacturers, and display equipment manufacturers.

2. GENERAL DESCRIPTION OF AN
ALPHANUMERIC DISPLAY TERMINAL

An alphanumeric display terminal is typically a compact unit that resembles a small television set equipped with a keyboard. These terminals display data on the face of a cathode-ray tube. The data can be entered from a keyboard or received from a computer. Figure 2-1 illustrates a typical alphanumeric display unit.

Data displayed by an alphanumeric display terminal may be in the form of alphabetic letters, numeric digits, punctuation marks, and specialized symbols. Some units can display only a subset, such as numeric digits, of the character set mentioned. In this text, any displayed symbol is referred to as a character. Other, more sophisticated devices used to display graphs and other complex shapes are commonly referred to as line-drawing units.

Most commercially available alphanumeric terminals can be connected either directly to a computer input/output channel or remotely via an appropriate controller or adapter at the computer site and a communications line.

The basic function of alphanumeric terminals is to provide rapid, easy access to data stored in a computer system or to the computational facilities of the computer. Two general types of operation well suited for alphanumeric display terminals are—

1. Obtaining information on a particular account or subject, such as credit, bank balance, inventory, or seating availability. Data files maintained at the central computer site serve as the source of information.

3

Fig. 2-1. Typical Alphanumeric Display Unit

These files can be quickly updated from the remote display stations as events and transactions take place.

2. Providing convenient man-machine "conversations" that permit the operator of the remote display station to base his inquiries upon prior results calculated by the computer and displayed on the screen. This type of application allows programmers, engineers, designers, and others to create and execute programs in a step-by-step fashion while being informed of programming errors and intermediate results at each step.

Programming of the computer at the central site will be a major portion of the implementation task for nearly every display system. Manufacturers of commercial computers are beginning to provide software support for the types of applications described.

Important characteristics of alphanumeric display terminals, which transmit to and receive data from remote computers over communications lines, include—

1. Transmission characteristics such as speed, code, and synchronization technique.
2. General input/output capabilities of the display device and any auxiliary equipment.
3. Cost.
4. Display characteristics.
5. Editing capabilities.
6. Control, including buffering and configuration limitations.

3. HISTORICAL DEVELOPMENT OF THE DISPLAY INDUSTRY

CATHODE-RAY TUBE

In 1879, Sir William Crookes performed studies in the area of electric discharges within gases, which led to the development of the Crookes tube. The modern cathode-ray tube (CRT) evolved from the Crookes tube development.

OSCILLOGRAPHY, RADAR, AND TELEVISION

The first significant use of the CRT was for oscillography. This use of a CRT allows one to see the nature of electric signals on the CRT screen. Oscilloscopes were available at the beginning of World War II, and they were quickly adapted to another use—radar. Radar uses the CRT to show the reflections of electromagnetic signals from targets, which appear on the CRT screen as irregularities or bright spots. Also at this time, television transmission was made possible by the continuous scanning of the cathode ray across the face of the tube; by varying its intensity, a picture was formed that showed movement in real-time. Television was demonstrated at the New York World's Fair in 1939. All three of these early uses of the CRT prevail today.

FIRST COMPUTER-DRIVEN DISPLAYS

By 1950, the electronic computer was five years old, but the only devices available to recover information from computers for immediate human use were teletypewriters and electric typewriters. These devices were effective for many uses and indeed are still used today for computer output. But faster means of computer output were needed, and in 1951 MIT utilized CRT's on the output of the Whirlwind I computer. The CRT was used in a very simple manner. The computer could put spots on the face of the CRT at any point on a matrix of 1024 x 1024 positions. This was good enough to plot equations and other patterns. At the same time, the University of Illinois operated CRT outputs in conjunction with the ILLIAC computer and used it for problems for which the human operator applied a trial-and-error process to find solutions. The most significant computer-driven CRT's were developed at MIT as part of the SAGE system. This development carried out in cooperation with Stromberg Carlson, now Stromberg DatagraphiX, Inc., a subsidiary of General Dynamics Corporation. These CRT's were used by air defense controllers as part of a real-time computer system to track aircraft in America's first large computer-oriented air defense system. The extensive man-machine interaction required by this application was fairly well developed in the SAGE system, but only now, almost two decades later, has this degree of interaction been accepted by commerce and industry.

COMPUTER STATUS DISPLAYS

In the early 1950s a CRT display was used on the ORDVAC computer at the Aberdeen Proving Grounds. This display operated in the same manner as the ones on Whirlwind I except that the spots were used to show the status of memory locations. Soon thereafter the LGP 30 and RPC 4000 used small CRT's as status displays. Later, computers used indicator lights instead, and this became standard for approximately ten years. When the CDC 6600 came on the market in late 1965, CRT's were used again for computer status displays, and they are in common use today.

EMERGENCE OF THE ALPHANUMERIC DISPLAY

Early CRT displays driven by computers required very laborious programming and extensive output from the computer to form images on the screen. Each dot position had to be addressed and intensified. Since the persistence of the dot on the screen was much less than a second, the process had to be repeated so that the image did not appear to go on and off, or flicker. Therefore the image on the screen was "refreshed" at a high rate (e.g., 40 times a second). Thus there was no noticeable flicker in these displays. However, the early computers had to allow enough space in their memories to hold the information while it was being refreshed on the screen. For the computer to form alphanumeric characters directly from the spots was a very inefficient process. Therefore, in the middle 1950s, the alphanumeric display generator appeared as a part of certain CRT devices. This generator used coded inputs and produced alphanumeric characters anywhere desired on the face of the CRT, obviating the necessity to hold a complex of dots in the computer for each character. Then a CRT display "now memory" was added in a control unit associated with the CRT device so as not to use up the computer's memory. Assuming, for example, that 3 bytes are needed to specify a location on the CRT, a computer-refreshed system would require about 45 bytes to hold the necessary complex of dots, whereas a display generator requires a total of only 4 bytes to specify and locate a character. For these displays, the computer needed to send information to the CRT device only one time for a new or updated display image. These CRT devices became the first alphanumeric displays, and today's displays are very much like them. One of the first to appear on the market was built by Digital Data, Inc., or DDI, later acquired by CDC (Centronics Data Computer). Teleregister also produced a CRT display, which became the basis for its small display when it was later acquired by the Bunker-Ramo Corporation.

FIRST SIGNIFICANT SALES

The first significant sales of alphanumeric displays using CRT's for a commercial application was to the brokerage industry for stock quotation. Teleregister, and now Bunker-Ramo Corporation, still have the highest installed base of alphanumeric displays.

International Business Machines Corporation was fairly late in bringing out an alphanumeric display, and the IBM 2260 did not appear until June 1966. This device is installed in an environment of a cluster of units connected to a controller, where the refresh memory for all units resides. It was not until the end of the 1960s that IBM had installed a significant number of these units. They now have an installed base, which is second only to Bunker-Ramo's, and have a heavy concentration in the airline reservation systems. Finally, 1968 and 1969 saw the advent of the standalone CRT display, which includes the CRT electronics and refresh memory in one unit. These stand-alone units were designed to be connected either directly to a computer or from a remote location through voice telephone lines to a computer. In April 1969, IBM brought out a stand-alone unit, the IBM 2265.

4. RELATED TECHNOLOGIES AND PRODUCTS

The development of display devices was important to many related technologies, and products in a number of diversified areas utilize their capabilities.

TELEVISION

Television is related to alphanumeric displays in a number of ways. First of all, the increased use of the CRT and related circuits owes a great deal to television. The low price of displays has been brought about, in part, by the mass production techniques developed for television sets. In addition, the TV raster scan, which also has been developed for mass production and is therefore inexpensive, may also be used for displays. The newer, smaller companies in the computer field use this technique more than any other. Some display companies use a commercial TV set for display. For example, Computer Communications, Inc., uses a Sony set as its display medium and provides a switch so the user can switch to broadcast TV when he is not using his display for computer access. Furthermore, the most prevalent method of generating color displays is by using television techniques and the ordinary TV three-gun shadow-mask CRT. These displays simply color-code the characters that are used to generate the display. Red, green, blue, and yellow are generally the only colors used.

INDICATORS

Indicators are alphanumeric character devices used for adding machines, equipment readout devices, stock quote board displays, and the

9

like. One of the common indicators is the Burroughs' Nixie® tube indicator. Indicators are related to alphanumeric displays because some applications that require a limited set of alphanumeric and/or a few characters per display use either indicators or alphanumeric displays. In fact, the early stock quote terminals used indicators, and some are still in use today.

GRAPHIC DISPLAYS

Graphic displays are similar to alphanumeric displays except that they are much larger, can provide extensive line drawings, and can display many more numeric characters at one time than can an alphanumeric display. Because of the complexity of graphic displays, they are almost always directly associated with a computer (usually a minicomputer), whose function specifically is to operate the graphic display. Much of the early work in the development of display technology was aimed at perfecting graphic displays.

One type of graphic display competes in some applications with alphanumeric displays. This is a display centered around the direct-view storage tube (DVST). The storage-tube display provides alphanumerics and graphics (i.e., complex line drawings) much more cheaply than the graphic displays previously described. Storage-tube displays are made by a number of new firms that specialize in this field, but because of their limitations, there are only certain applications where they can be used effectively. Where some graphics are required, but extensive interaction between the human operator and computer is not required, the storage-tube display can be very effective. Although priced much lower than most graphic displays, the storage-tube displays cost more than most alphanumeric displays (approximately $10,000 to $20,000).

LARGE AREA DISPLAYS

Large area displays, typically, are those used to show train and plane arrivals and departures in terminal buildings. In some cases, menu boards are used with closed-circuit TV, and monitors are placed around as enunciators for these applications. Alphanumeric displays can be used in the same way. For example, those that are TV-generated usually have the capability of driving more than one monitor. Thus, several TV monitors can be slaved to one display and used as an annunciation system. Other large area displays consist of very bright CRT tube displays, projected through special optics onto a screen. The circuits and other parts of such displays are similar to those used in alphanumeric displays.

PRINTERS

Printers are related to displays because in many cases they offer an alternative to a computer-output device. In other cases, they offer an auxiliary capability to alphanumeric displays.

PLOTTERS

Plotters are computer-driven devices that draw lines on paper much as graphic displays scan light lines on a CRT. Plotters are related to alphanumeric displays only in a general sense. They offer a type of computer output that might be used instead of, or in conjunction with alphanumeric displays.

COMPUTER OUTPUT MICROFILM

Computer output microfilm (COM) is related to displays in three ways:
1. A CRT is used as the imaging device for many of these units to get alphanumerics onto film, using the same general techniques as in displays.
2. A storage tube display is used with many (COM) units to provide a preview of the image to be registered microfilm.
3. The COM device may be considered as an alternative output device for computer displays.

AUDIO RESPONSE UNITS

Audio response units are used with computers to obtain output, usually by telephone, to an inquiry posed usually by Touch-Tone® code-key input. Portable terminals for use in audio-response systems might be considered for some application alternatives to displays. For example, a quick inquiry to the data base of a central computer system, remotely located, could be provided by either an audio-response terminal or an alphanumeric display terminal. Note that some alphanumeric display manufacturers—e.g., Applied Digital Data Systems, Inc., Computer Communications, Inc., and Logitron, Inc. (recently acquired by Bendix)—provide a portable display unit.

5. DISPLAY FEATURE DESCRIPTIONS

To the nontechnical potential display system user, what current-day displays will do for him is the paramount concern; to the purchaser of a display system, the actual capabilities of that display are more relevant than all the technical theories and problems. That is not to say that these people should not be interested in or become familiar with technical considerations and problems, but the technically unsophisticated users still have the problem of determining which of all these factors are actually relevant to their needs. There is also the problem of separating what is from what could be.

DEFINITIONS

The following definitions of terms and concepts provide an overview of computer display capabilities available today. The relevancy of any particular item depends upon the particular application with which the display will be associated.

Brightness

Brightness is the measure of light intensity and is generally measured in units called foot-lamberts. Brightness of the display must be considered relative to the environmental lighting within which the display will operate and the anticipated refresh rate at which the display will be refreshed. The brighter the environmental lighting, the brighter must be the display for easy viewing. On the other hand, as brightness is increased, flicker becomes more noticeable, thus requiring a higher refresh rate to maintain a flicker-free display. (See "flicker" in next section.)

Contrast

A number of definitions of contrast are in common use. Two of those frequently used are—

1. Contrast ratio. This is the ratio of the brightest to darkest portions of the display. It is employed where the gray scale is significant, as in television.

2. Brightness contrast or percentage contrast. The brightness contrast is equal to image brightness minus background brightness divided by background brightness. The percentage contrast is simply the brightness contrast multiplied by 100.

Still another type of contrast is that of color. Although brightness contrast is far better for detail, color contrast can be used effectively for indicating different classes of information or for enhancing contrast in marginal situations. For example, the afterflow of long-persistent phosphors has a high content of orange component. The contrast can be increased by using blue ambient lighting, provided the marked contrast does not lead to undesirable psychological reactions.

Cursor

A cursor is a special character that may appear on a CRT. It is used as a pointer, usually in connection with some interactive facility. Virtually all alphanumeric displays include a cursor that is used to designate the next character position or line at which data will be displayed. This enables the operator to keep track of positional information such as how far he has progressed through a line during typing, to designate active screen areas, or to point to character positions at which corrective action is to be applied. In graphic displays, cursors are associated with joysticks and trackballs. The cursor is not usually displayed at all times, but appears on operator command. Manual manipulation of the joystick or trackball by the operator causes a corresponding movement of the cursor on the CRT. Additional operator action, such as pressing a button, then can cause a hit.

Editing Facilities

The editing facilities provided for the operator's use govern the ease and flexibility of entering data and modifying or correcting previously displaced data. All currently available commercial display units use a visible cursor or entry marker to indicate to the operator the position where the next character will be displayed when entered. Normally, control keys are included within the keyboard layout to allow the operator to position the cursor for data entry at specified locations.

Editing facilities provided in some display units include—

1. Horizontal tabulation: This allows the operator to set specified stops within a display and later to skip to these stops in the same manner as on a typewriter.

2. Line erase: The operator can erase a whole line or selected portion of a line with a single key depression.

3. Line insertion: The operator can insert data within a line, with the previously displayed data being automatically shifted.

4. Transmission of partial display: This allows transmission of a selected portion of the total display, in contrast to having to transmit the full display each time.

5. Split screen: Allows retention of previously displayed data while new data are being entered or received. In practice, this may take the form of filling in a displayed format or displaying a series of operator inquiries and computer responses. With some units the operator can be prevented from modifying the previous data.

Refresh

Cathode-ray tube displays must be "refreshed" or regenerated periodically to produce persistent displays. The persistence of the particular phosphor used in the CRT is the principal factor that determines the required rate of refreshment. Most phosphors have exponential decay rates, with typical decay times ranging from 1 to 100 milliseconds. There are phosphors with decay times in the microsecond range, however, and there is one slow phosphor that lasts 16 seconds.

A flicker-free image is one that appears steady and stable to the viewer. The refresh rate required to produce a "flicker-free" display will vary with the sensitivity of the viewer, the brightness and contrast of the display, and the type of information being displayed. Older operators tend to exhibit a greater tolerance of flicker and will accept lower repetition rates as flicker-free. As brightness and contrast are increased, flicker becomes more noticeable, thus requiring a higher refresh rate to avoid the flicker effect. Finally, alphanumeric data will show flicker more readily than will graphic data. In general, 50 to 60 repetitions per second is a safe lower limit for flicker-free display of all types of data to all viewers. Repetition rates of 6 to 15 cycles per second should be avoided, as this range produces the most objectionable flicker.

Screen Configuration

In display systems, the master screen is the primary screen to which all display output is directed. The master screen is generally mounted on the display console, and usually the interactive devices of the system are associated with the master screen. Contrasted to slave and repeater screens (see below), the master is the primary screen to which display output is directed. It therefore need not be specifically addressed, as is the case with a slave for turning on and off under program control. Also, the master can be individually controlled which a repeater cannot.

Slave screens are displays associated with a graphic display system that can be individually turned on or off under program control. Slave screens differ from master screens in that they must be specifically addressed in order to be turned on or off. Slave screens differ from repeaters in that they are specifically addressable, whereas repeaters merely mimic the associated display.

Split screen is an operating characteristic of many alphanumeric displays. During split-screen operation the display is composed of two fields, one active and one passive. The passive field generally contains formatting or other information used by the operator or information that is stable during some other data manipulation. The active field contains the data being manipulated and generally only the data of the active area are transmitted between the display and the computer.

There are basically two types of split-screen operation: block and fill-in-the-blank. In the block type, the active viewing area is bracketed and must be a single contiguous area. All of the viewing area preceding and following the bracketed area is passive. For the fill-in-the-blank type, active and passive areas may generally be mixed in any order. This enables design and display of a basic form or format such that the operator need only fill in the active data.

Split-screen operation is extremely useful in many types of alphanumeric data manipulation. Further, by transmitting only the active data, the communications load is reduced over that which would otherwise be necessary. It should be noted that not all alphanumeric display terminals that provide split-screen operations restrict data transmission to active data only.

Multidrop

"Multidrop" is the capability for connecting more than one remote controller (multiunit or independent) to a single communications line. This capability requires that control logic be provided for controller address recognition to enable selective transmission to individual display units. This capability can be used to expand the number of display units at a single location or to permit units located at geographically separate locations to share the same line. The object of either arrangement is to reduce line costs. Careful analysis should be made when planning multidrop configurations to ensure that one line will provide adequate transmission capacity.

Operating Modes

Many display systems are programmable in a manner similar to the programming of a general-purpose digital computer. That is, each word fetched from storage represents an instruction (or an operand of an instruction) that must be decoded and its component fields distributed among the logic elements and registers of the control unit in order to obtain the desired action. In such a system, each instruction includes an operation code that defines the fields of the instruction and implies the required distribution and interpretation of data.

While the field makeup and data interpretation may vary from instruction to instruction, the operation code is a fixed field that occurs in every instruction. Generally, instructions are complete self-contained entities such that a trained systems programmer can select any instruction at random and describe the system interpretation and reaction to execution of the instruction.

In some display systems, it is often the case that the number of bits required by the instructions exceeds the number of bits available in a word of memory. The use of two words per instruction would, however, be wasteful of memory and would lengthen instruction execution time. The solution has been to implement a mode register that effectively contains all or part of the instruction operation code.

A control state, control mode, or control instruction having the capability, among others, to set explicit values into the mode register is usually provided. The control instruction(s) may be identified by a bit in the instruction that designates control or no control, or may also depend upon mode register settings. In the latter case, all no-control instructions generally include an escape indicator that will automatically set the mode register to control if the escape indicator is present. The mode register may contain the entire operation code or only a portion. In the former case, the instructions fetched include no operation code field, and for each operating mode there is only one acceptable instruction format. In the latter case, each instruction may also include an operation code and numerous instruction formats, decoding and interpretation of which are still dependent upon the mode register setting.

Thus, the use of a mode register and operating modes is a technique to increase instruction size without increasing either the word size or the number of words per instruction. Instructions are therefore not entirely self-contained in that the mode setting is part of the instruction but is not explicitly contained in the instruction.

Scrolling

Scrolling is a technique used to scan or manipulate textual data. The normal version of scrolling is to eliminate the top line of displayed data, move all lines of data up the screen one line, and insert a new line at the bottom. Scrolling is generally provided in both forward and backward direction in systems where it is provided at all. Two methods of scrolling are generally considered: single line and continuous. In single-line scrolling an explicit operator action, such as depressing a function switch, is required for each line of scrolling action. For continuous scrolling, an explicit operator action is required to start scrolling, after which the textual data is scrolled at a predefined rate until another operator action stops scrolling or a program-recognized sentinel such as End Of Text causes scrolling to stop automatically.

6. ALPHANUMERIC DISPLAY TECHNOLOGY

The alphanumeric display industry has experienced many changes during the past few years. These changes have resulted in an increasing number of new firms, new products, new system design concepts, and substantial price reductions. In effect, display units have become general-purpose, price-competitive devices that are potential alternatives for both peripheral equipment and remote nondisplay terminal equipment. Display improvements and price reductions are the result of perfecting display technology and incorporating new technological developments. The semiconductor industry has supplied the most significant of these technical developments, particularly with regard to integrated circuits for display memory, character generation, and control.

The performance, quality, usability, and price of an alphanumeric display device depend on many factors that relate to the construction of the display unit.

DISPLAY SYSTEM COMPONENTS

In general, a display system consists of four categories of operating components: the CRT, the display-control hardware, the memory, and the computer or processing system to which the display is connected. Component packaging varies so that numerous hardware configurations are possible. In some systems, all controls and memory may be placed in a separate controller, which is used to operate more than one display screen.

18

The layout of a typical display unit configuration is illustrated in Figure 6-1.

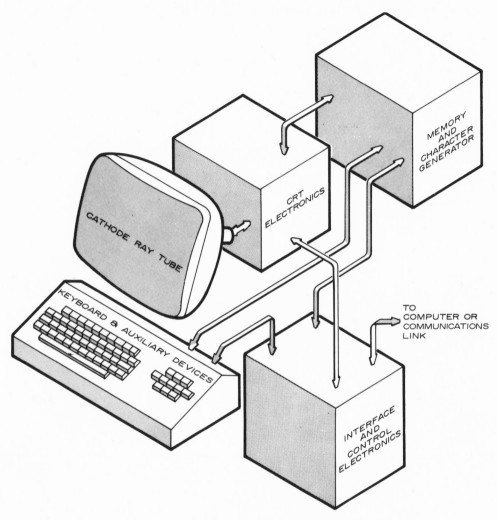

Fig. 6-1. Basic Alphanumeric Display Components

Cathode-Ray Tubes

The CRT is common in today's world as the picture tube of commercial television sets. All CRT's incorporate a basic set of components: the tube enclosure, a cathode, an electron-gun assembly, a processing structure, deflection electrodes or an external deflection assembly, and a phosphor coating on the viewing surface. Figure 6-2 illustrates the arrangement of basic components in a cathode-ray tube.

In the operation of the CRT, the cathode emits a stream of electrons that are accelerated and focused into a beam aimed at tube center by the

electron-gun assembly. The beam impacts on the phosphor-coated surface to form a spot of light. The specific location of impact at any time
depends upon the amount of beam bending induced by deflection control
settings. The beam is deflected along horizontal and vertical axes by deflection amplifier circuits, which receive analog signals that have been
generated in accordance with the digital pulses provided by the computer.
Intensity controls located outside the tube determine the energy of the
beam.

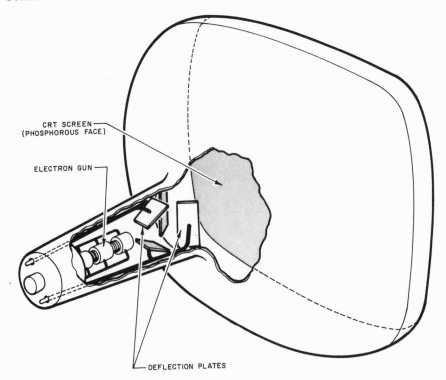

CRT SCREEN
(PHOSPHOROUS FACE)

ELECTRON GUN

DEFLECTION PLATES

Fig. 6-2.   Construction of the Cathode-Ray Tube (CRT)

Two basic methods of focus and deflection control are possible,
namely, electromagnetic and electrostatic. An electromagnetic system
consists of two pairs of yoke coils that rest on opposite sides of the tube
and generate perpendicular magnetic fields in proportion to the current
flow through the coils. Together, the magnetic fields exert both a horizontal and vertical deflection force on the electron beam. In the electrostatic
system, two pairs of electrically charged plates interact with the beam to
cause deflection in both the horizontal and vertical directions. Of the two
methods, electromagnetic deflection is normally less expensive, but electrostatic action usually provides more accurate control.

Departing from the custom of employing one technique to the exclusion of the other, many graphic display systems use a tube that relies upon electromagnetic deflection as the primary control but supplements with a minor electrostatic deflection control for the display of alphanumeric characters.

As the electrons fall upon the screen, they transfer their energy to the phosphor coating. The phosphor converts some of this energy into light upon impact and stores the remainder; this initial emission of light is called fluorescence. Once the beam has passed a particular section of phosphor, the phosphor continues to radiate through the conversion of its stored energy. This phenomenon is called phosphorescence, and the period during which it lasts is called the persistence of the phosphor. The decay rate specifies the rate at which the stored energy decreases.

Changing the electrostatic and/or electromagnetic field between the deflection plates permits the use of one of two basic deflection schemes in alphanumeric display units:

1. *Raster scan.* The electron beam is moved in a regular pattern across the face of the CRT. It can be best described by picturing the electron beam as being positioned at the upper left-hand corner of the CRT. The beam is then moved rapidly in the horizontal direction. When it reaches the end of the screen it is reset to the left of the screen, displaced downward slightly, and moved again in the horizontal direction. This pattern is continued until the beam is in the lower right-hand corner. While the beam is going through this scanning process, it can be modulated in intensity to form an image—in this case, alphanumeric characters. This scan technique typically matches an ordinary TV scan, which consists of 525 horizontal scanning lines. The complete pattern is repeated 30 times a second.

2. *Directed beam.* The electron beam is moved across the face of the CRT while it is turned off. It can be moved simultaneously in the horizontal and vertical directions to arrive at a particular position on the face of the CRT, the major positioning. Once at this position, the beam may be turned on or modulated while it is repositioned or moved to write or stroke characters. In this manner an alphanumeric character or symbol is "drawn" on the screen.

The type of phosphor used in a CRT determines the amount of energy that can be delivered to the phosphor without damage, the color of light emitted during fluorescence and phosphorescence, and the persistence. These factors in turn determine the brightness of the display and the rate at which the picture must be refreshed in order to remain stable.

The charactron is a special type of CRT; it is constructed as a regular

CRT but includes a stencil in which the shapes of characters, and other symbols are etched. The electron beam is extruded through a shaped-character aperture and assumes this shape when focused on the screen. Since no time is spent in deflecting the beam to form the character, this method is faster than techniques that require deflection.

A video display is another special kind of CRT. With this type, the beam systematically scans the entire face of the tube. The picture is generated by continuously varying the intensity of the beam in accordance with the video intelligence to be presented. Television is perhaps the best known example of a video display.

A storage tube is a video display device with a memory element that has the ability to control the beam intensity during the scan. Thus, a storage tube is a special type of CRT that combines the scanning function of a video display with a storage element. The advantages of the storage tube are its greater brightness and persistence. The latter reduces the memory requirements for refreshing the screen.

Control Hardware

At the heart of any display device is hardware that must convert input data and control information into output signals that control the CRT. Control hardware varies significantly from one type of display to another, according to the CRT element used and the display capability to be provided.

Intensity, deflection, and focusing amplifiers are found in virtually every display system. These circuits adjust the output of the cathode (intensity) and control the CRT deflection and focus. On the screen, the actions are interpreted as brightness, sharpness, and position of an image. In addition, a display using a charactron tube contains a stencil control that positions the stencil in order to transmit the beam through the desired character.

Character Generators

Character generators are hardware devices that accept codes and furnish a set of deflection controls as output that controls the CRT beam. The three basic categories of character generators are stroke, dot matrix, and monoscope. The stroke type of character generator controls the beam in short-line drawing movements so that the sequence of movements generates a character.

The matrix type uses a matrix of dots that is typically five wide by seven high. Illumination of selected dots forms the character. The matrix type of character translates each character code into a 35-bit control word in which each bit corresponds to a dot and indicates whether intensity is on or off for that dot. The bits are interpreted by the logic to determine whether the electron beam should be blanked or unblanked at the instant when the beam would fall upon the dot or execute the stroke. Actual beam movement may be accomplished by incrementing the beam from one coordinate position to the next until the end is attained or by sweeping the beam in brush-stroke fashion to the designated end point. Lines generated by these two methods are illustrated in Figure 6-3. Vector generators moving from one coordinate position to the next are called incremental vector

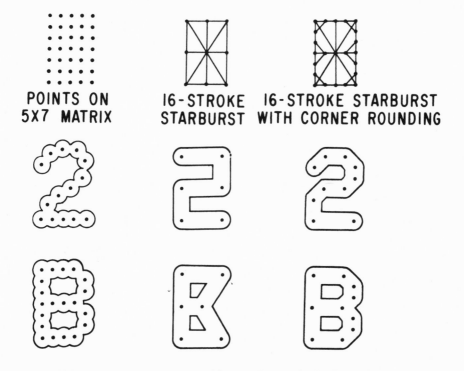

POINTS ON 5X7 MATRIX **16-STROKE STARBURST** **16-STROKE STARBURST WITH CORNER ROUNDING**

Fig. 6-3. Lines Generated by Stroke Method (above) and
Increment Methods (below)

generators. The lines they produce are not entirely straight and only approximate the desired line, but the deviation is seldom noticeable. Each increment is a quantum step in either the direction of the X or Y axis, or both. Thus, all lines are composed of straight-line segments that are horizontal, vertical, or sloped at 45 degrees.

The beam-sweeping type of vector generator, called a stroke vector generator, causes the total of changes specified in each axis to occur simultaneously in order to draw the indicated line. Even in this case, the line may not be straight but may appear to bend. This curvature develops if the changes are not truly simultaneous or are not evenly distributed over the time interval.

The monoscope technique employs a separate scanning tube that contains a plate with all displayable characters etched into it. The scan generates signals that control the movement of the electron beam in the display tube. Any symbol shape or type style can be generated with this technique.

Character generators are used in virtually all alphanumeric displays, but vector generators are rarely employed in such displays. Additional control hardware for alphanumeric displays are cursor, edit, and buffer controls.

A cursor is a special symbol that nearly always appears on the viewing screen of alphanumeric displays. This pointer indicates the character position into or from which the next character of data will be moved. Cursor controls enable the cursor to be repositioned by the operator.

Although cursors may be used on graphic displays, they are generally associated with interactive devices. Their function is to point to a specific location on the screen. In this case, the appearance of the cursor on the screen and its position are controlled by the operator through manipulation of the device with which the cursor is associated.

Edit controls provide a data manipulation capacity. At a minimum, the edit controls provide the capability to place the last character of input into the character position designated by the cursor. These controls may also include numerous other features such as insert and delete character as well as insert and delete line operations.

Comparison of Character Generation Techniques

Television

TV with Dot Characters

Description.   A television raster scan either duplicates that used in broadcast television or uses the same techniques to form a continuous pattern of horizontal lines on the CRT screen base of the tube. As each line is being scanned, the display memory is being accessed. Either the code for a character is found in memory and converted to dots for given places on the scan lines, or the data are stored in memory as dots and merely used to intensify given places on the scan lines.

Advantages.   An advantage of the dot characters is that ordinary television sets can be used for displays. Thus, TV character generation is probably the least expensive of any. Polarity reversal is possible for black-on-white, or white-on-black characters. Monitors slaved to the master alphanumeric display can be used with ordinary TV monitors. Color is possible, using ordinary TV shadow-mask tubes, for very effective displays at

15 to 25 percent increase in cost over black and white.

Disadvantages.   The quality of characters using a 5 x 7 dot matrix is not so good as many others. If a 7 x 9 matrix is used, this requires too many scan lines and the total number of characters on the display are limited. The scanning of tv-oriented displays must be synchronized with the memory used and incurs some additional cost.

Random Placement of Dots/Line Segments/Strokes (Vector Placement)

Description.   Random-placement character generation provides for the positioning of the electron beam to the desired place where a character is to be drawn. Then the character code from the memory is used to select from a table of characters the one desired. This table of vectors is stored in the circuits, using semiconductor technology in many cases. Then the character is drawn on the CRT screen, according to the output from the table, in any one of a number of ways, which may be a dot matrix, small line segments, strokes straight and curved, or similar technique. Depending on the manufacturer, any one of these methods is used.

Advantages.   Advantages of random placement are that flexible display formatting can be easily used. Information from the computer can be immediately placed in the correct position, for example. Use of protected formatting and editing features are less complex to supply than with some other methods. Dots have the same disadvantages as tv character generation. However, the area on the display screen can be more efficiently used. With dot patterns (7 x 9 or over), line segments, or strokes, good-quality characters can be produced.

Disadvantages.   The primary disadvantage of random placement has been that a random access memory is most effective with random placement character generation, and this has increased the cost of these displays. However, as memory costs decrease, this disadvantage is becoming less important. To form the higher-quality characters requires many dots, line segments, or strokes. The circuitry to supply these is more expensive than other methods.

Scan Placement of Dots/Line Segments/Strokes

Description.   In this method a type of scanning is used on the face of the CRT. As each possible character position is reached, the memory is accessed to find the corresponding character code. This character is decoded in the same manner as in random placement and then drawing of the character is the same as random placement.

Advantages.   Advantages of this method are primarily that a simplified storage access is possible and delay lines or MOS shift registers can be used for the memory quite effectively. This type should be less expensive than the random placement method.

Disadvantages. Disadvantages of scan placement are primarily linked with the memory type used. To gain the cost advantage by using delay line or MOS shift registers, it may be necessary to reduce the flexibility or increase the control and thus the cost of the display.

Monoscope

Description.   Monoscope display devices contain two CRT's. One CRT is the main one, as for the other types. The second one is the *monoscope*, which is a small CRT with a target at the end. This target has etched on it the complete character set to be used, in the font or style desired. Either random placement or scan placement may be used to direct the electron beam to the point where the character is to be drawn. Then the small electron beam in the monoscope scans the proper character on its target at the same time that the electron beam in the main CRT does. The signal from the small monoscope causes the character to appear on the screen just as it does on the template in the monoscope.

Advantages.   The primary advantage of the monoscope character generator is that the quality of character is very high. The characters can be designed to fit any normal or abnormal character set.

Disadvantages.   The disadvantages are primarily the cost of the unit and the inability to change the character set very readily. To change even one character, the monoscope has to be replaced.

Shaped Beam

Description.   In the shaped-beam character generation method a template is mounted inside the main CRT. The electron beam is directed through the proper character in this template and appears on the screen in the shape of the character.

Advantages.   The primary advantage is in the character quality, as in the monoscope character generator. Another advantage is the simplicity of the device, which could lower its price.

Disadvantages.   The most important disadvantage of this method is that the entire CRT must be changed if the character set is to be changed. Also, the electronic control of the CRT must be an almost precision-designed circuitry and is therefore sensitive to malfunction in rugged environments. The comparative higher cost of the circuitry might make it less desirable than the lower-cost, simplified, character generation method.

Memory and Buffer Controls

Memory requirements in support of the display are important. Two categories exist, and both must be taken into account and should be accounted for separately. The first memory requirement is refresh memory, used directly by the display. This memory is usually an integral part of the display for almost all alphanumeric displays.

The second type is memory used to perform display-related processing, including the processing of raw data into display commands, as well as memory required for programming needed in support of interactive devices.

The display capacity of alphanumeric displays is normally limited by the size of the refresh memory and is relatively easy to ascertain. However, the quantity of data that can be processed is somewhat more difficult to determine and depends upon the type of processing to be performed. In general, the amount of data that must be transmitted between the dis-

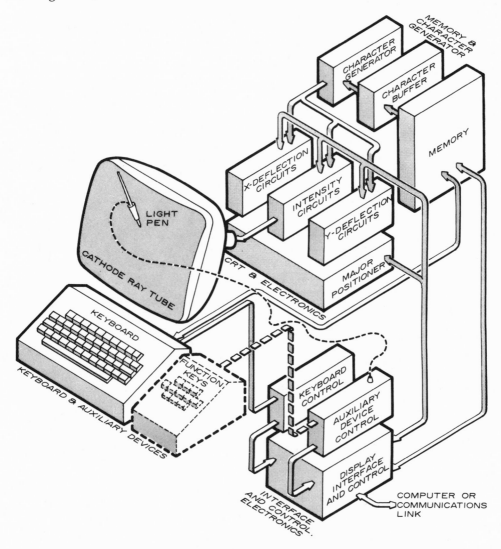

Fig. 6-4. Relationship of Display Components to Character Generation

play and the processing system in order to accomplish a required task provides a reliable indicator of the amount of data that can be processed. The relationship, however, is inverse, and the greater the transmission requirements, the smaller the amount of processing that can be accomplished.

The buffer controls handle transmission of data between the refresh memory and other components such as the display, the keyboard, and the associated computing system. These controls provide such features as split-screen operation, forms projection, and selected data transmission. Figure 6-4 illustrates the sequence of controlled operations required of CRT components in generating an alphanumeric character from the keyboard.

Phosphors receive and absorb energy while being bombarded by an electron beam. This energy is converted to light both at impact by the electrons and after the electron beam passes. To produce a constant picture, the phosphors must be refreshed. Typical refresh rates range from 30 to 60 times per second, and a memory must hold the data required to support the refresh cycle.

In storage-tube displays this memory is situated within the tube itself; however, in almost all alphanumeric displays it is contained in the display system and consists of core or delay line memory providing one character of storage for each character that appears on the screen.

A character buffer holds a code (for each alphanumeric character or symbol as it comes from memory) long enough to allow the character generator to produce the character on the screen. Memory is used to hold enough data to fill the entire screen in order to refesh (reproduce) the alphanumeric characters and symbols on the screen. The display on the face of the CRT must be refreshed, since the phosphor will glow for only a short time (usually 50 microseconds) after being struck by an electron beam. The number of times per second that the display has to be refreshed depends on the type of phosphor, the brightness of the characters on the screen, and the person viewing the screen. In a typical display, a 30 to 60 refresh rate will usually ensure that the display will not flicker.

Character generators convert digital-coded alphanumeric data into the operator-readable form of alphanumeric characters and symbols shown on the sceen. The particular technique chosen for a display depends on a number of factors, such as cost, desired output quality, overall electronic design considerations, and the previous product bases. In effect, by controlling the deflection, intensity, and/or cross-sectional area of the electron beam, the character generator can produce dots, line segments (straight and curved), and template-shaped characters.

Dot characters are used in raster-scan deflection techniques. Although the raster scan is inexpensive, the quality of characters depends on the number of possible dot positions. Typically, 5 x 7 dot positions are used for the less expensive displays. Better quality, and hence more expensive, displays use either more dot positions (e.g., 7 x 9) or one of the other character generation techniques.

The direct view storage tube (DVST) has extra components (e.g., a grid of wires behind the CRT screen) to hold the displayed image on the screen until it can be erased. Typically, DVST's are used in inexpensive graphics (line drawing) displays and are seldom used in alphanumeric displays, for the following reasons:

1. The storage on the screen eliminates the display memory, but at the same time it eliminates temporary storage of messages that can be edited, corrected, and updated *before* transmission to the computer.

2. The DVST does not allow erasure or changing of individual characters or lines. The whole screen must be erased.

3. Erasure may take a second or more, which is annoying to many operators.

4. Some DVST's fade after a short time.

5. The price difference between a computer-readable memory and the DVST is not so significant as it once was because the price of memories is approaching the price of the DVST and at the same time computer memories are providing the extra control formerly available only in the DVST.

However, for some teletypwriter-compatible (unbuffered) displays, use of the DVST makes sense, since each key depression sends to the computer a character that can be shown on the screen as part of the whole message. The computer need not refresh the CRT in this case.

Another type of storage used with some teletypewriter-compatible (unbuffered) displays is the circulating delay-line storage. This type of storage is used with a raster-scan type of display (in some cases a normal TV set is used), and all scan lines on the display (e.g., 525 TV lines) are divided into dots that continually circulate through the delay line, which feeds back on itself. As the user depresses a key and sends the character to the computer, the character is formed into dots and stored in the proper place in the circulating delay line, which continuously refreshes the screen. This type of display is reasonably inexpensive, but has many of the same disadvantages as the DVST. The exception, and it is an important one, is that erasure changes or updates may be performed selectively on the screen as they are transmitted to the computer.

Comparison of Types of Display Memory

Delay Line

Description. Delay lines are electronic circuits that include an element (such as a magnetostrictive device or glass element) which allows electric signals as a series of bits to travel at acoustic speeds. The ends of the delay lines are connected together so that the electric signals continually circulate. By inserting signals representing 1s and other signals representing zeros, the circulating delay line becomes a memory with the information available as a series of 1s and zeros. The delay-line signals are synchronized with the scan pattern on the CRT screen and the 1s and zeros control the data appearing on the screen.

Advantages.   One of the advantages of delay lines is low cost; a delay line that stores around a hundred thousand bits may cost about a half a cent a bit. When used with scanning type displays, particularly TV, delay lines can be made to synchronize with scan lines of the display so that the bits are available when needed. These circuits are very rugged pieces of equipment and are easily used for extraction of data.

Disadvantages.   A disadvantage of delay lines is that storage of data into them is not easy because the storage of data must be synchronized with information circulation in a delay line. The cost of control circuits to do this may easily outweigh the lower cost of the delay line. Delay lines are somewhat susceptible to temperature changes and their integration into circuits must be designed to take this into account.

Magnetic Core

Description.   Magnetic cores used in alphanumeric displays are almost exactly like those used for the main frame memory of computers. Therefore they have been well developed and come in a wide variety of speeds and configurations. Most commonly used are random-access core memories at 2 microseconds READ/WRITE time for word lengths up to 50 bits.

Advantages.   The primary advantage of magnetic core memory is the flexibility of operation. Because any data in the memory can be accessed in microseconds, the storage and retrieval of data can be made to synchronize with a variety of operating methods. The price of magnetic core memories has been steadily decreasing.

Disadvantages.   Until recently the primary disadvantage of core memories for alphanumeric displays was the cost. On the other hand, semiconductor memories are now challenging core memories in every way, including cost.

Semiconductors

Description.   Two types of semiconductor memories are used in alphanumeric displays. One is the metal oxide semiconductor (MOS) used in a configuration of shift registers. These act similarly to delay lines except that they make it easier to access the data in a shift register. The other type is the monolithic semiconductor such as those announced by IBM for the System/370. These are used in a configuration more like magnetic core memories for less than microsecond random access in words of many bits.

Advantages.   A major advantage of semiconductor memories is that prices are already approaching three cents a bit and should be close to one cent a bit in the next year or two. The MOS shift register configuration is cheaper than monolithic semiconductors, but is less flexible in operation. Semiconductors also are the most compact type of memory available.

Disadvantages.   The primary disadvantage of semiconductor memories has been price, but this is decreasing so rapidly that its lower price is becoming an advantage.

Storage Tubes (Direct View Storage Tube, DVST)

Description.   Storage tubes are CRT's with special electronic elements within the tube that allow the image on the face of the tube to be held for long periods of time. Characters may be generated on the face of the storage tube in the same manner as on other CRT's, but they need not be repeated until updates or new data are to be written.

Advantages.   One advantage of the storage tube is that separate refreshed memory is not required for display. In addition, the computer can be used to operate the display directly because it needs to do this only when update or new data are required, eliminating some circuitry in the display device. Thus, not only alphanumeric data but also graphic (line drawing) data can be displayed on the storage tube at low cost.

Disadvantages.   The most important disadvantage is that all editing, changes, error correction, and the like must be done through computer access while on line. Erasure is not selective, and the entire storage-tube screen must be erased and new information written if any part of the screen is to be changed. Once information is stored on the screen, it must at the same time be sent to the computer because the screen is not computer readable.

COMPUTER COMPONENT

A display system can be useful only when connected to a computing system. In alphanumeric display applications the computer is generally required simply to process data needed in a particular application. Often the operator can place input data into the display and alter it in numerous ways without involving the computer in any way.

The amount of software support required by a passive alphanumeric display is little more than is required by a high-speed printer.

Display Interface

The interface connects the display unit to the communication/computer system. In effect, the interface has three functions:

1. To reorganize the computer data word into the word structure required by the display.
2. To convert the computer logic levels into display logic levels
3. To match the communication transmission and data structure of the display with those required by the communication facilities.

The type of interface used depends on the system into which the display is to be integrated. For teletypewriter-compatible displays, the interface is exactly like a teletypewriter. For IBM-compatible displays, the interface is exactly like an IBM 2260 interface. In fact, in both cases there are many plug-to-plug compatible units on the market.

If the displays are in the proximity of the computer to which they are attached, the interface usually allows the displays to connect to the computer input/output channels, typically at 500 or 1000-foot maximum-cable distances from the computer. If the displays are remote from the computer, the interface usually is compatible with, or includes, a data set. A data set is a modulator/demodulator, or modem, that allows the ON-OFF type data signals of the display to be transmitted over ordinary voice telephone lines.

Control Electronics

The control electronics provide the necessary sequence, timing, and operation signals so that the display unit can perform its various functions. In conjunction with the interface electronics, the control electronics provide the needed addressing circuits to allow each display to be individually serviced by the computer.

Control electronics and memory are sometimes shared by a number of displays in a cluster arrangement (e.g., the IBM 2260). Thus the larger the number of displays used, the less expensive each display becomes. In some cases the total memory is limited so that the maximum number of characters per display screen decreases as more displays are added to a controller.

AUXILIARY DISPLAY SYSTEM FEATURES

Once requirements have been defined, the problem centers on determining the features, capacity, and general applicability of each available display. Features are generally easy to determine, but the capacity, in terms of total data handling rather than simply the quantity that can be placed on the screen, is more difficult to establish. Features include the hardware capabilities such as the character generator, the keyboard, and edit capabilities. Some of these features may be offered as options.

The keyboard provides the mechanism for the operator to enter data into the computer system. The keyboard is similar to a typewriter keyboard, although it usually has additional keys for control and special functions. These keys allow the user to select the appropriate technique for his particular operation and application.

Keyboards are available in typewriter, teletypewriter, key punch, and adding-machine layouts. Solid-state circuitry is used, and two-key rollover (where two keys may be depressed in rapid succession) is generally available. Special control keys are added to initiate communication and perform editing operations. A keyboard is usually supplied with all aphanumeric displays, but some may be purchased without the keyboard for purely monitoring functions. Function keys are available, but not standard equipment, to allow the operator to designate special instructions to the computer. For example, a function key could designate that the numeric keys being depressed are the number of the record to be accessed. These keys are mounted on the keyboard or on the front panel of the CRT. In addition, some manufacturers provide coded, changeable overlays so that the designation of the function keys can be changed.

SPECIAL DEVICES

In addition to standard auxiliary services, custom modifications and special devices are sometimes available from manufacturers. These items are generally high-priced, but may still be economically feasible. Examples include substitution of a different tube, design of special devices, and incorporation of special features such as blinking.

A light pen is available on some alphanumeric display devices. This is a light-sensitive device that detects the presence of light on the screen. It is not used to emit light. The pen may use a photodiode or phototransistor as the light-sensitive element, or it may use a fiber optic bundle to pipe the light to a photomultiplier device in the display. The light pen can be used to point at information that already appears on the screen, or to designate a location at which information is to appear.

Other displays have special devices that position the cursor on the screen. This cursor, which usually designates where the next character is to be placed, may be positioned with pushbuttons, a trackball, a joystick, or similar devices.

SELECTING A DISPLAY

The problem of selection of displays is basically a problem of defining requirements and determining needs. At some point in the course of selection it is imperative to know which processes are display-dependent and would therefore affect the decision on the display component and which are processor-dependent and therefore relevant to processor selection. For example, the flexibility and ease of cursor movement are alphanumeric display-dependent characteristics, and the finest processor in existence cannot make up for poor cursor controls. On the other hand, the display is unable to compensate for poor file-search time.

It is usually advisable to list requirements in terms of display-dependent items, processor-dependent items, and trade-off or uncertain items. This procedure will enable a more accurate evaluation of the primary weak and strong points of each system relevant to needs and may also point up possible trade-offs that would otherwise not be apparent. As noted, the first problem is to identify display requirements. Primary items to be considered for the display are—

1. Type of data to be displayed
2. Quantity of data to appear on the screen
3. Amounts and types of operator interaction needed
4. Communications capabilities required

Response time and data processing speed may also be important, but these must be considered with respect to the processor, since they are processor-dependent and not display-dependent.

Knowing the capabilities and facilities available in various display systems and relating these to particular problems are the primary prerequisites to learning the potential for a display system within an application. The establishment of accurate, concise requirements is vital to realizing this potential. Actual selection of a display system becomes easier when the needed preliminary analysis has been performed.

7. MANUFACTURER COMPARISON CHARTS ON ALPHANUMERIC DISPLAY TERMINALS

Transmission characteristics, general input/output capabilities, costs, and important characteristics unique to commercially available display terminals are summarized in the comparison charts on the following pages.

ALPHANUMERIC DISPLAY TERMINALS

IDENTITY		Alphacom DW 33 Data Window Video Terminal	American Data Systems ADS-260 Video Communications Terminal	Atlantic Technology ATC 2000 Video Display Terminal					
REPORT NUMBER		—	—	6170					
DISPLAY UNIT	Identity	33	260	Stand-alone:		Multistation:			
				2265	2266	2263	2264	2265	2266
	Viewing Area, in.	8.5 wide; 6 high	9 (diagonal)	9.5 wide; 7.0 high		10.5 wide; 8.0 high			
	Char/Line	72-80	32; 64; 80	80; 64; 40	80; 64; 40	80; 40	80; 40	80; 64; 40	80; 64; 40
	Lines/Display	25	4-30	12; 15; 24	24; 30; 48	3; 6	6; 12	12; 15; 24	24; 30; 48
	Char Set	64	64	64	64	64	64	64	64
	Total Char/Display	2000	2400	960	1920	240	480	960	1920
	Char Generation Technique	5 x 7 dot matrix	Stroke	Stroke					
EDITING FACILITIES	Horizontal Tab	Optional	Yes	Yes					
	Line Erase	Optional	No	Yes					
	Line Insert	Optional	Optional	No					
	Partial Display Transmit	Yes	Yes	Yes					
	Split Screen	No	Optional	Yes					
	Other	Char insert/erase; scrolling; full cursor controls	Full cursor controls; page erase	Full cursor controls; char addressing; LF/CR; wraparound: char insert/delete; display erase					
CONTROL UNIT	Identity	Self-contained	Self-contained	Self-contained		Model 2000 Expansion Units:			
						4824	4848	4896	4819
	Type of Buffer Storage	Delay line/MOS	MOS	Delay line		Delay line			
	Buffer Capacity Char	2000	2400	960	1920	240	480	960	1920
	Max Devices/ Controller	1 display; up to 15 slave displays	16 via polling adapter	1	1	8	4	2	1
				Plus 1 printer per stand-alone unit		Plus 1 printer per expansion unit			
	Multi-Drop	—	Yes	Yes					
PERIPHERY	Printer	TTY 33 RO	All digital printer compatibility	Selectric®-type char printer; medium-speed line printer					
	Other	Mag tape cassette reader/recorder	—	—					
PURCHASE PRICE, $		3500	1790-3490	8250-10,000 (stand-alone); 3250-4250 (multistation); 8500 (controller); 4000 (expansion unit)					
MONTHLY RENTAL, $		100	—	240-275 (stand-alone); 75-100 (multistation); 200 (controller); 100 (expansion unit)					
COMMENTS		Auto CR/LF available in 72- or 80-char/line formats; provides conversational/batch operating modes; automatic answerback, format mode, acoustic coupler optional; TTY-compatible; up to 480 cps data rate NOTE: No longer available	Capable of key, batch, or key/batch transmissions	Transmission is synchronous or asynchronous, half-duplex, at 1200 or 2400 bps over voiceband line; 64 ASCII character set (96 optional); multiple variable data fields; 7680-char buffer (includes 4 expansion units with 1920 char each); compatible with IBM 2260/2848 Display System; protected format feature; serviced by and leased/purchased from MAI Equipment Corp					

®, registered trademark

ALPHANUMERIC DISPLAY TERMINALS

IDENTITY		Beehive Electrotech Alpha 101 Computer Display Terminal	Beehive Electrotech Alpha 103 Computer Display Terminal	Beehive Electrotech Alpha 105 Computer Display Terminal	Bunker-Ramo BR-700 Information System	Bunker-Ramo Series 2200 Data Display System (Single Station)
REPORT NUMBER		—	—	—	—	—
DISPLAY UNIT	Identity	101	103	105	BR-720; BR-721; BR-722	2205/17
	Viewing Area, in.	7.5 wide; 6.0 high	7.5 wide; 6.0 high	7.5 wide; 6.0 high	8.75, 18, or 20 wide; 6.25, 13, or 15 high	8.75 wide; 6.25 high
	Char/Line	40	40	80	80	80
	Lines/Display	20	20	20	12	24
	Char Set	64	64	64	89	62; 92
	Total Char/Display	800	800	1600	960	960
	Char Generation Technique	5 x 7 dot matrix	5 x 7 dot matrix	5 x 7 dot matrix	5 x 7 dot matrix	5 x 7 dot matrix
EDITING FACILITIES	Horizontal Tab	Yes	Yes	Yes	Yes	Yes
	Line Erase	Yes	Yes	Yes	Yes	Yes
	Line Insert	No	No	No	Yes	No
	Partial Display Transmit	Yes	Yes	Yes	Yes	Yes
	Split Screen	Yes	Yes	Yes	Yes (with 2 cursors, 1 for each screen)	Yes
	Other	Char delete; full cursor controls; formatting (optional); clear screen	Char delete; full cursor controls; formatting (optional); clear screen/ tab; home	Char delete; full cursor controls; formatting (optional); clear screen/ tab; home	Full cursor controls; dual-screen display mode; page insert; line/page delete	Full cursor controls; char erase/insert; blink
CONTROL UNIT	Identity	Self-contained	Self-contained	Self-contained	BR-701	2221/2223 Control Unit
	Type of Buffer Storage	MOS	MOS	MOS	Magnetic drum (up to 518-page total storage)	Delay line
	Buffer Capacity Char	800	800	1600	1 960-char p (display); 1 p (prntr); 384 pp (common file); 102 pp (I/O buffer)	1032 (single station)
	Max Devices/ Controller	1 display; 1 printer	1 display; 1 printer (optional)	1 display; 1 printer (optional)	16 displays; 16 printers; repeater displays as required	1
	Multi-Drop	Optional	Optional	Optional	Yes	—
PERIPHERY	Printer	TTY 33	TTY 33	TTY 33	Modified TTY 35 RO (80-character platen)	TTY 33/35, KSR/ASR/RO
	Other	Paper tape reader/ punch (send/receive)	Paper tape reader/ punch (send/receive)	Paper tape reader/ punch (send/receive)	Paper tape pnch/rdr; interfaces any cmptr/ data lines; special devices as rqrd	TTY CX Paper Tape Reader/DRPE Paper Tape Punch
PURCHASE PRICE, $		3495; See Note	3495; See Note	3995	—	6895 (2205/17, 2221); 8600 (2205/17, 2223) See Note
MONTHLY RENTAL, $		120 (3-yr lease)	120 (3-yr lease)	See Note	—	
COMMENTS		Typewriter keyboard; standard programmable control keys (3), printer interface, remote keyboard, and composite video/remote drive; optional parallel interface; half-duplex; 8-level ASCII; asynchronous, up to 2400 bps	TTY keyboard; options include printer interface, remote keyboard, composite video/remote drive, and parallel interface; half-/full-duplex; 8-level ASCII; asynchronous, up to 2400 bps	TTY keyboard; options include printer interface, remote keyboard, composite video/remote drive, and parallel interface; half-/full-duplex; 8-level ASCII asynchronous, up to 2400 bps	Provides I/O buffer (3-page input/3-page output message) for each of 16 stations/communications interface module; external devices can also access 384-page files; designed for off-line operation to its own local data base without software; TTY/ Bell System Data-Phone interface std	Various display format combinations available; char/longitudinal parity checking; half-duplex transmission at 600-2400 bps over voice-band line; processor parallel transfer rate up to 55,000 cps
		NOTE: No longer available	NOTE: No longer available	NOTE: No longer available		NOTE: No longer in production

ALPHANUMERIC DISPLAY TERMINALS

IDENTITY		Bunker-Ramo Series 2200 Data Display System (Multistation)	Bunker-Ramo Series 200 Data Display System			Burroughs Input and Display System
REPORT NUMBER		6061	6060			6071
DISPLAY UNIT	Identity	2212	203/204	211	212	9351-4
	Viewing Area, in.	4.75 wide; 3.75 high	7.75 wide; 5.50 high	4.75 wide; 3.75 high	4.75 wide; 3.75 high	12 wide; 9 high
	Char/Line	37	8-64	8-42	8-42	80
	Lines/Display	12	2-12	2-12	2-12	25
	Char Set	62	39 (plus 15 optional)	14 (plus up to 12 optional)	40 (plus up to 12 optional)	66
	Total Char/Display	444	32-768	32-384	32-384	1018; 506; 250 (2000 display positions)
	Char Generation Technique	5 x 7 dot matrix	5 x 7 dot matrix	5 x 7 dot matrix	5 x 7 dot matrix	Stroke
EDITING FACILITIES	Horizontal Tab	Yes	No			Yes
	Line Erase	Yes	Yes			Optional
	Line Insert	No	No			Optional
	Partial Display Transmit	Yes	Yes			Yes
	Split Screen	Yes	Optional			No
	Other	Full cursor controls; char erase/insert; blink	Full cursor controls; CR/LF; blink; wraparound; char erase			Full cursor controls; char insert/delete; controlled format; programmed cursor
CONTROL UNIT	Identity	2222 Control Unit	222		223/224	Control I, II, or IIA
	Type of Buffer Storage	Delay line (9)	Delay line		Delay line	Magnetic core
	Buffer Capacity Char	9288 (multistation)	768-2304		768-6912	1024
	Max Devices/ Controller	18	Up to 36 (depending on display size)		Up to 96 (depending on display size)	1 display per Control I; 4 displays per Control II/IIA
	Multi-Drop	—	Optional		Optional	Yes
PERIPHERY	Printer	TTY 33/35 KSR, ASR, RO	TTY Model 33/35 KSR, RO			TTY Model 33 RO (1 per controller)
	Other	TTY CX Paper Tape Reader; DRPE Paper Tape Punch	TTY CX Paper Tape Reader; DRPE Paper Tape Punch			Modem expander
PURCHASE PRICE, $ **MONTHLY RENTAL, $**		7965 (2222); 1770 (2212) 231 (2222); 72 (2212)	2310 (203);2815 (204); 1300 (211); 1370 (212); 8950 (222); 10,800 (223); 12,900 (224); 850-4000 (expansion unit) 77 (203); 88 (204); 56 (211); 58 (212); 243 (222); 270 (223); 318 (224); 26-107 (expansion unit)			9460 (I); 14,300 (II); 4400 (IIA); 2640 (monitor); 880 (keyboard) 215 (I); 325 (II); 100 (IIA); 60 (monitor); 20 (keyboard)
COMMENTS		Char/longitudinal parity checking; half-duplex transmission at 600-2400 bps over voiceband line; processor parallel transfer rate up to 55,000 cps	Various arrangements of number of lines/display and char/line available; all displays must have same arrangement; different models of display units/auxiliary devices can be intermixed on same control unit; polling/ nonpolling operation; synchronous/asynchronous; 7-level, 8-/10-unit ASCII; half-duplex at 1200/1800 bps (120/180 cps) or 2000/2400 bps (250/300 cps)			Up to 4 Control IIs/12 Control IIAs can be multiplexed to 1 data set; synchronous/ asynchronous; 8-level ASCII (parity); half-duplex at 150, 300, 1200, 1800, 2000, or 2400 bps

ALPHANUMERIC DISPLAY TERMINALS

IDENTITY		Burroughs B 9352-1/B 9352-2 Input and Display Terminal	Compucord Data Sense 5000 Video Display/Mag Tape Terminal	Computek Series 100 CRT Terminal	Computer Communications CC-30 Communications Station	Computer Communications CC-33 Teletype Oriented Display Station
REPORT NUMBER		—	—	—	6125	6126
DISPLAY UNIT	Identity	B 9352-1/B 9352-2	DS 5000	100	CC-300 Model II (b/w); Model XII (color)	CC-300 Model II (b/w); Model XII (color)
	Viewing Area, in.	8 wide; 12 high	4 wide; 4 high	9.5 wide; 7.25 high	8 wide; 6.5 high	8 wide; 6.5 high
	Char/Line	40; 80	25	50; 73; 80	40	40
	Lines/Display	24; 12	16	20; 15; 13	20; 24 (optional)	20; 24 (optional)
	Char Set	66	64	64	64; 96 (optional)	64; 96 (optional)
	Total Char/Display	960	400	1100	800; 960 (optional)	800; 960 (optional)
	Char Generation Technique	5 x 7 dot matrix	5 x 7 dot matrix	7 x 9 dot matrix	5 x 7 dot matrix	5 x 7 dot matrix
EDITING FACILITIES	Horizontal Tab	Yes	Yes	Optional	Yes (1 fixed position)	Yes (1 fixed position)
	Line Erase	Yes	No	Optional	No	No
	Line Insert	No	No	Optional	No	No
	Partial Display Transmit	Yes	No	Optional	Yes	Yes
	Split Screen	No	No	Optional	Yes	Yes
	Other	Controlled format; full cursor controls	Full cursor controls; erase display/line/char	Full cursor controls; read-only memory microprograms; char transpose; char over-strike	Full cursor controls; char addressing; fixed format; screen erase; 4-color displays available; switch-selectable char/block transmission modes	Full cursor controls; CR/LF; display erase; char addressing; wrap-around; 4-color displays available
CONTROL UNIT	Identity	Self-contained	Self-contained	Self-contained	CC-301 Model II TV Display Controller	CC-301 Model III TV Display Controller
	Type of Buffer Storage	Delay line	MOS	Delay line/MOS	Magnetic core	Magnetic core
	Buffer Capacity Char	960	400	1100	1024	1024
	Max Devices/Controller	—	1 display; 1 printer; 1 mag tape unit	4	1 display; up to 6 slave displays (without amplification); up to 7 local I/O devices	1 display; up to 6 monitors (without amplification); up to 7 local I/O devices
	Multi-Drop	Yes	Optional	Yes	Yes	Yes
PERIPHERY	Printer	TTY 33 RO (1 per control)	Compucord PM 1600 Page Printer	132-char impact line printer	Impact/nonimpact line printers; TTY 33/35 RO, KSR, ASR Card readers; light pen; other devices on request	Impact/nonimpact line printers; TTY 33/35 RO, KSR, ASR Card readers; light pen; other devices on request
	Other	Modem expander	CompuPac Magnetic Tape Cassettes			
PURCHASE PRICE, $		8775	3500	5200	195–565 (display); 6300–6800 (controller); 550 (keyboard)	195–565 (display); 7200 (controller); 550 (keyboard)
MONTHLY RENTAL, $		195	98.50	—	—	—
COMMENTS		Up to 9 terminals can be connected via direct cable to single/multi-line control; up to 16 terminals can be connected to a modem at 1 location	2 integrated read/write mag tape units provide off-line, key-to-tape/tape-to-screen operations; synchronous/asynchronous; 8-level ASCII; up to 2400 bps over half-duplex, voice-band line; printed output at 100 lpm	TTY-compatible; self-contained, general-purpose, micropro-grammed processor allows editing via read-only memory/controls several peripherals; 8-level ASCII; asynchronous; half-/full-duplex; up to 1,000,000 bps max parallel data rate; 2400, 3600, 4800 bps syn-chronous rates opt	6 display sizes from 8–23 in.; asynch, 8-level ASCII; half-duplex; 110–9600 bps; Model II Controller portable; can accept external synch; 4M bps max parallel rate; channel interfaces for IBM 1130, System/360, XDS Sigma, CDC 3000/6000, PDP 8/-12	Switch-selectable data rates at 110, 600, 1200 bps; full-duplex over narrowband line; synchronous/asynchro-nous; 7-level, 8-/11-unit ASCII; plug-to-plug TTY-compatible; can accept external synch

ALPHANUMERIC DISPLAY TERMINALS

IDENTITY		Computer Consoles 520/724 Data Terminal System	Computer Displays ARDS 100A Advanced Remote Display Station	Computer Optics CO:70 Display System	Computer Terminal Datapoint 3300 Display Terminal	Computer Terminals TK-340 Display Terminal
REPORT NUMBER		—	—	—	—	—
DISPLAY UNIT	Identity	520	100A	CO:70	3300	TK-340
	Viewing Area, in.	11.25 wide; 5.75 high	6.5 wide; 8.5 high	9.5 wide; 7.5 high	11 wide; 8 high	8.75 wide; 7.375 high
	Char/Line	80	80	100	72	48
	Lines/Display	12; 24 (optional)	50	30	25	4; 8; 16
	Char Set	60	96	88	64	63
	Total Char/Display	960	4000	3000	1800	192; 384; 768
	Char Generation Technique	5 x 7 dot matrix	7 x 9 dot matrix	Stroke	5 x 7 dot matrix	9 x 11 dot matrix
EDITING FACILITIES	Horizontal Tab	Yes	Yes	Yes	Yes	No
	Line Erase	Yes	No	Yes	Yes	No
	Line Insert	Yes	No	Yes	—	No
	Partial Display Transmit	Yes	No	Yes	—	Yes
	Split Screen	Yes	No	Yes	No	No
	Other	Full cursor controls; char insert/delete; scrolling; variable fields; end of line/screen erase	Software/graphic input controlling cursor; full cursor controls	Full cursor controls; line addressing; char insert/delete; variable fields; end of line/screen erase; clear display; wraparound	Scrolling; fixed format; full cursor controls; line/screen erase	Send line; programmable blinking; full cursor controls
CONTROL UNIT	Identity	724	Self-contained	Self-contained	Self-contained	C-340
	Type of Buffer Storage	Magnetic core	Storage tube	Delay line	MOS	Magnetic core
	Buffer Capacity Char	960; additional 240 required for printer	4000	3000	1800	768
	Max Devices/Controller	6	6	1 master/2 slave displays (1000 char each)	1 display; 1 printer; 1 mag tape unit	4
	Multi-Drop	—	—	Yes	—	Yes
PERIPHERY	Printer	Yes	—	Yes	Yes	—
	Other	Magnetic tape (556/800 bpi)	Digital cassette recorder; mouse; joystick	Mag tape/paper tape I/O	3300T Magnetic Tape Unit	HCR-345 Hard Copy Recorder; V/M-256 Microfilm Video Input
PURCHASE PRICE, $		12,000	7950	8750 (master); 3250 (slave); 1775 (adapter)	4500 (display); 250 (high-speed buffer); 2250 (3300T)	15,000 (includes 4 stations, 1 controller/interface)
MONTHLY RENTAL, $		250	See Note	250 (master); 92 (slave); 50 (adapter)	145 (display); 7 (high-speed buffer); 85 (3300T)	175; see Note
COMMENTS		IBM-compatible via 2701 adapter; detachable typewriter keyboard; 15-cps printer; 280,000-char local mag tape storage unit reads/writes at 1600 cps; half-duplex; 1200/2400 (optional) bps; 7-level ASCII; compatible with Bell System Data Set 202C	Operates in symbol/graphic modes; TTY-compatible; graphic vectors/special symbol set std; operates half-/full-duplex; 8-level, 10-/11-unit ASCII; asynchronous, up to 1200 bps; compatible with Bell System Data Sets 103A/202C NOTE: No longer available	IBM-compatible via 2701 adapter; format mode (access all memory data)/data mode (access variable data); remote data adapter interfaces up to 32 displays/printers to 1 data set; asynchronous up to 2400 bps; half/full-duplex; 7-level, 10-unit ASCII; compatible with Bell System Data Set 201B1	Compatible with TTY 33; optional 240-cps read/write mag tape unit stores 800,000 char/cassette; half-/full-duplex; asynchronous at 110–600 bps std/1200–4800 bps optional; 8-level ASCII; compatible with Bell System Data Sets 103/202	Interfaces to accommodate 1200, 1800, 2000, 2400, or 4800 bps available; contention/polled modes; auto retransmit on parity error (polled mode); 8-level, 10-unit ASCII; asynchronous; half-duplex; 11 internal/19 external control codes NOTE: No longer in production

ALPHANUMERIC DISPLAY TERMINALS

IDENTITY		Conrac 201 Data Display Terminal	Control Data 200 User Terminal	Control Data 210 Entry Display System	Control Data 211-4 Multi-Station Entry/Display Terminal	Control Data 214 Single Station Display Terminal
REPORT NUMBER		—	6160	—	—	—
DISPLAY UNIT	Identity	201	217-2	211F	211-4	214
	Viewing Area, in.	11/7.5 wide; 7.5/8.5 high	8 wide; 6 high	8.0 wide; 6.0 high	8 wide; 6 high	8 wide; 6 high
	Char/Line	80; 40	50; 80	50	50	50
	Lines/Display	12; 24	20; 13	20	20	20
	Char Set	Up to 71	64	64	64	64
	Total Char/Display	960	1000; 1040	1000	1000	1000
	Char Generation Technique	5 x 7 dot matrix	5 x 7 dot matrix	5 x 7 dot matrix	5 x 7 dot matrix	5 x 7 dot matrix
EDITING FACILITIES	Horizontal Tab	Yes	Yes	No	Optional	No
	Line Erase	Yes	Yes	No	Optional	No
	Line Insert	No	Yes	No	Optional	No
	Partial Display Transmit	Yes	Yes	Yes	Yes	Yes
	Split Screen	No	Yes	No	No	No
	Other	Full cursor controls; fixed format; char insert/delete	Full cursor controls; CR/LF	Full cursor controls	Full cursor controls	Full cursor controls
CONTROL UNIT	Identity	Self-contained	Self-contained	216 Remote Controller	216-4 Remote Controller	214 Remote Controller
	Type of Buffer Storage	Delay line	Delay line	Delay line	Delay line	Delay line
	Buffer Capacity Char	960	1000; 1040	1000 char/display	1000	1000
	Max Devices/ Controller	1 display; 1 printer	1 display; 1 printer; 1 card reader	Up to 12 display units/ printers (6 printers max)	Up to 12 display units/ printers (6 printers max)	1
	Multi-Drop	No	Yes	Yes	Yes	Yes
PERIPHERY	Printer	TTY 33/35 (via optional adapter)	222-1/222-2 Line Printer; 218-1 Typewriter Printer	IBM Selectric Typewriter	IBM Selectric Typewriter	Yes
	Other	—	224-2 Card Reader	No	No	No
PURCHASE PRICE, $		7500-8500 (OEM only)	12,720	—	18,550 (216-4); 4455 (211-4)	6250
MONTHLY RENTAL, $		—	275-305 (1- to 5-yr lease)	135 (display); 725 (controller); 270 (printer)	320 (216-4); 115 (211-4)	140
COMMENTS		Options include poll/ select, twisted pair, nonstd data rate modules; longitudinal/ vertical parity checking std; half-/full-duplex; asynchronous up to 2400 bps; compatible with Bell System Data Sets 202C/202D (103/ 201 optional)	Remote batch processing and off-line card-/ display-to-print applications; operates half-duplex at 2000/ 2400 bps; synchronous; 7-level ASCII; compatible with Bell System Data Sets 201A (2000 bps)/201B (2400 bps); 300-lpm line printer, 15-cps char printer, 330-cpm card reader optional	Display format of 13 80-char lines; direct computer I/O channel interfaces available; 15-cps print speed; operates half-duplex; 6-bit BCD (data)/ ASCII (control); synchronous at 2000/ 2400 bps; compatible with Bell System Data Sets 201A/201B	Display format of 13 80-char lines available with 1024-char storage capacity; interfaces available for local operation	Display format of 13 80-char lines available with 1024-char storage capacity

ALPHANUMERIC DISPLAY TERMINALS

IDENTITY		Control Data 217 Video Display Station	Control Data 241-1 Remote Graphic Subsystem	Courier Terminal Systems Executerm I Remote Data Terminal	Courier Terminal Systems Executerm 60 Remote Data Terminal	Data Disc 6200 Series Television Display System
REPORT NUMBER		—	—	—	—	—
DISPLAY UNIT	Identity	217	241-1	I	60	6250
	Viewing Area, in.	8 wide; 6 high	12 wide; 12 high	6.4 wide; 4.8 high	6.4 wide; 4.8 high	9.75 wide; 7.25 high
	Char/Line	50	86; 64	40	40	85; 64
	Lines/Display	20	64; 43	15	6; 12 (optional)	48; 40
	Char Set	64	64; 128 (optional)	64; 96 (optional)	64	64
	Total Char/Display	1000	Approx 3000	256; 512 (optional)	240; 480 (optional)	4080; 2560
	Char Generation Technique	5 x 7 dot matrix	Stroke	7 x 8 dot matrix	7 x 8 dot matrix	5 x 7/7 x 10 dot matrix
EDITING FACILITIES	Horizontal Tab	No	Yes	Yes	Yes	Yes
	Line Erase	No	Yes	No	No	Yes
	Line Insert	No	Yes	No	No	Yes (under program control)
	Partial Display Transmit	Yes	Yes	Yes	Yes	Yes (requires ASCII readback option)
	Split Screen	No	Yes	Yes	—	Yes
	Other	Full cursor controls	As programmed	Clear display/end of screen; char insert/delete; full cursor controls; blink; scrolling; fixed format	Full cursor controls; scrolling; char insert/delete; clear end of line; protected format; clear display/end of screen	Overlay; blink; selective erase; full programmable cursor editing features
CONTROL UNIT	Identity	Self-contained	241-1	Self-contained	Self-contained	6200 Series Controller
	Type of Buffer Storage	Delay line	Magnetic core	MOS	MOS	Row buffer/disc memory
	Buffer Capacity Char	1000	4000 std (expandable to 12,000)	256; 512 (optional)	240; 480 (optional)	85 (row buffer); 4080 (disc memory)
	Max Devices/ Controller	1	1	1 display; 1 printer	1; up to 8 displays (via optional adapter); 1 printer	128
	Multi-Drop	Yes	No	No	No	Yes (up to 10/channel)
PERIPHERY	Printer	No	Yes	Execuprint I	Execuprint I	TTY 33 ASR
	Other	No	Card reader; magnetic tape	No	No	Color display; keyboard multiplexor; graphic tablet; track ball; light pen; printer
PURCHASE PRICE, $		12,000	71,020	3800	5500 (single station); 4800 (multistation)	25,000
MONTHLY RENTAL, $		—	1415	137	250 (single station); 175 (multistation)	See Note
COMMENTS		Display format of 13 80-char lines available; up to 5 display units can be multiplexed onto 1 data set	Contains internal processor; adaptable for local operations; peripherals can be attached if optional I/O channel included in subsystem; all editing facilities are function of software	IBM-compatible; variable-data entry/transmission; conversation/edit modes; 8-level ASCII; half-/full-duplex; up to 110, 150, 300, 1200 bps; asynchronous; Execuprint I (RO) prints 10 cps, on 80-char line, from CRT, computer memory ($80/mo); char parity checking; TTY keyboard	Single station is IBM 2265-compatible; multistation, IBM 2260-compatible (requires adapter); Execuprint I (RO) prints 10 cps, on 80-char line, from CRT, computer memory ($80/mo); char parity/longitudinal redundancy checking; half-duplex; synchronous; 1200/2400 bps; 8-level ASCII	Dedicated display processor option available; disc memory stores video signal (1 channel per terminal); each display point addressable for presentation of complex graphic displays; can intermix black and white/color; 4 programmable char sizes NOTE: No longer available

ALPHANUMERIC DISPLAY TERMINALS

IDENTITY		Data Disc 6500 Series Graphic Display System	Stromberg-DatagraphiX 1100 Inquiry Display System	Stromberg-DatagraphiX 1110 Interactive Display System	Delta Data Systems Delta I Video Display Terminal	Delta Data Systems 2000 Color Display Terminal
REPORT NUMBER		—	—	—	6180	—
DISPLAY UNIT	Identity	6512	C560 Station	SD 1110	1020	2000
	Viewing Area, in.	7.25 high; 9.75 wide	5.0 wide; 3.0 high	10 wide; 10 high	9 wide; 7 high	14 wide; 9.5 high
	Char/Line	85; 42	50	80	40	40
	Lines/Display	51; 25	10	35	24	24
	Char Set	64	61 (selected from 78)	64	64; 96 (opt); line drawing opt	64; 96 (opt); line drawing opt
	Total Char/Display	4335; 2142; 2125; 1050	500	1066	960	960
	Char Generation Technique	5 x 7 dot matrix	5 x 7 dot matrix	Charactron shaped-beam tube	5 x 7 dot matrix	5 x 7 dot matrix
EDITING FACILITIES	Horizontal Tab	Yes	No	Yes	Yes	Yes
	Line Erase	Yes	No	Yes	Yes	Yes
	Line Insert	Yes	No	Yes	Yes	Yes
	Partial Display Transmit	Yes	Yes	Yes	Yes	Yes
	Split Screen	Yes	No	Yes	Yes	Yes
	Other	Overlay; blink; selective area erase; full programmable cursor editing features	Full cursor controls	Char insert/delete; display erase; variable erase; full cursor controls	Full cursor controls; char addressing; blink; char insert/delete; transmit char/line; display/end of screen erase	Char insert/delete; clear message/line/page; full cursor controls; blink
CONTROL UNIT	Identity	6501 Controller	C310 Station Controller	Self-contained	Self-contained	Self-contained
	Type of Buffer Storage	5200 Series Parallel Disc Memory	Delay line (in each display unit)	Delay line	Magnetic core	Magnetic core
	Buffer Capacity Char	4335 per display	500 per display	1079	1024	1024
	Max Devices/Controller	32	24 displays; 4 printers	22	1 printer; slave monitors; 1 TTY; 1 cassette	1 printer; slave monitors; 1 TTY; 1 cassette
	Multi-Drop	Yes (up to 10 per channel)	No	Yes	Yes	Yes
PERIPHERY	Printer	TTY 33/35 ASR	Yes	Yes	TTY	TTY
	Other	Keyboard; color display; graphic tablet; track ball; light pen; printer	No	Paper tape reader/punch	Cassette tape recorder; card reader	Cassette tape recorder; card reader
PURCHASE PRICE, $		11,000-12,000 (2-/4-chnnl); 35,000-36,000 (16-/32-chnnl)	See Note	—	5500	10,200
MONTHLY RENTAL, $		—	98 (C560 display); 320-555 (C310 controller)	—	—	—
COMMENTS		Disc memory stores video signal; up to 16 full-resolution (262,144 pts/display) or 32 half-resolution (131,072 pts/display) displays; 4 programmable char sizes; options include keyboard multiplexor, video disc file, switching unit, dedicated display processor, auxiliary program storage unit	Display width can be adjusted from 3.0-6.5 inches; height from 1.0-3.5 inches; half-/full-duplex; 8-level ASCII; synchronous/asynchronous up to 2400 bps NOTE: No longer in production	IBM System/360 compatible; synchronous/asynchronous transmission at 2000/2400 bps; additional display formats operational; multistation controller can handle up to 22 displays; optional data set distributor configuration can include up to 12 stand-alone units/modem	Remote programmed cursor control; asynchronous operation up to 15-kHz word rates; 7-level ASCII; full-duplex; compatible with IBM 2265 display	Data can be displayed in 4 colors; remote programmed cursor control/char addressing; IBM 360-compatible (via 2701) in polled/unpolled or contention modes; synchronous/asynchronous up to 15-kHz word rate; full-duplex; 7-level ASCII; compatible with Bell System Data Sets 103, 201, 202

ALPHANUMERIC DISPLAY TERMINALS

IDENTITY		Harris-Intertype Harris 1100 Editing and Proofing Terminal	Digital Scientific 2102 TV Terminal Controller	Ferranti Electric TDM 2008 Remote Terminal Display	Ferranti Electric TDM 2020 Remote Terminal Display	Ferranti Electric TDM 2020C Remote Terminal Display
REPORT NUMBER		—	—	—	—	—
DISPLAY UNIT	Identity	1100	Std TV monitor	2008	2020	2020C
	Viewing Area, in.	8.5 high; 11.0 wide	Variable	9.45 wide; 7.09 high	9.45 wide; 7.09 high	9.45 wide; 7.09 high
	Char/Line	40 (double column); 80 (single column)	32	64	64	64
	Lines/Display	50 (double column); 25 (single column)	25	12	32	32
	Char Set	100; 118 (optional)	64	64	64	64
	Total Char/Display	2000	800	768	2048	2048
	Char Generation Technique	11 x 15 dot matrix	5 x 7 dot matrix	10 x 14 dot matrix	10 x 14 dot matrix	10 x 14 dot matrix
EDITING FACILITIES	Horizontal Tab	No	Optional	Yes	Yes	Yes
	Line Erase	Yes	No	Yes	Yes	Yes
	Line Insert	Yes	No	No	No	No
	Partial Display Transmit	Yes	Yes	Yes	Yes	Yes
	Split Screen	Yes	No	Optional	Optional	Optional
	Other	Insert/delete char, line, par, block; resequence text; wraparound; single line/continuous scroll up/down to 8000 char	Cursor positioning from keyboard/processor; char/line addressing	Full cursor controls; new line; overwrite; char insert/delete; erase message; clear display	Full cursor controls; new line; overwrite; char insert/delete; erase message; clear display	Full cursor controls; new line; overwrite; char insert/delete; erase message; clear display
CONTROL UNIT	Identity	Self-contained	2102 TV Terminal Controller	Self-contained	Self-contained	TDC 2000 Display Controller
	Type of Buffer Storage	MOS	Delay line	Magnetostrictive delay line	Delay line	Magnetostrictive delay line
	Buffer Capacity Char	2000; 6000 (optional)	800 min	768	2048	2048
	Max Devices/Controller	1 display; 1 paper tape reader/punch	1 display; 1 printer/controller	1	1	64
	Multi-Drop	Yes	Yes	No	No	No
PERIPHERY	Printer	No	TTY 33, 35, or 37 RO	TTY 33 ASR (optional)	TTY 33 ASR (optional)	TTY 33 ASR (optional)
	Other	CX/BRPE paper tape reader/punch, emulator (120 cps/60 cps)	—	No	No	No
PURCHASE PRICE, $		14,500	4495	4000 (OEM only)	4500 (OEM only)	6000 (TDC 2000); 3500 (TDM 2020C); OEM only
MONTHLY RENTAL, $		—	120 (see Note)	—	—	—
COMMENTS		Designed for text/function code proofreading in editing/typesetting application; 110-cps punch opt; 6-level paper tape; TTS code std; ASCII/EBCDIC opt; up to 1200 cps line speed; compatible with Bell 202D; off-line operation capability; full cursor controls	Standard serial/parallel interfaces available up to 4800 bps; up to 32 terminal controllers per line are individually addressable; uses any standard 64-char code set NOTE: No longer in production	Display format of 9 80-char lines available; raster char generation displayed via 10-line horiz/14-element vert resolutions; conversational mode; char parity checking; half-duplex; 8-level ASCII; asynchronous (std) up to 1200 bps/synchronous (opt) at 2400 bps	Display format of 26 80-char lines available; raster char generation displayed via 10-line horiz/14-element vert resolutions; conversational mode; char parity checking; half-duplex; 8-level ASCII; asynchronous (std) up to 1200 bps/synchronous (opt) at 2400 bps	Display format of 26 80-char lines available; raster char generation displayed via 10-line horiz/14-element vert resolutions; conversational mode; char parity checking; half-duplex; 8-level ASCII; asynchronous (std) up to 1200 bps/synchronous (opt) at 2400 bps

ALPHANUMERIC DISPLAY TERMINALS

IDENTITY		Foto-Mem Foto-Vision Display Terminal	Honeywell Datanet-760 Keyboard/Display Subsystem (formerly GE)	Honeywell Datanet-765 CRT Communications Terminal (formerly GE)	Honeywell Datanet-775 CRT Communications Terminal (formerly GE)	Honeywell Datanet-785 CRT Communications Terminal (formerly GE)
REPORT NUMBER		—	6321	—	—	—
DISPLAY UNIT	Identity	Foto-Vision TV Receiver	DMU 761	DMU 761	DMU 761	DMU 761
	Viewing Area, in.	9.75 wide; 7.25 high	8.0 wide; 6.3 high	8.0 wide; 6.3 high	8.0 wide; 6.3 high	8.0 wide; 6.3 high
	Char/Line	80	46	46	46	92
	Lines/Display	24	4; 8; 16; 26	22	22	22
	Char Set	64	64	64	64	64
	Total Char/Display	1920	184; 368; 736; 1196	1012–2024	1012–2024	2024
	Char Generation Technique	5 x 7 dot matrix	5 x 7 dot matrix	5 x 7 dot matrix	5 x 7 dot matrix	5 x 7 dot matrix
EDITING FACILITIES	Horizontal Tab	Yes	Yes	Yes	Yes	Yes
	Line Erase	Yes	No	No	No	No
	Line Insert	Yes	No	No	No	No
	Partial Display Transmit	Yes	Yes	Yes	Yes	Yes
	Split Screen	Yes	No	Yes	Yes	Yes
	Other	Full cursor controls; scrolling; char blink; protected format; char insert/delete; wrap-around	Full cursor controls; special symbols facilitate tables; char addressing	Wraparound; display erase; char addressing; full cursor controls	Wraparound; display erase; char addressing; full cursor controls	Wraparound; display erase; char addressing; full cursor controls
CONTROL UNIT	Identity	Self-contained	DCU 760	DCU 765/766	DCU 775/776	DCU 785/786
	Type of Buffer Storage	MOS	Delay line	Delay line	Delay line	Delay line
	Buffer Capacity Char	1920	Up to 5888 (in units of 1472)	1012–2024	1012–2024	2024
	Max Devices/ Controller	32 displays; slave printers	32 display units/ printers; 4 printers max	2 displays; 5 slave displays	2 displays; 5 slave displays	2 displays; 5 slave displays
	Multi-Drop	Yes	Optional	Yes	Yes	Yes
PERIPHERY	Printer	Foto-Print 30 Data Printing Terminal	TTY 33/35 RO	TermiNet 300; TTY 33/35	TermiNet 300; TTY 33/35	TermiNet 300; TTY 33/35
	Other	Paper tape read/punch; mag tape read/write	No	No	No	No
PURCHASE PRICE, $		3495	1010 (display); 1010 (keyboard); 14,000 (controller)	—	—	—
MONTHLY RENTAL, $		—	83/terminal (32-terminal configuration)	170 (2-terminal configuration)	170 (2-terminal configuration)	170 (2-terminal configuration)
COMMENTS		Acoustic coupler option ($320) requires TTY interface ($215); available as monitor without keyboard; keyboard interchangeable with Photo-Print 30; 8-level ASCII; asynchronous up to 2400 bps	DMU 761/Electronic Keyboard (EKB 761) replaces DTU 760 Display Terminal Unit; slave display/printer monitors available; half-/full-duplex; 8-level ASCII; synchronous at 2000/2400 bps or asynchronous up to 1200 bps	1012-char buffer option expands total controller capacity to 2024; asynchronous up to 1200 bps; 8-/16-key multipurpose keyboards opt; printed output at 10, 15, or 30 cps; compatible with Bell System Data Set 202C; options include page printer adapter, poll/select feature	1012-char buffer option expands total controller capacity to 2024; synchronous at 2000, 2400, 4800 bps; 8-/16-key multipurpose keyboards opt; printed output at 10, 15, or 30 cps; compatible with Bell System Data Sets 201A, 201B, 203; options include printer adapter, poll/select feature	Controllers available without displays; single station only; synchronous at 2000, 2400, 4800 bps; 8-/16-key multipurpose keyboards opt; printed output at 10, 15, or 30 cps; compatible with Bell System Data Sets 201A, 201B, 203; options include printer adapter, poll/select feature

ALPHANUMERIC DISPLAY TERMINALS

IDENTITY		Honeywell VIP 200 Series Visual Information Projection System			Honeywell VIP 2300 Series Visual Information Projection System	
REPORT NUMBER		6384			—	
DISPLAY UNIT	Identity	303/304/317	311	312	2323 (single station)	2317 (multistation)
	Viewing Area, in.	7.75 wide; 5.50 high	4.75 wide; 3.75 high	4.75 wide; 3.75 high	9 wide; 6.25 high	9 wide; 6.25 high
	Char/Line	8–64	8–42	8–42	80	37; 80
	Lines/Display	2–12	2–12	2–12	12	6; 24
	Char Set	39 (plus 15 optional)	14 (plus up to 12 optional)	40 (plus up to 12 optional)	62; 92	62
	Total Char/Display	32–768	32–384	32–384	960	222; 960
	Char Generation Technique	5 x 7 dot matrix	5 x 7 dot matrix	5 x 7 dot matrix	5 x 7 dot matrix	5 x 7 dot matrix
EDITING FACILITIES	Horizontal Tab	No			Yes	
	Line Erase	Yes			Yes	
	Line Insert	No			No	
	Partial Display Transmit	Yes			Yes	
	Split Screen	Optional			Yes	
	Other	Full cursor controls; display erase; CR/LF; char insert/delete			Char insert/delete; clear display; fixed format; variable erase	
CONTROL UNIT	Identity	323			Self-contained	2317 Controller
	Type of Buffer Storage	Delay line			Delay line	Delay line
	Buffer Capacity Char	768–6912			960	960
	Max Devices/ Controller	Up to 96 (max actual number depends on display size)			1	36
	Multi-Drop	Optional			—	—
PERIPHERY	Printer	TTY 33/35 KSR, RO			Teletype 33/35 KSR, RO	
	Other	TTY CX Paper Tape Reader/DRPE Paper Tape Punch			—	
PURCHASE PRICE, $		1840–3020 (display unit); 14,690–51,800 (controller/expansion units)			10,500 (CRT, keyboard, controller, interface)	4200 (keyboard/CRT); 16,800 (controller, interface)
MONTHLY RENTAL, $		50–92 (display unit); 293–1230 (controller/expansion units)			—	—
COMMENTS		Manufactured by Bunker-Ramo; various arrangements no. of lines/display and char/line available; all displays must have same arrangement; different models of display units/auxiliary devices can be intermixed on same control unit; half-duplex; 8-level ASCII; synchronous/asynchronous at 1200, 2000, 2400 bps over voiceband line			Manufactured by Bunker-Ramo; half-duplex at 1200/2400 bps; char/longitudinal parity checking	

ALPHANUMERIC DISPLAY TERMINALS

IDENTITY		Hendrix Electronics Series 5100 Display Terminal	Infoton Vista Basic Display Terminal	Infoton Vista Standard Display Terminal	Infoton Vista Plus Display Terminal	IBM 2260 Display Station
REPORT NUMBER		—	—	—	—	6456
DISPLAY UNIT	Identity	5200	Basic	Standard	Plus	2260
	Viewing Area, in.	10 wide; 12 high	10 wide; 7 high	10 wide; 7 high	10 wide; 7 high	9 wide; 4 high
	Char/Line	Adjustable right, left margins	32; 64	40; 80	40; 80	40; 80
	Lines/Display	32	10; 20	10; 20	10; 20	6; 12
	Char Set	128	64; 96 (optional)	64; 96 (optional)	64; 96 (optional)	64 (36 alphanumeric; 28 special)
	Total Char/Display	3072	1280	1600	1600	240; 480; 960
	Char Generation Technique	11 x 13 dot matrix	5 x 7 dot matrix	5 x 7 dot matrix	5 x 7 dot matrix	5 x 7 dot matrix
EDITING FACILITIES	Horizontal Tab	Yes	No	No	Yes	No
	Line Erase	Yes	No	Yes	Yes	No
	Line Insert	Yes	No	No	Yes	No
	Partial Display Transmit	Yes	No	No	Yes	Yes
	Split Screen	Yes	No	No	Yes	Yes
	Other	Full cursor controls; char insert/delete; protected format; blink; rolling; display, word, sent, par erases	Full cursor controls; blinking; page/roll mode; CR/LF; blink	Full cursor controls; CR/LF; blink; erase to end of line	Full cursor controls; protected format; CR/LF; blink	Ltd cursor control with basic unit; full range of controls opt; erase to end of line/ to end of screen
CONTROL UNIT	Identity	Self-contained	Self-contained	Self-contained	Self-contained	2848
	Type of Buffer Storage	MOS	MOS	MOS	MOS	Delay line
	Buffer Capacity Char	4096	1280	1600	1600	7680
	Max Devices/ Controller	53 displays, printers, I/O devices	1	1	1	24 displays; 1 printer
	Multi-Drop	Yes	No	No	Yes	No
PERIPHERY	Printer	IBM 735 Selectric Typewriter	TTY RO; NCR, TI thermal printers	TTY RO; NCR, TI thermal printers	TTY RO; NCR, TI thermal printers	IBM 1053 Model 4
	Other	Mag tape	Magnetic tape	Magnetic tape	Magnetic tape; badge reader	No
PURCHASE PRICE, $		7500	1995–2595	2195–2995	2845–3395	1570 (2260); 34,920 (2848)
MONTHLY RENTAL, $		—	—	—	—	30–50 (2260); 360–775 (2848)
COMMENTS		Separate TTY keyboard; IBM-compatible; limited graphics; keyboard lockout; auxiliary drum storage; operator-/ program-controlled send/receive; up to 2400 bps; asynchronous; ASCII; switch-selectable half-/full-duplex/ echoplex modes; multiplexing/polling units available; text editor	Plug-to-plug TTY replacement; half-/full-duplex; 7-level ASCII; asynchronous up to 8000 bps	Half-/full-duplex; 7-level ASCII; asynchronous up to 800 bps	Executes data compression in transmit mode; half-/full-duplex; 7-level ASCII; asynchronous up to 800 bps	Mdl 1 attaches to 2848 mdl 3, displays up to 960 char; Mdl 2 attaches to 2848 mdl 1, 2, 21, 22, displays up to 240 or 480 char; 1053 Printer requires adapter; opt numeric inset, nondestructive cursor; remote S/360 interface via 2701 DAU; asynch; 1200-/2400 bps; 7-level, 10-unit ASCII; half-duplex

ALPHANUMERIC DISPLAY TERMINALS

IDENTITY		IBM 2265 Display Station	ITT Data Equipment and Systems Alphascope 3100 Display			IRA Systems Irascope Display Terminal
REPORT NUMBER		6459	—			—
DISPLAY UNIT	Identity	2265	3100A			Irascope
	Viewing Area, in.	10.4 wide; 4.8 or 3.12 high	7.5 wide; 4.37 high			9.5 wide; 7 high
	Char/Line	64; 80	80			64
	Lines/Display	15; 12	16 (plus program line)	16 (plus program line)	16 (plus program line)	32
	Char Set	64 (36 alphanumerics; 28 special)	67	67	67	64
	Total Char/Display	960	1360	1360	1360	1200
	Char Generation Technique	Stroke	5 x 7 dot matrix	5 x 7 dot matrix	5 x 7 dot matrix	Monoscope
EDITING FACILITIES	Horizontal Tab	No	Yes			Yes
	Line Erase	No	Yes			Yes
	Line Insert	No	No			Yes
	Partial Display Transmit	Yes	Yes			Yes
	Split Screen	Yes	No			Yes
	Other	Full cursor controls, line addressing optional	Repeat feature; full cursor controls; protected field format; char insert/delete; end of screen/end of line erase			Char insert/delete; fixed format; full cursor controls
CONTROL UNIT	Identity	2845	3101 (stand-alone)	3104	3108	Self-contained
	Type of Buffer Storage	Delay line	Delay line	Delay line	Delay line	Magnetostrictive delay line
	Buffer Capacity Char	960	1360 per display	1360 per display	1360 per display	1200
	Max Devices/ Controller	1 display; 1 printer	1	4	8	1
	Multi-Drop	Yes (up to 16)	Yes	Yes	Yes	Yes
PERIPHERY	Printer	1053 Model 4	ITT 3010 Envoy Electronic Dataprinter			Yes
	Other	No	ITT 3100B Slave Monitor			—
PURCHASE PRICE, $		5430 (2265); 900 (keyboard); 8295 (2845)	6900 (stand-alone)	22,410 (1 controller per 4 displays)	28,290 (1 controller per 8 displays)	5995
MONTHLY RENTAL, $		170 (2265); 29 (keyboard); 170 (2845)	203	625	812	See Note
COMMENTS		Two format arrangements available; each display requires 1 2845; 1053 Printer requires adapter; S/360 remote interface via 2701 DAU; asynch; 7-level, 10-unit ASCII; 1200/ 2400 bps; half-duplex; up to 16 2265/2845 units can be multi-dropped on 1 line	TV mix feature permits entry of variable data; program keys access specific CPU program for examination of display data; plug-to-plug compatible with IBM 2260/2848; high-speed adapters available for direct computer connection; multiplexer feature connects up to 8 controllers in local/remote applications; serial interface at 1200/2400 bps; asynchronous; 7-level, 10-unit ASCII; half-duplex (4-wire); compatible with Bell System Data Sets 202D (1200)/201B (2400)			Char/line field adjustable from 40 to 80; opt parallel interface; serial data rate up to 1200 bps; modified 7-level ASCII

NOTE: No longer available |

ALPHANUMERIC DISPLAY TERMINALS

IDENTITY		Interactive Terminals Logiport/1 Portable CRT Computer Terminal (formerly Logitron)	Philco-Ford D-20 Alphanumeric Color Display Unit	Philco-Ford D-21 Alphanumeric Display Unit	Philco-Ford D-22 Alphanumeric Display Unit	Philco-Ford D-30 Rack-Mounted Graphic Display Unit
REPORT NUMBER		—	6650	6651	—	—
DISPLAY UNIT	Identity	Logiport/1	D-20	D-21	D-22	D-30
	Viewing Area, in.	7 wide; 5 high	10.5 wide; 7.4 high	10.7 wide; 9 high	Any std monitor	12 wide; 16 high
	Char/Line	32	32	64	32; 48; 64	72
	Lines/Display	16	24	24	12; 20; 24	48
	Char Set	64	60	62	50; 63; 63	59
	Total Char/Display	512	768	1536	384; 960; 1536	3456
	Char Generation Technique	5 x 7 dot matrix	5 x 7 dot matrix	5 x 7 dot matrix	5 x 12, 7 x 9, 5 x 7 dot matrix	5 x 7 dot matrix; 8 x 10 (special symbols)
EDITING FACILITIES	Horizontal Tab	No	No	No	No	No
	Line Erase	No	No	No	Yes	No
	Line Insert	No	No	No	No	No
	Partial Display Transmit	Yes	Yes	Yes	Yes	Yes
	Split Screen	No	No	Yes	No	No
	Other	Full cursor controls; rolling; home	Full cursor controls; display erase; char insert/delete	Full cursor controls; line addressing; fixed format; display erase; char insert/delete	Blink; scrolling	Full cursor controls; blink
CONTROL UNIT	Identity	Self-contained	Self-contained	Self-contained	Self-contained	Self-contained
	Type of Buffer Storage	MOS	Magnetostrictive delay lines	Magnetostrictive delay lines	Magnetic core	Magnetostrictive delay lines
	Buffer Capacity Char	512	768	1536	3072; 7680; 12,288	3456
	Max Devices/ Controller	1 display; 1 printer	1; 30 (using 8-bit parallel I/O)	1; 30 (8-bit parallel interface)	8	30 (8-bit parallel interface)
	Multi-Drop	No	No	Yes	Yes	No
PERIPHERY	Printer	Yes	No	TTY 37 RO	No	No
	Other	—	Keyboard	Keyboard	No	Track ball; light pen; keyboard
PURCHASE PRICE, $		2950	7200	9200	—	25,000-40,000 (display, computer interface, track ball)
MONTHLY RENTAL, $		150 (with coupler); 135 (without coupler)	See Note	See Note	—	—
COMMENTS		Direct TTY-compatible; portable; integral acoustic coupler; operates in local (edit)/on-line (conversation) modes; transmits/receives data over public telephone network up to 110/300 bps (switch-selectable); asynchronous; 8-level ASCII; half-/full-duplex	Displays color-coded data intermixed in red, green, blue, white; also available as electronics-only, rack-mounted unit without monitor; half-duplex; 8-level ASCII; synchronous, up to 110 bps NOTE: No longer available	Compatible with IBM 2260 message format; also available as electronics-only, rack-mounted unit without monitor; half-duplex; 8-level ASCII; asynchronous, up to 1200 bps NOTE: No longer available	Options include 8-bit parallel I/O and Bell System 202D1 Data-Phone Data Set interface; compatible with IBM 2260; available as rack-mount only or stand-alone keyboard/monitor; accommodates 1 edit channel, 7 display channels	Includes limited graphic capability; can display 1-line diagrams; special characters available; 8-bit parallel I/O std; color combinations include black and white/red, green, blue, white

ALPHANUMERIC DISPLAY TERMINALS

IDENTITY		RCA 8750 Modular Video Data System							RCA 8752-100 Video Data Terminal	RCA 8752-200 Video Data Terminal
REPORT NUMBER		6703							6702	–
DISPLAY UNIT	Identity	8750-10, -11, -12							8752-100	8752-200
	Viewing Area, in.	4.0w; 2.8h	8.0w; 1.4h	4.0w; 5.6h	8.0w; 2.8h	8.4w; 1.7h	8.0w; 5.6h	8.4w 3.4h	8.0 wide; 5.6 high	8 or 5.6 wide; 8.5 or 3.8 high
	Char/Line	27	5.4	27	54	80	54	80	54; 80; 81	50; 54; 81
	Lines/Display	10	5	20	10	6	20	12	20, 14	32; 22; 20; 14
	Char Set	96	96	96	96	96	96	96	64	96
	Total Char/Display	270	270	540	540	480	1080	960	1080, 1134	1080, 1134, 1600, or 1782; 2268 (dbl page)
	Char Generation Technique	Monoscope							Monoscope	Monoscope
EDITING FACILITIES	Horizontal Tab	Yes							Yes	Yes
	Line Erase	Yes							Yes	Yes
	Line Insert	Yes							Yes	Yes
	Partial Display Transmit	Yes							Yes	Yes
	Split Screen	Yes							Yes	Yes
	Other	Full cursor controls; fixed format; char insert/delete; display/ variable data erase							Full cursor controls; char insert/delete; fixed format; screen erase	Full cursor controls; char insert/delete; selective display suppress
CONTROL UNIT	Identity	8759 Video Data Controller (contains up to 6 video data generators)							Self-contained	Self-contained
	Type of Buffer Storage	Magnetostrictive delay lines contained in video data generator							Delay line	Delay line
	Buffer Capacity Char	2160 per Video Data Generator; up to 6 VDGs per video data controller							1280	1080; 1134; 1600; 1782
	Max Devices/ Controller	8 per 8756-11 VDG; 4 per 8756-21 VDG; 2 per 8756-31 VDG							Up to 8 displays can be multiplexed on 1 line via 8755 Switch; 1 printer per display	1 display; 1 printer
	Multi-Drop	Optional							Yes	Yes
PERIPHERY	Printer	8754 Data Display Copier							TTY 33/35 RO	Any printer up to 120 cps
	Other	No							No	3 electronic keyboards
PURCHASE PRICE, $		15,040–22,560 (VDC 8759); 7500–10,340 (VDG 8756); 2820 (VDT 8751)							6400 (8752); 5900 (8755)	8325
MONTHLY RENTAL, $		315–475 (VDC 8759); 160–220 (VDG 8756); 65 (VDT 8751)							110 (8752); 111 (8755)	190
COMMENTS		8750 system includes 8759 Controller, up to six 8756 Video Data Generators, and up to eight 8751 Video Data Terminals per VDG; display arrangement and number of terminals is function of 8756 VDG model employed; full-duplex; 8-level ASCII (parity); synchronous at 2400 bps; operates in nonpolling/multistation, poll/address environment; compatible with Spectra 70 Series computers; 299 arrays available							Replaces RCA 6050 Video Data Interrogator; each display contains own control logic; half-duplex; 8-level ASCII; asynchronous up to 1200 bps; 8755 Video Data Switch allows multiple 8752s	Dual memory provides two 1134-char pages (display/nondisplay); can operate on same line with Spectra 70 Modular Video Data System; synchronous asynchronous; operator/processor or unattended print operation; processor-controlled auto retransmit

ALPHANUMERIC DISPLAY TERMINALS

IDENTITY		Ann Arbor Terminals A^{2}T202 Video Display Terminal	Data Access Systems VST 2000 Video Data Terminal	Sanders 620 Stand-Alone Data Display Terminal	Sanders 720 Data Display Terminal	Sanders 920 Tabular Display System
REPORT NUMBER		—	—	6744	6745	—
DISPLAY UNIT	Identity	A^{2}T202	2000	6220	708	920-102
	Viewing Area, in.	9 (diagonal on rectangular tube)	10.5 wide; 8.0 high	7.5 wide; 9.5 high	7.5 wide; 9.5 high	15 wide; 11 high
	Char/Line	32 std; 64 opt	72	52	52	81
	Lines/Display	8 std; 16 opt	18	40	40	24
	Char Set	64 (ASCII)	64 (ASCII)	64	64	96+
	Total Char/Display	256 std; 512, 1024 opt	1296 (screen); 1296 (storage)	768; 2080 display positions	256, 512, or 1024; 2080 display positions	1944
	Char Generation Technique	5 x 7 dot matrix	5 x 7 dot matrix	Stroke	Stroke	Stroke
EDITING FACILITIES	Horizontal Tab	No	No	Optional	Yes	Yes
	Line Erase	No	Yes	No	Yes	Yes
	Line Insert	No	Optional	No	Yes	Yes
	Partial Display Transmit	No	Optional	Yes	Yes	Yes
	Split Screen	No	Optional	Yes	Yes	Optional
	Other	Full cursor controls; carriage return; clear screen; home; switch-selectable page/roll modes	Full cursor controls; page erase; page flip; home	Full cursor controls; vertical tab; CR/LF; fixed format	Vertical tab; full cursor controls; CR/LF; fixed format	Full cursor controls
CONTROL UNIT	Identity	Self-contained	Self-contained	Self-contained	701	Self-contained
	Type of Buffer Storage	MOS	Delay line	Delay line	Delay line	Delay line
	Buffer Capacity Char	1024	2592 (2 pages); opt to 7776 (6 pages)	781	1024; 2048; 3072	1944
	Max Devices/ Controller	1 display; up to 10 slave displays	1 display; 4 printers; multiple slave monitors	1 display unit; 1 printer	12 display units; 1 printer can share each display buffer segment	1
	Multi-Drop	Opt (128 addresses)	No	Yes	Yes	Yes
PERIPHERY	Printer	TTY 33	Any ASCII serial input printer	TTY 33/35 RO	TTY 33/35 RO	No
	Other	—	Magnetic tape cassette	No	TTY CX Paper Tape Reader; DRPE Paper Tape Punch	No
PURCHASE PRICE, $		695 (display driver); 110 (9-in. monitor)	2,870; 295 (modem); 395 (auto answer)	5400-9000	2550 (display); 475 (keyboard); 6000-9000 (controller)	25,000
MONTHLY RENTAL, $		—	179; 20 (modem); 22 (auto answer)	180-200	100 (display) 20 (keyboard); 238-339 (controller)	—
COMMENTS		TTY add-on; 7-level ASCII; async up to 1200 bps; TTY interface, composite video/remote drive std; options: TV output, various display formats, acoustic interface, auto LF on CR, video synchronous output; serial/parallel interface, RO input available	TTY-compatible; modified Video Systems VST Series; integral acoustic/hardwire modem; RS232B/TTY interface; selectable speeds up to 2400 bps; half-/full-duplex; 128-char ASCII generation/recognition; programmable cursor	Horizontal format also available with 32 64- to 84-char lines; up to 20 terminals can share 1 line; half-duplex; 8-level ASCII; asynchronous up to 100/1800 bps or synchronous at 2000/2400 bps	Various keyboard arrangements available; 9.5 x 7.5 display available with 32 64-char lines (2048 positions); half-/full-duplex; 8-level ASCII; synchronous at 2000/2400 bps or asynchronous up to 110, 1000, 1200, 1800 bps	Includes 16 function keys; status indicators

ALPHANUMERIC DISPLAY TERMINALS

IDENTITY		Sugarman Laboratories T6 Video Terminal	Time-Sharing Terminals TST Datapoint 3300 Data Terminal	TEC 540 Display Terminal	TEC 550 Display Terminal	TEC 560 Display Terminal
REPORT NUMBER		—	—	—	—	—
DISPLAY UNIT	Identity	T6 TV Monitor	3300	540	550	560
	Viewing Area, in.	10 wide; 6.5 high	11 wide; 8 high	9 wide; 6.5 high	9 wide; 6.5 high	9 wide; 6.5 high
	Char/Line	80	72	32	32	50
	Lines/Display	20	25	8	16	20
	Char Set	64	64	67	67	67
	Total Char/Display	1600	1800	256	512	1000
	Char Generation Technique	5 x 7 dot matrix	5 x 7 dot matrix	Stroke	Stroke	Stroke
EDITING FACILITIES	Horizontal Tab	Yes	Yes	Yes	Yes	Yes
	Line Erase	Yes	Yes	Yes	Yes	Yes
	Line Insert	No	—	Yes	Yes	Yes
	Partial Display Transmit	Yes (char/line/block)	—	Yes	Yes	Yes
	Split Screen	Yes	No	Yes	Yes	Yes
	Other	Full cursor controls; rolling; char insert/delete; blinking; fixed format; wraparound	Full cursor controls	Full cursor controls; char insert/delete; blink; rolling; wraparound; fixed format	Full cursor controls; char insert/delete; blink; rolling; wraparound; fixed format	Full cursor controls; char insert/delete; blink; rolling; wraparound; fixed format
CONTROL UNIT	Identity	Self-contained	Self-contained	Self-contained	Self-contained	Self-contained
	Type of Buffer Storage	MOS	MOS	Magnetic core	Magnetic core	Magnetic core
	Buffer Capacity Char	1600	1800	256	512	1000
	Max Devices/Controller	1 printer; unlimited slave displays	1 display; 1 printer; 1 magnetic tape unit	1 display; 1 printer	1 display; 1 printer	1 display; 1 printer
	Multi-Drop	No	—	—	—	—
PERIPHERY	Printer	TTY	Yes	TTY 33	TTY 33	TTY 33
	Other	Magnetic tape read/record unit	Magnetic tape cassette (optional)	—	—	—
PURCHASE PRICE, $		6000	4500	4450	4450	4700
MONTHLY RENTAL, $		—	195	See Note	—	—
COMMENTS		TTY-compatible; operates in Character (conversation)/Block (edit) Modes; can execute any control function via control escape char/text char; microprogrammed controller (ROM); data rates switch-selectable 110 to 2400 bps; asynchronous; half-/full-duplex; 8-level, 11-unit ASCII	TTY 33-compatible; 240-cps char/sec mag tape unit, optional; std TTY keyboard; auxiliary 10-key numeric keyboard; half-/full-duplex; 110 to 4800 bps data rate; 8-level ASCII; compatible with Bell System Data Sets 103/202	Up to 32 software-driven annunciator-type messages opt; page/segment modes; data rates up to 4800 bps (async, 7-level, 10-/11-unit ASCII) or 2000/2400/4800 bps (sync, 8-level ASCII); 8-bit parallel interface up to 38,500 cps	Up to 32 software-driven annunciator-type messages opt; page/segment modes; data rates up to 4800 bps (async, 7-level, 10-/11-unit ASCII) or 2000/2400/4800 bps (sync, 8-level ASCII)	Up to 32 software-driven annunciator-type messages opt; page/segment modes; data rates up to 4800 bps (async, 7-level, 10-/11-unit ASCII) or 2000/2400/4800 bps (sync, 8-level ASCII)
				NOTE: No longer available	NOTE: Not in production; available as returned	NOTE: Not in production; available as returned

ALPHANUMERIC DISPLAY TERMINALS

IDENTITY		TEC 555 Display Terminal	Ultronic Systems Videomaster 7000 Display Terminal	Univac Uniscope 100 Display Terminal	Univac Uniscope 300 Visual Communication Terminal	Video Systems VST 1000 Video Data Terminal
REPORT NUMBER		—	6851	6866	6864	—
DISPLAY UNIT	Identity	555	7212; 7223	100	300	1000
	Viewing Area, in.	9 wide; 6.5 high	9.5 wide; 7.5 high	10 wide; 5 high	10 wide; 5 high	10.5 wide; 8.0 high
	Char/Line	32	64; 80	80; 32; 64	64	36 (72 folded)
	Lines/Display	16	15; 12	6; 12; 16	8; 16	18 (2 pages)
	Char Set	67	64	64; 96 (optional)	56; 61; 96	64
	Total Char/Display	512	960	480; 512; 960; 1024	1024; 512	1296
	Char Generation Technique	Stroke	5 x 7 dot matrix	Stroke	Stroke	5 x 7 dot matrix
EDITING FACILITIES	Horizontal Tab	Yes	Yes	Yes	Yes	No
	Line Erase	Yes	Yes	No	Yes	Yes
	Line Insert	Yes	No	No	Yes	No
	Partial Display Transmit	Yes	Yes	Yes	Yes	Yes
	Split Screen	Yes	Optional	Yes	Yes	Yes
	Other	Full cursor controls; char insert/delete; blink; rolling; wrap-around; fixed format	Full cursor controls; char insert/delete; line addressing; display erase; keypunch mode; format mode	Char insert/delete; blink; display erase	Full cursor controls; char insert/delete; screen erase; blinking; scrolling	Full cursor controls; selective transmit; page erase; page flip; home
CONTROL UNIT	Identity	555 Controller	7016; 7018; 7026; 7028	Self-contained	Multistation Control Unit (MSCU)	Self-contained
	Type of Buffer Storage	Magnetic core	Magnetostrictive delay line	Magnetic core	Magnetic core	Delay line
	Buffer Capacity Char	8000	960	1024	8192; 16,384; 24,576	1296
	Max Devices/ Controller	16 displays; 16 printers	1 display; 1 printer	1 (single station); up to 31 via multiplexer (multistation)	24; 48	1 display; 4 printers; unlimited slave displays (std TV monitors)
	Multi-Drop	—	Yes	Yes	Yes	No
PERIPHERY	Printer	TTY 33	Yes (30 cps, nonimpact printer)	Univac Communications Output Printer	No	Any serial ASCII input printer
	Other	—	—	TTY 33/35	No	Serial incremental mag tape unit
PURCHASE PRICE, $ MONTHLY RENTAL, $		2900 (keyboard/display); 18,700 (controller) See Note	350 (display); 4200 (control); 430 (kybd) 15 (display); 117 (control); 24 (kybd)	2950-3450 60-70	15,140 (300S); 4130 (300M); 32,625 (MSCU) 410 (300S); 135 (300M); 850 (MSCU)	2990 75-129
COMMENTS		Up to 32 software-driven annunciator-type messages opt; page/segment modes; data rates up to 4800 bps (async, 7-level, 10-/11-unit ASCII) or 2000/2400/4800 bps (sync, 8-level ASCII); 8-bit parallel interface up to 38,500 cps NOTE: No longer available	Operates in half-duplex mode at 1200/2400 bps; 7-level ASCII; vertical/ longitudinal parity checking; IBM 2265/ 2845-compatible via 2701 DAU	Up to 31 units can operate on 1 line; half- (single station)/full-duplex (multistation); modified 7-level ASCII; synchronous at 2000 (switched)/2400 (leased) bps; compatible with Bell System Data Sets 201A (2000)/ 201B (2400); data rates up to 4800/9600 bps possible	300S Terminal contains 1 display station/1 integral controller; 122 overlays for 35 opt function keys automatically identified; half-duplex; modified 7-level ASCII; synchronous at 2000 (switched)/2400 (leased) bps; full-duplex opt; compatible with Bell System Data Sets 201A (2000)/201B (2400)	TTY-compatibility opt; data rates at 110, 150, 300 bps; folded logical 72-char line with 2-page screen/storage capacity (eighteen 36-char lines/page); TTY keyboard std; 8-level ASCII; asynchronous; half-/full-duplex; even parity checking; integral coupler

ALPHANUMERIC DISPLAY TERMINALS

IDENTITY		Wyle 600 Computerminal	Xerox Data Systems 7550/7555 Multipurpose Keyboard Display	Delta Data Systems Telterm I Computer Display Terminal	Delta Data Systems Telterm II Computer Display Terminal	Delta Data Systems Telterm III Computer Display Terminal
REPORT NUMBER		—	—	—	—	—
DISPLAY UNIT	Identity	600	7550/7555	I	II	III
	Viewing Area, in.	6 wide; 4.5 high	10 wide; 7 high	11 wide; 6 high	11 wide; 6 high	11 wide; 6 high
	Char/Line	32	86	80	80	80
	Lines/Display	8	32	27	27	27
	Char Set	64	96	64; 96 opt;	64; 96 (opt); line drawing opt	64; 96 (opt); line drawing opt
	Total Char/Display	1024	2048; 2752 char positions	2160	2160	2160
	Char Generation Technique	Stroke	Monoscope	7 x 9 dot matrix	7 x 9 dot matrix	7 x 9 dot matrix
EDITING FACILITIES	Horizontal Tab	Yes	No	Yes	Yes	Yes
	Line Erase	Yes	Yes	No	Yes	Yes
	Line Insert	Yes	Yes	No	Yes	Yes
	Partial Display Transmit	Yes	Yes	No	Yes	Yes
	Split Screen	Yes	No	Yes	Yes	Yes
	Other	Char insert/delete; erase display	Char insert/delete; erase display; scrolling	Blink; format; paging; fully addressable cursor	Edit; format; blink; margin set; paging; fully addressable cursor	Edit; format; blink; margin set; paging; fully addressable cursor
CONTROL UNIT	Identity	Self-contained	Self-contained	Self-contained	Self-contained	Self-contained
	Type of Buffer Storage	Magnetic core	Magnetostrictive delay line	MOS	MOS	MOS
	Buffer Capacity Char	1024	2285	3000	3000	3000
	Max Devices/ Controller	1 display; 1 printer	1	1 display; remote monitors; 1 printer; 1 cassette; 1 light pen	1 display; remote monitors; 1 printer; 1 cassette; 1 light pen	1 display; remote monitors; 1 printer; 1 cassette; 1 light pen
	Multi-Drop	Yes	No	Optional	Optional	Optional
PERIPHERY	Printer	TTY 33/35	TTY 35/37 RO	10, 15, 165 cps	10, 15, 165 cps	10, 15, 165 cps
	Other	Magnetic tape cassette recorder	7553 Hard Copy Output (optional)	Cassette tape; light pen	Cassette tape; light pen	Cassette tape; light pen
PURCHASE PRICE, $		OEM only	10,000 (7550); 12,500 (7555)	3000	3500	4500
MONTHLY RENTAL, $		—	265 (7550); 330 (7555)	80	90	110
COMMENTS		Operates in full-duplex; asynchronous up to 1200 bps; 8-level ASCII; up to 23 units can be multidropped on 1 line; vertical/longitudinal parity checking; compatible with Bell System Data Set 202D; addressable memory; polled transmission; parallel interface opt; serial rates up to 2400/4800 bps available	Compatible with TTY 37; operates in full-duplex mode at 150 bps (Model 7750)/optionally at 1800 bps (Model 7555); operates in char/echo or message mode modes; half-duplex optional; compatible with Bell System Data Set 202	TTY replacement; numeric pad; storage in excess of display data via paging; integral coupler; switch-selectable line rates, parity; audible alarm; std key layout; options: direct memory access, high-speed buffers	Block mode transmission; TTY replacement; numeric pad; storage in excess of display data via paging; integral coupler; switch-selectable line rates, parity; audible alarm; std key layout; options: direct memory access, high-speed buffers	IBM 2265 replacement; block mode transmission; numeric pad; storage in excess of display data via paging; integral coupler; switch-selectable line rates, parity; audible alarm; std key layout; options: direct memory access, high-speed buffers

ALPHANUMERIC DISPLAY TERMINALS

IDENTITY		American Terminal Systems Series 765 Video Communication Terminal	American Terminal Systems Series 766 Video Communication Terminal	American Terminal Systems Series 767 Video Communication Terminal	Applied Digital Data Systems Envoy 600 Portable CRT Terminal	Applied Digital Data Systems Envoy 640 Portable CRT Terminal
REPORT NUMBER		–	–	–	–	–
DISPLAY UNIT	Identity	765–10/–20/–30/–40	766–10/–20/–30/–40	767–10/–20/–30/–40	600	640
	Viewing Area, in.	9 (tube diagonal)	9 (tube diagonal)	12 (tube diagonal)	3.5 wide; 2.25 high	3.5 wide; 2.25 high
	Char/Line	32	64	80	32	64
	Lines/Display	4; 8; 15; 16; 30	4; 8; 16; 30	4; 8; 16; 30	16	16
	Char Set	64; 96 (optional)	64; 96 (optional)	64; 96 (optional)	64	64
	Total Char/Display	128; 256; 480; 512; 960	256; 512; 1024; 1920	320; 640; 1280; 2400	256	1024
	Char Generation Technique	9 x 14 filled–stroke matrix	9 x 14 filled–stroke matrix	9 x 14 filled–stroke matrix	5 x 7 dot matrix	5 x 7 dot matrix
EDITING FACILITIES	Horizontal Tab	Yes	Yes	Yes	Yes (fixed stop at each eighth position)	Yes (fixed stop at each eighth position)
	Line Erase	Optional	Optional	Optional	No	Yes
	Line Insert	Optional	Optional	Optional	No	No
	Partial Display Transmit	Optional	Optional	Optional	No	Yes
	Split Screen	Optional	Optional	Optional	No	Yes
	Other	Char/page erase; CR/LF; scroll; full cursor controls	Char/page erase; CR/LF; scroll; full cursor controls	Char/page erase; CR/LF; scroll; full cursor controls	Full cursor controls; CR; home; screen erase	Full cursor controls; CR; home; screen erase; char insert/delete; fixed format; blink
CONTROL UNIT	Identity	Self–contained	Self–contained	Self–contained	Self–contained	Self–contained
	Type of Buffer Storage	MOS	MOS	MOS	MOS semiconductor	MOS semiconductor
	Buffer Capacity Char	128; 256; 480; 512; 960	256; 512; 1024; 1920	320; 640; 1280; 2400	256	1024
	Max Devices/ Controller	4, 8, 12, or 16 (15 if printer interface required) displays per polling adapter	4, 8, 12, or 16 (15 if printer interface required) displays per polling adapter	4, 8, 12, or 16 (15 if printer interface required) displays per polling adapter	1 display	1 display
	Multi–Drop	Optional	Optional	Optional	No	No
PERIPHERY	Printer	ADS Series 715 Printer	ADS Series 715 Printer	ADS Series 715 Printer	No	No
	Other	ADS Mag Tape Cassette	ADS Mag Tape Cassette	ADS Mag Tape Cassette	–	–
PURCHASE PRICE, $		1,900–2,400	2,500–3,500	2,700–3,900	3,195	3,895
MONTHLY RENTAL, $		125 max (see Note)	175 max (see Note)	200 max (see Note)	See Note	–
COMMENTS		IBM 2845/2265 replacement via 360/2701; half–/full–duplex; sync/async; serial up to 75, 110, 150, 300, 600, 1200, 2400, 4800, 9600 bps; 15,000 cps parallel NOTE: No longer available	IBM 2845/2265 replacement via 360/2701; half–/full–duplex; sync/async; serial up to 75, 110, 150, 300, 600, 1,200, 2,400, 4,800, 9,600 bps; 15,000 cps parallel NOTE: No longer available	IBM 2845/2265 replacement via 360/2701; half–/full–duplex; sync/async; serial up to 75, 110, 150, 300, 600, 1,200, 2,400, 4,800, 9,600 bps; 15,00 cps parallel NOTE: No longer available	Portable; built–in acoustic coupler; TTY compatible; data compression; local edit in conversation mode; async; ASCII; half–duplex; 110/300 bps (selectable) NOTE: No longer available	Portable; built–in acoustic coupler; TTY compatible; data compression; local edit in conversation mode; async; ASCII; half–duplex; 110, 300 bps (selectable); limited graphics

ALPHANUMERIC DISPLAY TERMINALS

IDENTITY		Applied Digital Data Systems Consul 800 Stand-Alone CRT Terminal	Applied Digital Data Systems Consul 840 Stand-Alone CRT Terminal	Applied Digital Data Systems Consul 880 Stand-Alone CRT Terminal	Hazeltine 1760 Desk-Top Video Display Terminal	Hazeltine 2000 Desk-Top Video Display Terminal
REPORT NUMBER		—	—	—	—	—
DISPLAY UNIT	Identity	800	840	880	1760	2000
	Viewing Area, in.	6 wide; 4 high	12 (tube diagonal)	12 (tube diagonal)	6.48 wide; 6.48 high	10 wide; 5.5 high
	Char/Line	32	64	80	55	74
	Lines/Display	16	16	20-24	32	27
	Char Set	64	64	64	64	64
	Total Char/Display	256	1024	1,920	1,760	1,998
	Char Generation Technique	5 x 7 dot matrix	5 x 7 dot matrix	5 x 7 dot matrix	5 x 7 dot matrix	5 x 7 dot matrix
EDITING FACILITIES	Horizontal Tab	Yes (fixed stop at each eighth position)	Yes (fixed stop at each eighth position)	Yes (fixed stop at each eighth position)	Yes (also vertical/diagonal)	Yes
	Line Erase	No	Yes	Yes	Yes	Yes
	Line Insert	No	No	No	Yes	Yes
	Partial Display Transmit	No	Yes	Yes	Yes	Yes
	Split Screen	No	Yes	Yes	Yes	Yes
	Other	Full cursor controls; CR; home; screen erase	Full cursor controls; CR; home; screen erase; char insert/delete; fixed format; blink	Full cursor controls; CR; home; screen erase; char insert/delete; fixed format; blink; limited graphics	Full cursor controls; char insert/delete; fixed format; variable roll-up	Full cursor controls; char insert/delete; fixed format; variable roll-up
CONTROL UNIT	Identity	Self-contained	Self-contained	Self-contained	Self-contained	Self-contained
	Type of Buffer Storage	MOS semiconductor	MOS semiconductor	MOS semiconductor	Magnetic core	Magnetic core
	Buffer Capacity Char	256	1024	1,920	2,048	2,048
	Max Devices/ Controller	1 display, printer, cassette unit	1 display, printer, cassette unit; slave monitors	1 display, printer, cassette unit; slave monitors	1 display, printer/ cassette; slave monitors	1 display, printer/ cassette; slave monitors
	Multi-Drop	No	No	No	Yes	No
PERIPHERY	Printer	Yes	Yes	Yes	Yes	Yes
	Other	Mag tape cassettes	Mag tape cassettes	Mag tape cassettes	Mag tape cassette; remote monitors	Mag tape cassette; remote monitors
PURCHASE PRICE, $		2,995	2,650	2,990	2,995 (1-24 units)	2,995 (1-24 units)
MONTHLY RENTAL, $		See Note	—	150	108 See Note	88 (plus $20 maintenance)
COMMENTS		Desktop version of ADDS Envoy 600; hard-copy interface; built-in acoustic/hardwired modem (Bell System 103 equivalent); TTY compatible; data compression; local edit in conversation mode; async; ASCII; half-duplex; 110/300 bps (selectable) NOTE: No longer available	Desktop version of ADDS Envoy 640; hard-copy interface; built-in acoustic/hardwired modem (Bell System 103 equivalent); TTY compatible; data compression; local edit in conversation mode; async; ASCII; half-duplex; 110, 300, 1200, 1800, 2400 bps (selectable)	Desktop version of ADDS Envoy 640 with increased char capacity; hard copy interface; built-in acoustic/hard-wired modem (Bell System 103 equivalent) TTY compatible; data compression; local edit in conversation mode; async; ASCII; half-duplex; 110, 300, 1200, 1800, 2400 bps (selectable)	Asynchronous; serial rates to 110, 150, 300, 600, 1,200 bps (switch-able); adjustable to 9,600 bps plus; half-duplex; solid state removable keyboard; 8-level ASCII; 32 control codes; modular CRT can be remoted; computer addressable cursor NOTE: No longer available	TTY compatible; asynchronous; serial rates to 110, 150, 300, 600, 1,200 bps (switchable) adjustable to 9,600 bps plus; half-/full-duplex solid state TTY removable keyboard; 8-level ASCII; 32 control codes; computer addressable cursor; keyboard functions program controllable; batch mode

ALPHANUMERIC DISPLAY TERMINALS

		Honeywell 316/516-7210 Alphanumeric Display Terminal	Imlac PDS-1 Programmable Display System	Incoterm SPD 10/20 Stored Program Display (formerly International Computer Terminals)	Mark Computer Systems DD-70 Data Display Terminal	
IDENTITY						
REPORT NUMBER		—	—	—	—	
DISPLAY UNIT	Identity	7215; 7216	PDS-1	SPD 10/20	DD-70M	DD-70L
	Viewing Area, in.	10.0 wide; 5.0 high	8.5 wide; 7.5 high	9.5 wide; 7.0 high	7.0 wide; 4.5 high	8.3 wide; 6.0 high
	Char/Line	64	Up to 128	64	32	32/64
	Lines/Display	16	Up to 64	1-30 (programmable)	8	16/32
	Char Set	64	As programmed; see Comments	64	64	64
	Total Char/Display	1,024	1,200 (40 frames/sec)	1,920	256	1,024
	Char Generation Technique	Closed stroke	Vector stroke	7 x 10 dot matrix	5 x 7 dot matrix	5 x 7 dot matrix
EDITING FACILITIES	Horizontal Tab	Yes	Yes	Yes (any combination)	Yes	Yes
	Line Erase	Yes	Yes	Yes	Repeat char erase	Repeat char erase
	Line Insert	Yes	Yes	Yes	Repeat char insert	Repeat char insert
	Partial Display Transmit	Yes	Yes	Yes (including fields)	Yes	Yes
	Split Screen	No	Yes	Yes (horizontally/vertically)	No	No
	Other	Full cursor controls; data protect/tab; char insert/delete	Full cursor controls; keyboard graphics editing	Full cursor controls; programmed for application-oriented functions	Full cursor controls; char insert/delete	Full cursor controls; char insert/delete
CONTROL UNIT	Identity	Self-contained	PDS-1	Self-contained	Self-contained	Self-contained
	Type of Buffer Storage	Magnetic core	Magnetic core	Magnetic core	MSI	MSI
	Buffer Capacity Char	1,048	1,440	1,920	256	1,024
	Max Devices/Controller	1	No hardware limit; software limited by function of application	1 display, printer	1 display, printer	1 display, printer
	Multi-Drop	—	Optional	Yes	—	—
PERIPHERY	Printer	Optional (via 7217 interface)	Optional	Yes (30 cps, 132-char line)	TTY ASR 33; Inktronic 2101	TTY ASR 33; Inktronic 2101
	Other	7217 interface accommodates badge reader/other devices	Paper/mag tape; discs (opt)	Tape cassette; TTY; microfilm viewer	—	—
PURCHASE PRICE, $		4,950 (display); 500 (serial interface); 300 (keyboard)	8,845 (basic)	5,300 (51-unit quantity)	3,500	4,400
MONTHLY RENTAL, $		124 (display); 13 (serial interface); 8 (keyboard)	300	96 (51-unit quantity, 5-yr lease)	80.50-107.75 (depending on options)	101.20-118.45 (depending on options)
COMMENTS		Displays operate with any Series 16 communication options (asynchronous/synchronous, up to 9,600 bps); can be driven from multi-line controllers/in polled environment	91 alphanumeric, 36 graphic char generation subroutines in std text/graphics editing program; any software-defined char/symbols can be programmed/controlled by any key; includes 16-bit processor; 4K core; opt horizontal orientation; serial rates to 9,600 bps; any 5- to 8-level code	Contains small programmable 2,048-word core memory computer; multiplexor available to connect/address 16 displays on 1 line; 75-4,800 bps serial rate; sync/async; ASCII; half-/full-duplex; 16 special function keys	Various arrangements include horizontal/vertical CRT, hardwired/keyboard-variable format, auxiliary files, insert/delete edit, blink/intensity called-up char, attached/separate keyboard, internal 2-wire modem, RS232B/TTY interface; 5,000-cps display output; 19 max control keys; parity checking; recognize reverse error code; 1,000-50,000 bps line speed (voice-/broadband); modified ASCII; 2-wire half-duplex (voice)/simplex (broad); asynchronous	

ALPHANUMERIC DISPLAY TERMINALS

IDENTITY		Photophysics Series 45 Model 20 CRT Data Terminal	Spiras Systems Irascope Series UL	Spiras Systems Irascope Series UL	Spiras Systems Irascope Series TY	Spiras Systems Irascope Series TY
REPORT NUMBER		—	—	—	—	—
DISPLAY UNIT	Identity	45 std TV monitor	DBEC-A/N-UL	DBEC-A/N-UL-360	DBEC-A/N-TY	DBEC-A/N-TY-360
	Viewing Area, in.	8.5 wide; 6.25 high	9.5 wide; 7 high	9.5 wide; 7 high	9.5 wide; 7 high	9.5 wide; 7 high
	Char/Line	40	64	64	64	64
	Lines/Display	25	32	32	32	32
	Char Set	96	64	64	64	64
	Total Char/Display	1,000	1,028 (less 6 char/line)	1,028 (less 6 char/line)	1,028 (less 5 char/line)	1,028 (less 5 char/line)
	Char Generation Technique	5 x 7 dot matrix	Monoscope	Monoscope	Monoscope	Monoscope
EDITING FACILITIES	Horizontal Tab	Yes	Yes	Yes	Yes	Yes
	Line Erase	Yes	Yes	Yes	Yes	Yes
	Line Insert	Yes	Yes	Yes	Yes	Yes
	Partial Display Transmit	Yes	Yes	Yes	Yes	Yes
	Split Screen	Yes	Yes	Yes	Yes	Yes
	Other	Full cursor controls; CR/LF; clear page; char insert/delete; double space; char blink; line recall, clear; repeat; frame roll	Full cursor controls; char insert/delete; format protect	Full cursor controls; char insert/delete; format protect	Full cursor controls; char insert/delete; format protect; page roll	Full cursor controls; char insert/delete; format protect; page roll
CONTROL UNIT	Identity	Self-contained	Self-contained	Self-contained	Self-contained	Self-contained
	Type of Buffer Storage	MOS semiconductor	Magnetostrictive delay line	Magnetostrictive delay line	Magnetostrictive delay line	Magnetostrictive delay line
	Buffer Capacity Char	1040	1028	1028	1028	1028
	Max Devices/ Controller	1 display with integral copier	1 display (plus peripherals)	1 display (plus peripherals)	1 display (plus peripherals)	1 display (plus peripherals)
	Multi-Drop	Optional	Yes	Yes	Yes	Yes
PERIPHERY	Printer	Integral Quantafax Copier	Yes	Yes	Yes	Yes
	Other	Magnetic tape cassette systems	Magnetic tape, paper tape, cassette	Magnetic tape, paper tape, cassette	Magnetic tape, paper tape, cassette	Magnetic tape, paper tape, cassette
PURCHASE PRICE, $		9,900	5,745	7,245	4,995	6,495
MONTHLY RENTAL, $		340	See Note	See Note	See Note	See Note
COMMENTS		TTY-compatible; 110, 150, 300, 600, 1200 bps; synch/asynch; ASCII; integral electrophotographic printer for 5 x 5-in. hard copy of displayed data in 5 sec (add'l copies at 2-sec intervals) on keyboard-/software command; up to 16 units per modem via Modem I/O Expander	Char/line field adjustable from 40 to 80; half-duplex; opt parallel interface; serial data rate up to 1,200 bps; modified 7-level ASCII \n\nNOTE: No longer available	Char/line field adjustable from 40 to 80; half-duplex opt parallel interface; serial data rate up to 1,200 bps; modified 7-level ASCII; IBM 360 remote capability via 2701 Data Adapter Unit \n\nNOTE: No longer available	Max 80 char/line; double-key roll-over/lockout; page roll starts at 833rd char/33rd line; Message mode permits editing (block transfer from cursor to EOM); TTY-compatible (char-key transfer); ASCII; half-duplex \n\nNOTE: No longer available	Max 80 char/line; double-key roll-over/lockout; Message mode permits editing (block transfer); TTY-compatible (char-key transfer); ASCII; half-duplex; IBM 360 remote capability via 2701 \n\nNOTE: No longer available

ALPHANUMERIC DISPLAY TERMINALS

IDENTITY		Spiras Systems Irascope Series TY	Spiras Systems Irascope Series TY	TEC Series 400 Model 430 Data-Screen Terminal	TEC Series 400 Model 440 Data-Screen Terminal	TEC Series 400 Model 450 Data-Screen Terminal
REPORT NUMBER		—	—	—	—	—
DISPLAY UNIT	Identity	DBC-A/N-TY	DBC-A/N-TY-360	430	440	450
	Viewing Area, in.	9.5 wide; 7 high	9.5 wide; 7 high	9 wide; 6.5 high	9 wide; 6.5 high	9 wide; 6.5 high
	Char/Line	64	64	32	40	50
	Lines/Display	32	32	Up to 24	Up to 24	Up to 24
	Char Set	64	64	64	64	64
	Total Char/Display	1,028 (less 5 char/line)	1,028 (less 5 char/line)	768	900	1,200
	Char Generation Technique	Monoscope	Monoscope	5 x 7 dot matrix	5 x 7 dot matrix	5 x 7 dot matrix
EDITING FACILITIES	Horizontal Tab	No	No	Yes	Yes	Yes
	Line Erase	No	No	Yes	Yes	Yes
	Line Insert	No	No	Yes	Yes	Yes
	Partial Display Transmit	No	No	Yes	Yes	Yes
	Split Screen	No	No	Yes	Yes	Yes
	Other	Without Message/Edit logic assembly	Without Message/Edit logic assembly	Full cursor controls; char insert/delete; blink; protected format; roll-up/-down	Full cursor controls; char insert/delete; blink; protected format; roll-up/-down	Full cursor controls; char insert/delete; blink; protected format; roll-up/-down
CONTROL UNIT	Identity	Self-contained	Self-contained	410	410	410
	Type of Buffer Storage	Magnetostrictive delay line	Magnetostrictive delay line	MOS	MOS	MOS
	Buffer Capacity Char	1,028	1,028	As required	As required	As required
	Max Devices/ Controller	1 display (plus peripherals)	1 display (plus peripherals)	31	31	31
	Multi-Drop	Yes	Yes	—	—	—
PERIPHERY	Printer	Yes	Yes	TTY	TTY	TTY
	Other	Magnetic tape, paper tape, cassette	Magnetic tape, paper tape, cassette	—	—	—
PURCHASE PRICE, $		4,495	5,995	1,486 (basic)	1,486 (basic)	1,769 (basic)
MONTHLY RENTAL, $		See Note	See Note	See Note	See Note	See Note
COMMENTS		Max 80 char/line; double-key roll-over/ lockout; char-key transfer only; TTY-compatible; ASCII; half-duplex; opt Model E-1 Message/Edit logic assembly costs $650, converts unit to Model DBEC-A/N-TY NOTE: No longer available	Max 80 char/line; double-key roll-over/ lockout; char-key transfer only; TTY-compatible; ASCII; half-duplex; IBM 360 remote capability via 2701; CC-1 Cluster Controller polls/ multiplexes up to 31 displays (groups of 8), 1 printer NOTE: No longer available	Options include I/O adapters (sync/async/ parallel/TTY), editing, printer adapter, 96-char set, edit/ nonedit keyboards; stand-alone/multistation models available; char/line addressing; modified ASCII; 75-9,600 bps serial; half-/full-duplex NOTE: No longer available	Options include I/O adapters (sync/async/ parallel/TTY), editing, printer adapter, 96-char set, edit/ nonedit keyboards; stand-alone/multistation models available; char/line addressing; modified ASCII; 75-9,600 bps serial; half-/full-duplex NOTE: No longer available	Options include I/O adapters (sync/async/ parallel/TTY), editing, printer adapter, 96-char set, edit/ nonedit keyboards; stand-alone/multistation models available; char/line addressing; modified ASCII; 75-9,600 bps serial; half-/full-duplex NOTE: No longer available

ALPHANUMERIC DISPLAY TERMINALS

IDENTITY		TEC Series 400 Model 460 Data-Screen Terminal	Video Systems VST 1200 Video Data Terminal	Video Systems VST 2000 Video Data Terminal	Video Systems VST 5000 Video Data Terminal	Video Systems VST 7000 Video Data Terminal
REPORT NUMBER		—	—	—	—	—
DISPLAY UNIT	Identity	460	1200	2000	5000	7000
	Viewing Area, in.	9 wide; 6.5 high	10.5 wide; 8.0 high	10.5 wide; 8.0 high	10.5 wide; 8.0 high	10.5 wide; 8.0 high
	Char/Line	64	72	72	72	72
	Lines/Display	Up to 24	18 (1 page)	18 (2 pages)	18 (4 pages)	18 (6 pages)
	Char Set	64	64; upper-/lowercase optional	64; upper-/lowercase optional	64; upper-/lowercase optional	64; upper-/lowercase optional
	Total Char/Display	1,536	1,296	2,592	5,184	7,776
	Char Generation Technique	7 x 7 dot matrix	5 x 7 dot matrix	5 x 7 dot matrix	5 x 7 dot matrix	5 x 7 dot matrix
EDITING FACILITIES	Horizontal Tab	Yes	No	No	No	No
	Line Erase	Yes	Yes	Yes	Yes	Yes
	Line Insert	Yes	No	No	No	No
	Partial Display Transmit	Yes	Yes	Yes	Yes	Yes
	Split Screen	Yes	Yes	Yes	Yes	Yes
	Other	Full cursor controls; char insert/delete; blink; protected format; roll-up/-down	Full cursor controls; selective transmit; page erase; page flip; home; protected format optional	Full cursor controls; selective transmit; page erase; page flip; home; protected format optional	Full cursor controls; selective transmit; page erase; page flip; home; protected format optional	Full cursor controls; selective transmit; page erase; page flip; home; protected format optional
CONTROL UNIT	Identity	410	Self-contained	Self-contained	Self-contained	Self-contained
	Type of Buffer Storage	MOS	Delay line	Delay line	Delay line	Delay line
	Buffer Capacity Char	As required	1,296	2,592	5,184	7,776
	Max Devices/ Controller	31	4 printers; multiple monitors	4 printers; multiple monitors	4 printers; multiple monitors	4 printers; multiple monitors
	Multi-Drop	—	No	No	No	No
PERIPHERY	Printer	TTY	Any ASCII serial input printer	Any ASCII serial input printer	Any ASCII serial input printer	Any ASCII serial input printer
	Other	—	Any serial incremental mag tape unit	Any serial incremental mag tape unit	Any serial incremental mag tape unit	Any serial incremental mag tape unit
PURCHASE PRICE, $		2,051 (basic)	2,670	2,870	3,990	4,990
MONTHLY RENTAL, $		See Note	77–145	79–155	119–185	149–215
COMMENTS		Options include I/O adapters (sync/async/ parallel/TTY), editing printer adapter, 96– char set, edit/nonedit keyboards; stand– alone/multistation models available; char/line addressing; modified ASCII; 75–9,600 bps serial; half–/full–duplex NOTE: No longer available	TTY-compatible (opt); built-in coupler (hard– wired); any ASCII coding of function switches for remote positioning of cursor; parity checking; full–/ half-duplex; up to 1,200 bps; 2,400 opt; TV-compatible	TTY-compatible (opt); built-in coupler (hard– wired); any ASCII coding of function switches for remote positioning of cursor; parity checking; full–/ half-duplex; up to 1,200 bps; 2,400 opt; TV-compatible	TTY-compatible (opt); built-in coupler (hard– wired); any ASCII coding of function switches for remote positioning of cursor; parity checking; full–/ half-duplex; up to 1,200 bps; 2,400 opt; TV-compatible	TTY-compatible (opt); built-in coupler (hard– wired); any ASCII coding of function switches for remote positioning of cursor; parity checking; full–/ half-duplex; up to 1,200 bps; 2,400 opt; TV-compatible

ALPHANUMERIC DISPLAY TERMINALS

IDENTITY		Beehive Medical Electronics Model I CRT Terminal	Beehive Medical Electronics Model II CRT Terminal	Beehive Medical Electronics Model III CRT Terminal	Beehive Medical Electronics Model IV CRT Terminal	Bunker-Ramo Series 2200 Data Display System (Multistation)
REPORT NUMBER		—	—	—	—	6061
DISPLAY UNIT	Identity	I	II	III	IV	2206/17
	Viewing Area, in.	8.8 wide; 5.9 high	8.8 wide; 5.9 high	8.8 wide; 5.9 high	8.8 wide; 5.9 high	4.75 wide; 3.75 high
	Char/Line	40; 80 (optional)	40; 80 (optional)	40; 80 (optional)	40; 80 (optional)	37; 80
	Lines/Display	20	20	20	20	6; 12; 24
	Char Set	64 (ASCII)	64 (ASCII)	64 (ASCII)	64 (ASCII)	62
	Total Char/Display	800; 1600 (optional)	800; 1600 (optional)	800; 1600 (optional)	800; 1600 (optional)	222; 444; 888; 960
	Char Generation Technique	5 x 7 dot matrix	5 x 7 dot matrix	5 x 7 dot matrix	5 x 7 dot matrix	5 x 7 dot matrix
EDITING FACILITIES	Horizontal Tab	No	Yes	Yes	Opt	Yes
	Line Erase	No	Yes	Yes	Opt	Yes
	Line Insert	No	No	Yes	No	No
	Partial Display Transmit	No	Yes	Yes	Yes	Yes
	Split Screen	No	No	Yes	Yes	Yes
	Other	Full cursor controls; home; clear; scroll	Full cursor controls; erase screen; home; clear; scroll	Char insert/delete; page insert/delete; erase screen; scroll	Full cursor controls; erase to end of line/ screen; erase display; wraparound; line addressing; variable data transmit via SOM/EOM symbols	Full cursor controls; char erase/insert; blink
CONTROL UNIT	Identity	Self-contained	Self-contained	Self-contained	Self-contained	2222
	Type of Buffer Storage	MOS	MOS	MOS	MOS	Delay line (9)
	Buffer Capacity Char	800; 1600 (optional)	800; 1600 (optional)	800; 1600 (optional)	800; 1600 (optional)	9288 (multistation)
	Max Devices/ Controller	1 display (plus peripherals)	1 display (plus peripherals)	1 display (plus peripherals)	1 display (plus peripherals)	36 (222-char displays)
	Multi-Drop	No	No	No	No	Yes
PERIPHERY	Printer	No	Serial ASCII printer	Serial ASCII printer	IBM 1053-M4; serial ASCII printer	TTY 33/35 KSR, ASR, RO
	Other	Magnetic tape cassette	Magnetic tape cassette	Magnetic tape cassette	Numeric Keyboard	TTY CX Paper Tape Reader/DRPE Paper Tape Punch
PURCHASE PRICE, $		2495	2767	2987	3495	7965 (2222); 1825 (2206/17)
MONTHLY RENTAL, $		—	—	—	—	231 (2222); 66 (2206/17)
COMMENTS		Plug-in opt for 80-char line; parallel I/O opt; parity checking; local mode; async up to 2400 bps; half-/full-duplex; model changes/ options field-installed; 5-way cursor control; 64-char ASCII subset; upper-/lowercase, multilevel blink opt	Interactive/block send (page-transmit) std; printer/cassette opt; plug-in opt for 80-char line; parity checking; local mode; async up to 2400 bps; half-/full-duplex; 5-way cursor control; 64-char ASCII subset; model changes/ options field-installed; upper-/lowercase, multilevel blink opt	Interactive/block send (page-transmit) std; printer/cassette opt; plug-in opt for 80-char line; parity checking; local mode; async up to 2400 bps; half-/full-duplex; 5-way cursor control; 64-char ASCII subset; model changes/ options field-installed; upper-/lowercase, multilevel blink opt	Direct hardware/soft-ware replacement for IBM 2265; requires IBM 2701/Type III adapter; 80-char line opt; LRC/VRC parity checking; selectable 1200 (async)/2400 (sync) bps; half-duplex; 8-level, 10-unit ASCII; Bell System 202D1/ 201B1 (C2)-compatible	Various display format combinations available; char/longitudinal parity checking; half-duplex at 600-2400 bps (voiceband line); parallel transfer rate up to 55,000 cps

ALPHANUMERIC DISPLAY TERMINALS

IDENTITY		Communitype Series 1000 Video Data Display Terminal		Computer Optics CO: 75 Display System	Data 100 73-1 Interactive Terminal	Data 100 73-2 Interactive Terminal
REPORT NUMBER		—		—	—	—
DISPLAY UNIT	Identity	1000 (std monitor/TV receiver)	1023 (std monitor/TV receiver)	CO:75	73-1	73-2
	Viewing Area, in.	12 (tube diagonal)	12 (tube diagonal)	9.5 wide; 7.5 high	9 wide; 6 high	9 wide; 6 high
	Char/Line	40	72	100	72; 80	72; 80
	Lines/Display	20	20	15	12	24
	Char Set	64 (ASCII)	64 (ASCII)	88	64	64
	Total Char/Display	800	1440	1500	864; 960	1728; 1920
	Char Generation Technique	5 x 7 dot matrix	5 x 7 dot matrix	16 x 18 dot matrix	5 x 7 dot matrix	5 x 7 dot matrix
EDITING FACILITIES	Horizontal Tab	Yes	Yes	Yes	Yes	Yes
	Line Erase	Yes	Yes	Yes	No	No
	Line Insert	Optional	Optional	Optional	No	No
	Partial Display Transmit	Yes	Yes	Yes	Yes	Yes
	Split Screen	Yes	Yes	Optional	No	No
	Other	Full cursor controls; char/end-of-page/ screen erase; page roll/scroll; char/line blink; char insert/ delete optional	Full cursor controls; char/end-of-page/ screen erase; page roll/scroll; char/line blink; char insert/ delete optional	Full cursor controls; char insert/delete; form fill-in; screen erase; underline	Full cursor controls; rolling; wraparound; std edit mode	Full cursor controls; rolling; wraparound; std edit mode
CONTROL UNIT	Identity	Self-contained	Self-contained	CO:75 Control Unit	Self-contained	Self-contained
	Type of Buffer Storage	MOS (static shift registers)	MOS (static shift registers)	Delay line	MOS	MOS
	Buffer Capacity Char	800 (expandable to 1600)	1440 (expandable to 2880)	1500	960	1920
	Max Devices/ Controller	Up to 50 slave monitors/terminal	Up to 50 slave monitors/terminal	32	1 display/combination of 2 peripherals (1 printer, 1 mag tape cassette)	1 display/combination of 2 peripherals (1 printer, 1 mag tape cassette)
	Multi-Drop	Optional (up to 32 terminals/line)	Optional (up to 32 terminals/line)	Yes	No	No
PERIPHERY	Printer	10/15/30 cps serial printer optional	10/15/30 cps serial printer optional	Optional	Optional	Optional
	Other	Mag tape cassette (300,000 char) optional	Mag tape cassette (300,000 char) optional	Magnetic tape/paper tape optional	Magnetic tape cassette (optional)	Magnetic tape cassette (optional)
PURCHASE PRICE, $		3350	3950	6100	3950	4750
MONTHLY RENTAL, $		143 (including maintenance)	159.50 (including maintenance)	—	118 (1-yr lease includ- ing maintenance)	138 (1-yr lease includ- ing maintenance)
COMMENTS		110, 150, 300, 1200 to 9600 bps interfaces available; ASCII std; Baudot (TTY 28 replace- ment)/EBCDIC codes available: high-speed (0.5 mHz) parallel I/O interface available; modular configuration allows separation of key- board/controller from display; half-/full- duplex; TTY-style/numeric cluster keyboard; odd/even char parity checking; 10/15/30 cps serial transfer rate; 60 cps opt; portable con- figuration (acoustic coupler interface) avail- able; protected data field feature opt; memory paging opt		IBM-compatible via 2701 Adapter; Format mode (access all memory data)/Data mode (access variable data); Remote Data Adapter controls up to 32 displays/printers; async; up to 2400 bps; 7-level, 10-unit ASCII; 201B1-compatible; 250,000 cps parallel transfer rate	TTY 33/35 inter- changeable; 10-key numeric keyboard, printer, mag tape cassette opt; operates in On-line (echoplex) mode/Edit mode (send keys cause line/display to be transmitted); 7- level, 10-/11-unit ASCII; half-/full-duplex; async; 110-1200 bps (selectable)	TTY 33/35 inter- changeable; 10-key numeric keyboard, printer, mag tape cassette opt; operates in On-line (echoplex) mode/Edit mode (send keys cause line/display to be transmitted); 7- level, 10-/11-unit ASCII; half-/full-duplex; async; 110-1200 bps (selectable)

ALPHANUMERIC DISPLAY TERMINALS

IDENTITY		A. B. Dick Videograph M9900 Display Control Unit	NCR 795 Data Display System	Raytheon DIDS-400 Digital Information Display System	Raytheon DIDS-400 Digital Information Display System	Raytheon DIDS-400 Digital Information Display System
REPORT NUMBER		—	—	—	—	—
DISPLAY UNIT	Identity	Any std monitor/TV receiver	795-300	401	401-3	402
	Viewing Area, in.	—	9.5 wide; 7.5 high	8.5 wide; 6.5 high	9 wide; 7 high	8.5 wide; 6.5 high
	Char/Line	24; 32; 48	64	40; 80; 65; 64	40; 80	40; 80; 65; 64
	Lines/Display	16	32	13; 13; 16; 23	12	13; 13; 16; 23
	Char Set	64 (ASCII)	64 (ASCII)	64	64	64 (96 optional)
	Total Char/Display	384; 512; 768	1024; 512; 256	520; 1040; 1500	480; 960; 1040	520; 1040; 1500
	Char Generation Technique	9 x 11 dot matrix	Stroke	Monoscope	Monoscope	Monoscope
EDITING FACILITIES	Horizontal Tab	No	Yes	Yes	Yes	Yes
	Line Erase	Yes	Yes	Yes	Yes	Yes
	Line Insert	Yes	Yes	No	No	No
	Partial Display Transmit	Yes	Yes	Yes	Yes	Yes
	Split Screen	Yes	Optional	Yes	Yes	Yes
	Other	Full cursor controls; new line; home; erase message; send line/message; blink; roll/crawl	Full cursor controls; char insert/erase; vertical tab; carriage return; blink	Full cursor controls; char insert/delete; screen erase; protected text	Full cursor controls; char insert/delete; screen erase; protected text	Full cursor controls; char insert/delete; screen erase
CONTROL UNIT	Identity	M9900 DCU	795-100	425	425	Self-contained
	Type of Buffer Storage	Magnetic core	Magnetostrictive delay line	Display line (in each display)	Delay line (in each display)	Delay line
	Buffer Capacity Char	512; 1024	1024; 2048; 3072	520, 1040, 1500 per display unit	480, 960, 1040 per display unit	520; 1040; 1500
	Max Devices/Controller	1 (16 lines)-16 (1 line); unlimited slave monitors	12 display units, 12 teleprinters	64 display consoles, printer adapters	12/64 display consoles, printer adapters	1; up to 8 display consoles can share 1 data set
	Multi-Drop	Yes	Yes	Yes	Yes	Yes
PERIPHERY	Printer	M9600 Videojet	TTY 33 RO	TTY 33/35 RO	TTY 33/35 RO	TTY 33/35 RO
	Other	M975 CRT Copier	—	Printer options at 10, 30, 40 cps	Printer options at 10, 30, 40 cps	Printer options at 10, 30, 40 cps
PURCHASE PRICE, $		7100 (excludes keyboard) to 8300	2450 (display); 525 (keyboard); 10,150-14,700 (cntrl)	4100 (401); 7000-12,000 (425)	4100 (301-3); 7000-12,000 (425)	6600 (includes printer, display/control)
MONTHLY RENTAL, $		—	70 (display); 15 (keyboard); 290-420 (cntrl)	125 (401); 350 (425); 75 (print control)	125 (401-3); 200-350 (425); 75 (print cntrl)	200 (includes printer, display/control)
COMMENTS		Keyboard opt; 8-level ASCII; asynchronous; 250 kHz max input/100 kHz max output; non-composite, composite with/without cursor; external sync/blanking; includes interface to Varian 620/i; each additional independent display (multistation) reduces format by 1 line per unit	2 keyboard arrangements available; half-/full-duplex; 8-level ASCII; 110/1000/1200/1800 bps	Synchronous at 2400 bps; DIDS-450 programmable general-purpose control unit available; half-duplex; 8-level ASCII; 300-cps max output to display; char/longitudinal parity checking; automatic retransmission; 60-key keyboard	Compatible with IBM S/360; 13th line opt; printer connects to display; 12-display control unit portable; asynch; half-duplex; up to 2400 bps; 8-level, 10-unit ASCII; char/longitudinal parity checking; automatic retransmission; 60-key keyboard	Stand-alone unit; asynchronous up to 1200 bps; synchronous at 2400 bps; can operate over voiceband line from DIDS-450 programmable control unit; 8-level ASCII; half-duplex; char/longitudinal parity checking; 60-key keyboard

ALPHANUMERIC DISPLAY TERMINALS

IDENTITY		Raytheon DIDS-400 Digital Information Display System	Sanders Data Systems 622 Stand-Alone Data Display System	Science Associates MSG/COM I Large Scale Alphanumeric Display (Receive Only)	Science Associates MSG/COM II Large Scale Alphanumeric Display (Receive Only)	Science Associates MSG/COM III Large Scale Alphanumeric Display (Receive Only)
REPORT NUMBER		—	—	—	—	—
DISPLAY UNIT	Identity	Data-Select Display Console	622	MSG/COM I	MSG/COM II	MSG/COM III
	Viewing Area, in.	6.5 wide; 8.5 high	7.5 wide; 9.5 high	60.39 wide; 47.5 high	60.39 wide; 21.5 high	95.5 wide; 27 high
	Char/Line	45	52	30	30	48
	Lines/Display	23	40	10	5	8
	Char Set	64	64 (ASCII)	64	64	64
	Total Char/Display	1035	1024	300	150	384
	Char Generation Technique	Monoscope	Stroke	5 x 13 dot matrix	5 x 13 dot matrix	5 x 7 dot matrix
EDITING FACILITIES	Horizontal Tab	Yes	Optional	No	No	No
	Line Erase	Yes	No	No	No	No
	Line Insert	No	No	No	No	No
	Partial Display Transmit	Yes	Yes	No	No	No
	Split Screen	Yes	Yes	No	No	No
	Other	Full cursor controls; char insert/delete; screen erase; tab/ protected text	Full cursor controls; vertical tab; CR/LF; fixed format; home	Internal/input-controlled format; automatic LF at EOL	Internal/input-controlled format; automatic LF at EOL	Input-controlled format; automatic LF at EOL
CONTROL UNIT	Identity	420 Control Unit	Self-contained	Electronic cabinet (stand-alone/integral) MOS	Electronic cabinet (stand-alone/integral) MOS	Electronic cabinet (stand-alone) MOS
	Type of Buffer Storage	Delay line (in each display)	Delay line			
	Buffer Capacity Char	1035	1024	130 (interface buffer); 300 (display storage)	130 (interface buffer); 150 (display storage)	143 (interface buffer); 384 (display storage)
	Max Devices/ Controller	64 display consoles	1 display; 1 printer	1 display	1 display	1 display
	Multi-Drop	No	Yes	Yes	Yes	Yes
PERIPHERY	Printer	TTY 33/35 RO; TI thermal printer	TTY 33/35 RO	No	No	No
	Other	—	No	TTY 33-compatible	TTY 33-compatible	TTY 33-compatible
PURCHASE PRICE, $		7000 (display); 15,000 (controller)	6100	9417	7755	12,050
MONTHLY RENTAL, $		—	199	325	285	384
COMMENTS		Identification card reader to right of tube; 20 line-select keys to left; printers connected directly to displays; controller interfaces directly to computer at 80,000 bps	Horizontal format available with 32 64-/84-char lines; 8-level ASCII; opt serial I/O at 110-1800 bps (async)/2000, 2400 bps (sync); format/ type option with 2 intensity fields; busy response to computer poll in Type mode; 2048 screen positions; detachable keyboard (10 ft); longitudinal redundancy checking	8-level ASCII/NYSE (6-level) Ticker Code; asynchronous; 135/ 270/540 bps (switch selectable); RS232-compatible; options available on char/ background colors; output of displayed data up to 60 cps; 1.5 x 2.12-in. char size; 175-ft viewing range	8-level ASCII/NYSE (6-level) Ticker Code; asynchronous; 135/ 270/540 bps (switch selectable); RS232-compatible; options available on char/ background colors; output of displayed data up to 60 cps; 1.5 x 2.12-in. char size; 175-ft viewing range	8-level ASCII; asynchronous; 110-300 bps; RS232/direct TTY 33-compatibility; options available on char/ background colors; output of displayed data up to 60 cps; 1.5 x 2.12-in. char size; 175-ft viewing range

ALPHANUMERIC DISPLAY TERMINALS

IDENTITY		Science Associates MSG/COM IV Large Scale Alphanumeric Display (Receive Only)	Tektronix T4002 Graphic Computer Terminal	Texas Scientific Entelekon 80 CRT Terminal System	Wyle 8260 Computerminal	Burroughs B 9353 Input and Display System
REPORT NUMBER		—	—	—	—	—
DISPLAY UNIT	Identity	MSG/COM IV	T4002	80	8260	B 9353
	Viewing Area, in.	56.5 wide; 15 high	8.25 wide; 6.0 high	6.5 x 9.5	9 wide; 4 high	108 sq. in. (rectangular)
	Char/Line	43	85	40; 64; 80	40; 80	80
	Lines/Display	6	39	6; 12; 16; 24	12	25
	Char Set	64	96 (ASCII, upper-/lowercase)	64; 96 opt	64	66
	Total Char/Display	258	3315	Multiple of char/line by lines/display	480; 960	2,000
	Char Generation Technique	5 x 7 dot matrix	7 x 9 dot matrix	5 x 7 dot matrix	5 x 7 dot matrix	Stroke
EDITING FACILITIES	Horizontal Tab	No	Yes	Yes	Yes	Yes
	Line Erase	No	No	Yes	Yes	Yes
	Line Insert	No	Yes	Yes	No	Yes
	Partial Display Transmit	No	Yes	Yes	Yes	Yes
	Split Screen	No	Yes	Yes	No	Yes (controlled format/forms)
	Other	Input-controlled format; automatic LF at EOL	Full cursor controls; screen erase; home; CR/LF; vertical tab	Char insert/delete; fixed format; full cursor controls; rolling; blinking; random access to any screen location from computer	Char insert/delete format protect; full cursor controls	Programmatic cursor controls; fixed/variable tab; paging; char insert/delete; partial screen/erase; clear/home
CONTROL UNIT	Identity	Electronic cabinet (stand-alone)	Self-contained	Terminal Control Unit (TCU)	8848 Display Control	B 9353-2
	Type of Buffer Storage	DTL	MOS	Solid state integrated circuits	Semiconductor	Magnetic core (nonspatial)
	Buffer Capacity Char	20 (interface buffer); 258 (display storage)	3315 (display storage); 84 (line buffer)	1:1 with max display format	960	1,024
	Max Devices/Controller	1 display	1 display and printer	1 (TCU); up to 64 via multiplexor (MTCU)	16	4 monitors/keyboards
	Multi-Drop	Yes	No	Yes	Yes	Yes
PERIPHERY	Printer	No	4601 Hard Copy	TTY 33/35	IBM 1053	TTY 33 RO (1 per controller)
	Other	TTY 32/33 compatible	4901 Interactive Graphic Unit; joystick	Any ASCII equipment	TTY 33/35	Modem expander (up to 4, 8, 12, 16 controls per line)
PURCHASE PRICE, $		5895	8800; 600 (serial interface)	4295 (display, TCU); 995 (MTCU)	OEM only	6,200–20,460
MONTHLY RENTAL, $		221	338.80	—	—	130–425
COMMENTS		5-level Baudot; 8-level ASCII; asynchronous; 60-110 bps; direct TTY 32/33-compatibility; options available on char/background colors; output of displayed data up to 60 cps; 1.5 x 2.12-in. char size; 100-ft viewing range	TTY-compatible subset; sync/async, half-/full-duplex interface opt; 2 programmable char sizes; 500-cps avg speed; includes point (1024 x 760)/ incremental plotting, vectors; 128-code ASCII keyboard; TTY I/O port interfaces to PDP-8, Nova, Supernova, HP 2100; up to 125K bps	Hardware/software-compatible with IBM 2260/2848, 2265 under QTAM, BTAM, TTAM; MTCU can directly interface System/360 multiplexor channel/ 2700 Series Adapter; data rates up to 250K cps; special functions I/O available	Hardware/software-compatible with IBM 2260/2848; asynchronous; up to 110/150/300/600/1200/2400 bps; half-duplex; 8-level, 10-/11-unit ASCII; char/longitudinal parity checking; auto retransmission; 480/960-char max message length	Includes on-/off-line control; poll/select operations opt; 8-level ASCII; half-duplex; up to 1,800 bps (async); 4,800 bps (sync); variable data length transmit; one 1,024-char/two 512-char/four 256-char shared memory modules; modems available

ALPHANUMERIC DISPLAY TERMINALS

IDENTITY		Corning Data Systems 904 Interactive Graphic Display	Courier Terminal Systems Executerm II Remote Data Terminal	Courier Terminal Systems Executerm 65 Remote Data Terminal	Four-Phase Systems System IV/70 Multiterminal Display Processing System	Hypertech GTU-1 Generalized Terminal Unit
REPORT NUMBER		—	—	—	—	—
DISPLAY UNIT	Identity	904	II	65	IV/70	GTU-1
	Viewing Area, in.	8.5 wide; 11 high	11.5 wide; 5.5 high	6.4 wide; 4.8 high	9 wide; 7 high	9 (tube diagonal)
	Char/Line	72	80	40; 80	48; 81	25
	Lines/Display	64	24	12; 6 (opt)	24; 12	12
	Char Set	96 (full ASCII)	64 (ASCII)	64 (ASCII)	120 (ASCII, BCD, TTY, EBCDIC;IBM2260, 2265)	64
	Total Char/Display	4,608	960; 1,920 (opt)	480/960; 240 (opt)	1,152; 972	300
	Char Generation Technique	5 x 7 dot matrix	7 x 8 dot matrix	7 x 8 dot matrix	8 x 10 dot matrix	5 x 7 dot matrix
EDITING FACILITIES	Horizontal Tab	Yes	Yes	Yes	Yes	Yes
	Line Erase	No	Yes	No	Yes	No
	Line Insert	No	Yes	No	Yes	No
	Partial Display Transmit	No	—	Yes	Yes	Yes
	Split Screen	No	No	Yes	Yes	Yes (3 divisions)
	Other	Full cursor controls via console/software; graphic input of cursor position via Read-Terminal function; display erase; wraparound	Full cursor controls; form fill-in; char blink; scroll; auto top line transmit on page roll opt	Full cursor controls; char blink; page roll; char insert/delete; clear display/end of screen; line address-ing opt	Full cursor controls; erase screen/end of line; format protect; page roll/scroll; char insert/delete; blink char/words; programmable functions	Format title storage; program control; lateral cursor controls; home
CONTROL UNIT	Identity	Self-contained	Self-contained	Self-contained	IV/70 Central Processing Unit	Self-contained
	Type of Buffer Storage	Photochromatic storage tube	MOS	MOS	MOS/LSI semiconductor random access memory	MOS shift register
	Buffer Capacity Char	4,608	960; 1,920 (opt)	480/960; 240 (opt)	24K bytes	600
	Max Devices/ Controller	1 display	1 display/printer	1 display/printer	32 video terminals plus 8 I/O channels; 64 devices/channel; see Comments	1
	Multi-Drop	—	Optional (polled network)	Yes	Yes	No
PERIPHERY	Printer	—	Execuprint I (10 cps; 80 char/line)	Execuprint I (10 cps; 80 char/line)	Char/line printers	Selectric (735); TTY 33/35
	Other	Mouse; joystick; paper tape reader/punch	—	—	Disc; mag tape; punched cards; synch/ asynch data sets	Mag tape cassette (2 integral read/write units; 100,000-char capacity each)
PURCHASE PRICE, $		19,650	4,370-4,560	5,150	12,100 (CPU); 980 (video terminal)	5,000-10,000
MONTHLY RENTAL, $		820 (1-year lease); 670 (4-year lease)	158-165	—	335 (CPU); 36 (video terminal)	Purchase only
COMMENTS		TTY-compatible; half-/ full-duplex; operation; 110, 150, 300 bps (switchable); compatible with Bell System Data Sets 103A/103A2/112A; char/vector generators; std unit includes hard copy, slide overlay, software support, win-dowing, zooming, per-spective transforma-tions handled via software	TTY-compatible; opt software-controlled modes include conver-sational, edit, format echo; 8-level ASCII; half-/full-duplex; parallel interface transfer to 500 cps; full programmable cur-sor controls; opt function keys/numeric key pad available	IBM System/360-com-patible; 2265/2845 replacement (under OS, DOS, QTAM, BTAM); char parity/longitudinal redundancy checking; variable data transmit via SOM/EOM framing symbols; 8-level, 10-unit ASCII; half-duplex; async up to 1,200 (202D)/2,400 (201B) bps	Combines medium-scale digital computer with up to 32 video ter-minals; simulates IBM 2260/2848; can perform local preprocessing (data validation, mes-sage reformatting, error checking, oper-ator cueing); fixed for-mats called from local storage; stand-alone display/processing capability	Low-speed I/O is TTY 33/35/37-compatible at 110, 150, 300 bps (103A); high-speed I/O at 600, 1,206, 2,400, 4,800 bps (202C); half-duplex; async via 7-level, 10-/11-unit ASCII; block transfer; CRC/ LRC with auto retrans-mit; unattended operation

ALPHANUMERIC DISPLAY TERMINALS

IDENTITY		TEC Series 400 DSP Data-Screen Display Terminal	TEC Series 400 DSA Data-Screen Display Terminal	TEC Series 400 DST Data-Screen Display Terminal	Terminal Communications TC-70 Video Display Terminal	Ultronic Systems Videomaster II Brokerage Display System
REPORT NUMBER		—	—	—	—	—
DISPLAY UNIT	Identity	DSP 5020/-8024	DSA 5020/-8024	DST 5020/-8024	TC-70	Videomaster II
	Viewing Area, in.	8 wide; 6 high	8 wide; 6 high	8 wide; 6 high	12 (tube diagonal)	9.5 wide; 7.5 high
	Char/Line	50; 80	50; 80	50; 80	32	80 (12 lines) 40 (12 lines) 40 (6 lines)
	Lines/Display	20; 24	20; 24	20; 24	16	12 (80 char); 12 (40 char) 6 (40 char); 24
	Char Set	64 (ASCII)	64 (ASCII)	64 (ASCII)	64	64 (ASCII)
	Total Char/Display	1000; 1920	1000; 1920	1000; 1920	512	1920; 960; 480; 240
	Char Generation Technique	5 x 7 dot matrix	5 x 7 dot matrix	5 x 7 dot matrix	5 x 7 dot matrix	7 x 10 dot matrix
EDITING FACILITIES	Horizontal Tab	Yes	Yes	Yes	Yes	Yes
	Line Erase	Yes	Yes	Yes	No	No
	Line Insert	Yes	Yes	Yes	No	No
	Partial Display Transmit	Yes	Yes	Yes	Yes	Yes
	Split Screen	Yes	Yes	Yes	Yes	As programmed
	Other	Full cursor controls; char insert/delete; field tab; blink; screen protect; page/ end of line erase	Full cursor controls; char insert/delete; field tab; blink; screen protect; erase page/to end of line	Full cursor controls; char insert/delete; field tab; blink; screen protect; page/ end of line erase	Full cursor controls; field delimiters; page erase; variable header; home	Full programmable cursor controls; operates in Quote mode/ Computer mode
CONTROL UNIT	Identity	Self-contained	Self-contained	Self-contained	Self-contained	Videomaster II Control Unit
	Type of Buffer Storage	MOS	MOS	MOS	MOS	Magnetostrictive
	Buffer Capacity Char	1000; 1920	1000; 1920	1000; 1920	512	1920; 960; 480; 240
	Max Devices/ Controller	1 display, keyboard, printer; up to 10 remote monitors	1 display, keyboard, printer; up to 10 remote monitors	1 display, keyboard printer; up to 10 remote monitors	1 display; 1 printer	8 (1920 char/display); 16 (960 char/display); 20 (480 char/display); 24 (240 char/display)
	Multi-Drop	No	Yes (up to 16)	No	Yes	Yes
PERIPHERY	Printer	Any TTY-compatible device	Any TTY-compatible device	Any TTY-compatible device	TC-35 (14.8 cps)	Receive-only (30 cps)
	Other	Remote monitors	Remote monitors	Remote monitors	—	TTY
PURCHASE PRICE, $		1850 (5020); 2050 (8024); 319 (keyboard)	2100 (5020); 2300 (8024); 319 (keyboard)	1850 (5020); 2050 (8024); 319 (keyboard)	4,490	Not available for purchase
MONTHLY RENTAL, $		—	—	—	175	
COMMENTS		Rack-mount/desktop units; high/low-speed parallel (char) interface to 800 kHz/10 kHz; Data-Panel with 16 software-driven incandescent legends	Rack-mount/desktop units; TTY compatible; serial interface; async; half-/full-duplex; 7-level, 10-/11-unit ASCII; 110-9600 bps; multiple units dropped at common site require only 1 modem (chained control); Data-Panel with 16 incandescent legends	Rack-mount/desktop units; serial interface; 110-2,400 bps; async; half-/full-duplex; 7-level, 10-/11-unit ASCII; Data-Panel with 16 software-driven incandescent legends; TTY compatible	Line control/code-compatible with IBM 2740; 6-level BCD; async; half-duplex; up to 1,200 bps; 15 function keys for cursor positioning in predefined data entry fields; packed transmission via variable-length field delimiters	Char set includes 7 fractions, 4 special char, 3 format char; std EIA RS232B interface; async; 1,200-2,400/4, 800-9,600 bps; half-duplex (2-/4-wire); VRC parity checking; IBM 360-based polling sequence (4-char word); 8 poll commands; IBM 2260/ 2848-compatible via 2701 DAU

ALPHANUMERIC DISPLAY TERMINALS

IDENTITY		Computer Communications Totelcom CC-335 Display Terminal	Computer Terminal Datapoint 2200 Display Terminal	Computek Series 400 CRT Display System		Video Systems VST 3712 Video Data Terminal
REPORT NUMBER		—	—	—		—
DISPLAY UNIT	Identity	CC-335	2200	400/12	400/15	VST 3712
	Viewing Area, in.	3.25 high; 8.75 wide	7 wide; 2.5 high	8.25 in. by 6.4 in.; see Comments	8.25 in. by 6.4 in.; see Comments	10.5 x 8.0
	Char/Line	72/80 (switch selectable)	80	85 (std orientation); 66 (vertical)	85 (std orientation); 66 (vertical)	72
	Lines/Display	12	12	40 (std orientation); 50 (vertical)	40 (std orientation); 50 (vertical)	18
	Char Set	64 (ASCII)	94 (ASCII)	96; 64 opt (ASCII)	96; 64 opt (ASCII)	96 (full ASCII)
	Total Char/Display	864/960	960	3400	3400	1296
	Char Generation Technique	5 x 7 dot matrix	5 x 7 dot matrix	Stroke (straight/curved)	Stroke (straight/curved)	5 x 7 dot matrix
EDITING FACILITIES	Horizontal Tab	Yes (next unprotected, every tenth position)	Yes	No (software only)	No (software only)	Optional
	Line Erase	Yes	Yes	No	No	Yes
	Line Insert	Yes	Yes	No	No	No
	Partial Display Transmit	Yes	Yes	No	No	Yes
	Split Screen	Yes (protected fields at half intensity)	Yes	No	No	Yes
	Other	Full cursor controls; char insert/delete; home; scrolling; margin set; clear display/memory	As programmed	Full cursor controls; CR/LF; erase display; 1-min display intensification	Full cursor controls; CR/LF; erase display; 1-min display intensification	Full cursor controls; selective transmit; page erase; home
CONTROL UNIT	Identity	Self-contained	Self-contained	Self-contained	Self-contained	Self-contained
	Type of Buffer Storage	MOS (dynamic shift registers)	Magnetic core	Storage tube	Storage tube	Delay line
	Buffer Capacity Char	960	960 (allocated memory)	3400	3400	1296
	Max Devices/Controller	1	1 display; 2 magnetic tape cassettes	Up to 3 additional keyboard/displays (independent/slave operation; individually addressable)	Up to 3 additional keyboard/displays (independent/slave operation; individually addressable)	1 display, 4 printers, multiple monitors
	Multi-Drop	No	Yes	No	No	
PERIPHERY	Printer	Optional	Impact or nonimpact (30 cps; 132 col.)	400/HCU Hard Copy Unit; any serial ASCII printer up to 100 bps	400/HCU Hard Copy Unit; any serial ASCII printer up to 100 bps	Any ASCII serial input printer
	Other	Magnetic tape cassette optional	2 integral magnetic tape cassettes	—	—	Any serial incremental mag tape
PURCHASE PRICE, $		4,250 (acoustic coupler); 3,950 (RS232B interface)	5550 (basic; 2K)	7,400 (basic); 3,750 (HCU printer) Third-party leasing	8,400 (basic); 3,750 (HCU printer) Third-party leasing	2,795
MONTHLY RENTAL, $		—	180 (basic); 95-135 (printer)			105
COMMENTS		Portable; TTY 33/35-replacement; 7-level, 10-/11-unit ASCII; async; half-/full-duplex; selectable 110, 150, 300, 600, 1200 bps; selectable odd/even char parity generation/checking; Line Transmit/Display Transmit modes; point-to-point operation over leased/switched line	Stand-alone unit includes keyboard, display, control logic, 2K memory (expandable to 8K); 8-bit words; entry direct to tape; programmable formatting; any code (ASCII, BCD, EBCDIC); program call on tape; transmit from tape	230-symbol char set capacity; 240-cps max sync display rate; 2000-cps max async rate; limited editing; flexible complex char generation; 4 char sizes available; increased char capacity; graphics-oriented, upgradable; 110-280,000 bps serial async line rate; odd/even parity	Point/vector generation via 1024 x 800 display points; graphic modes: absolute, incremental, scalable vector; 2-/4-byte vector formats; 240-cps max sync display rate; 2000-cps max async rate; complex char generation; 4 char sizes; 110-180,000 bps serial async line rate	TTY-compatible (opt); built-in coupler (hardwired); any ASCII coding of function switches for remote positioning of cursor; parity checking; full-/half-duplex; up to 1200 bps (2400 opt)

8. ALPHANUMERIC DISPLAY DEVICE FUNCTIONS

Alphanumeric displays can be used in four basic types of functions that define the degree of interaction between the user and the display device, and in turn, the computer. These functions include data entry, data retrieval, inquiry/response, and monitoring and control. Table 8-1 summarizes the distributon of displays according to function.

Displays are usually considered as general-purpose devices. However, specific display characteristics are used for each function to facilitate the information interchange between the operator and the computer. Not all characteristics or capabilities of a display are required for each function. Some manufacturers have developed basic displays with minimum capabilities that can be expanded to include a full range of optional features. This design strategy allows them to propose a lower-priced display equipped with only those features that are required for a specific purpose. Table 8-2 indicates the typical display characteristics for each type of function.

DATA ENTRY

Data entry systems and equipment are primarily concerned with the input of data to a computer system. The interaction between the user, terminal, and computer is one way—toward the computer. The computer does little more than acknowledge the receipt of the data. The only output is the display of data-entry forms or operational instructions for the operator.

Table 8-1 presents examples of some of the major applications within the data-entry function. These applications are used primarily to create or to update data files.

Table 8-1. Major Applications
Within Display Function Areas

DATA ENTRY	DATA RETRIEVAL	INQUIRY/RESPONSE	MONITORING AND CONTROL
Order entry	Credit checking	Inventory control	Process control
Production data collection	Seat availability checking	Reservation transaction	Numerical control
Account update	Stock quotation status	Account transaction	Cash flow monitoring
Transaction reporting	Record or file status	Problem solving	Annunciation
		Education	
		Text editing	
		Program development	
		Computer-aided instruction	
		Management information systems	

A relatively small screen, good data editing and format capabilities, and optional input techniques are required for the data-entry function. Transactions are usually 80 to 150 characters each, and therefore a larger screen is not required. Editing capability and local memory allow the operator to correct data errors prior to transmission to the computer, thereby decreasing computer operating costs and system overhead. Use of protected formats (those that do not change over a period of time) provides a guide for entering data. Then, when needed, the protected formats can be easily changed for a different use of data entry on the same terminal.

DATA RETRIEVAL

Data-retrieval systems and equipment are used to extract previously stored data from a file or a system. Data retrieval is basically one-way transmission from computer to terminal to user(s). Limited input data are used to identify the desired data for retrieval. Table 8-1 also presents ex-

Table 8-2. Display Characteristics According to Function

FUNCTION	SCREEN SIZE	NUMBER OF CHARACTERS	EDITING CAPABILITY	BUFFERED STORAGE	KEYBOARD FUNCTION (KEYS, LIGHT PEN)	FORMAT FEATURES	TYPICAL PRICE, $
Data entry	Small	800	Yes	Yes	Keys	Yes	2750–4000
Inquiry	Medium to large	500–1,000	No	No	Keys, Light pen	No	2500–3750
Inquiry/response	Large	1,000–2,500	Yes	Yes	Keys, Light pen	Yes	4000–6500
Monitoring	Small to large	200–1,000	No	No	Optional keyboard	No	1500–6500

amples of some of the major applications within the data-retrieval function. In effect, data retrieval is used when the operator wants specific data with regard to the current status of a file. Data retrieval does not change the data in the files.

The data-retrieval function usually results in a large amount of data being transmitted to the operator for a relatively small amount of input. Since the response may cover a wide range of applications that require significantly different output data volumes, the alphanumeric display screen usually must accommodate between 500 and 1000 characters. Optimal input techniques are also required to facilitate the selection of the desired data. Coded keys (e.g., function keys) are used for the rapid selection of major data items. A light pen is sometimes used in lieu of function keys for convenient selection of a desired item from a list of items displayed on the screen.

INQUIRY/RESPONSE

Inquiry/response systems and equipment are used to support extensive interaction between the computer and the operator. This function uses two-way transmission to aid the operator effectively in completing his particular task. It often uses the storage capacity of the computer system as well as the high-speed arithmetic capabilities afforded. Table 8-1 also presents examples of some of the major applications within the inquiry/ response function. These applications require extensive programming support and sophisticated computer systems. It is sometimes convenient to divide this function into the following subareas, each a significant function in its own right: access-to-data base, access to computation, method of training, and method of text manipulation.

The inquiry/response function covers a broad, diverse, and often complex spectrum of applications. Displays must have general-purpose facilities so that they can meet the requirements of the maximum number of potential applications. In effect, display devices incorporate the features of data entry and data retrieval described above. In addition, a larger screen is usually required to permit an effective dialogue between the operator and the computer.

MONITORING AND CONTROL

Monitoring and control systems and equipment provide status information on critical elements that affect system operation. This function automatically informs the user when changes occur and allows him to interrogate the status of various aspects of the operation. In turn, the user is provided with sufficient time to take corrective action. Transmission is essentially one way, from the computer to the user, for strict monitoring functions; transmission is both ways when control is also a function. Table 8-1 presents examples of some of the major applications for displays within this function.

The monitoring and control functions require a variety of display capabilities. The size of the screen and the use of many special keys are typical user considerations. In addition, some graphic or line-drawing capability is desirable in many applications. Where the graphic data required are simple, a "beefed up" alphanumeric display can be used. Otherwise, a more extensive graphic (line drawing) display must be employed.

9. SPECIFIC DISPLAY APPLICATIONS

One can imagine an almost endless list of potential end-user applications for alphanumeric displays. On-line programming, automated design, computer-aided instruction, file management, text editing, message composition, and source-data automation are just a few of the more promising display uses. The great majority of present and potential display applications, however, can be grouped into the four categories described in the subsequent paragraphs. The equipment capabilities that are necessary or desirable in a variety of specific display applications are summarized in Table 9-1.

ENGINEERING AND DESIGN

In this class of application, the user can be considered a "programmer" in the sense that a technical cross-conversation takes place between the system and the user. By means of the display console, the user engages in a flexible, interactive dialogue with the computer. Probably the most widely discussed application in this category is computer-aided design, in which the objective is to supply engineers with a set of tools that will help them—

1. To perform various detailed or tedious computations.
2. To see and compare the results of various design methods and parameters.
3. To gain access to textbook, historical, and other types of information.
4. To store the results of various designs for future reference.

Use	Number of Characters Displayed	Character Set	Special Inputs	Special Outputs	Plotting Ability	Screen Size	Color	Price Range, $
Engineering and Design								
Design Engineers and Mathematicians	High	AN	Yes	Maybe (1/N)	Yes	Large	Desir.	NC
Program Designers	Med.	AN	No	1/N	No	Med.	No	1-5K
Information, Flexible								
Industrial/Govt. Managers:								
Budgeting	Med.	AN	No	1/N	G & T	Med.	Desir.	1-3K
Process control	Low	AN	No	1/N	G & T	Med.	Desir.	1-5K
Production control	Low	AN	No	1/N	G & T	Med.	Desir.	1-5K
Inventory management	Low	AN	No	Hard Copy	No	Med.	No	1-3K
Military Commanders:								
Photo and map interpretation	High	AN	Yes	1/N (low N)	Yes	Large	Yes	10-15K
Cryptography and translation	Med.	Changeable AN	No	1/N	No	Med.	Desir.	2-5K
Planning and war gaming	High	AN	Cursor, light pen	1/N	Desir.	Large	Yes	5-10K
Scientific Research Engineers	Low	AN	No	1/N	No	Med.	No	1-5K
Banking and Finance Specialists	Low	AN	No	No	No	Med.	No	1-3K
Information, Structured								
Hospital Administrators and Nurses	Low	AN	No	1/N	No	Med.	No	1-3K
Airline Reservation Clerks	Low	AN	No	1/N	No	Small	No	1-3K
Auto Rental Dispatchers	Low	AN	No	1/N	No	Small	No	1-3K
Railroad Car and Shipment Disposition Controllers	Low	AN	No	1/N	No	Med.	No	1-5K
Fleet Vehicle Location and Content Controllers	Low	AN	No	Hard Copy	No	Med.	No	1-5K
Insurance Company Managers and Clerks	Low	AN	No	1/N	No	Med.	No	1-5K
Bank Tellers	Low	AN	No	No	No	Small	No	1-3K
Bank Managers	Low	AN	No	1/N	No	Med.	No	1-5K
Stock Brokers:								
Portfolio analysis	Low	AN	No	1/N	G & T	Med.	No	1-3K
Stock quotations	Low	AN	No	No	No	Med.	No	1-3K
Industrial Administrators (personnel records, etc.)	Low	AN	No	1/N	No	Med.	No	1-3K
Librarians:								
Library searching	Low	AN	No	1/N	No	Large	No	2-7K
Indexing and abstracting	High	AN	No	1/N	No	Med.	No	2-5K
Text Editors	Low	AN	No	No	No	Med.	No	1-3K
Military Administrators	Low	AN	No	1/N	No	Med.	No	1-5K
State and Local Government Personnel (vehicle license identification, etc.)	Low	AN	No	1/N	No	Small	No	1-5K
Educators (CAI, etc.)	Med.	AN	in some cases	No	in some cases	Med.	No	1-3K
Monitor Functions								
System Operators, Monitors, Paging Clerks, and Security Personnel	Low	AN	Video	1/N	No	Large	in some cases	1-3K
Communications								
Message Center Operators:								
Alphanumeric messages	High	AN	in some cases	1/N	No	Med.	No	About 2K
Graphical/pictorial data	High	AN	No	1/N	Yes	Large	Yes	About 5K

Number of Characters		Screen Size			
High:	5000 or more	Large:	about 20"	AN:	Alphanumeric plus symbols
Med.:	1000 to 4000	Med.:	about 15"	G & T:	Graphs and tables only
Low:	1000 or less	Small:	about 10"	Desir.:	Desirable but not essential
				NC:	Not critical
				1/N:	1 hard-copy output device per N displays

75

The software requirements for interactive engineering and design systems are particularly demanding. The language used for man/machine interaction must be a comprehensive one to permit flexible, efficient dialogues; yet it should be reasonably easy to learn and use. Often a "bootstrap" (self-teaching) course is programmed into the display software to aid in training men who will work with the consoles. The hardware, like the software, must be flexible enough to permit free interchanges of information and the use of whatever graphic representations are needed for the particular application. To eliminate the need for special keyboards, the display screen itself can often be used for structured dialogue; alternative choices are displayed, and the user makes his selection by means of a cursor or light pen.

Applications include—

1. Engineering and mathematics: research, design, and development.
2. Programming: program development and debugging.
3. Management planning (industry and government): forecasting, scheduling, and logistics.

INFORMATION—FLEXIBLE OR STRUCTURED INTERACTION

In these applications the main purpose of the display console is to provide quick, convenient access to information in a large, centrally located data base. In some cases the information in the data base is updated by means of messages entered by the display console users. In other cases, conventional batch-processing techniques are used to update the data base, and the display consoles are used only to access the information.

The applications in this category can be logically divided into two subclasses: flexible and structured. The "flexible" classification allows the same sort of flexible man/machine dialogues as in engineering and design, but here the goal is mainly to provide efficient access to a fixed, though complex, data base. The "structured" classification applies to those applications where the exact form of the information to be transferred, in both directions, is known beforehand and can be structured for maximum effectiveness with respect to cost, ease of operation, reliability, and other factors.

There are literally hundreds of potential applications in this category. The following list, subdivided into the flexible and structured classifications, includes the ones that seem most promising at this time.

1. Flexible interaction
   (a) Industrial and government management, planning, and oper-

ations: budgeting, process control, production control, inventory management

(b) Military command and control: strategy and planning, damage assessment and logistics, photo and map interpretation, cryptography and translation

(c) Scientific research: laboratory experiment monitoring, query and retrieval, psychological studies

(d) Banking and finance (in-depth customer service): credit analysis, account analysis, checking analysis, stock portfolio analysis

2. Structured interaction

(a) Hospital administration: patient record query and retrieval, nursing station aids to patient care, diagnosis analysis

(b) Transportation: airline reservations, auto rentals, railroad car and shipment disposition, fleet vehicle location and content control, hotel reservations

(c) Insurance: policy searching, claim adjustment, policy file maintenance

(d) Banking and finance (routine customer service): bank teller stations, bank management inquiries, stock quotations

(e) Industrial administration: personal records, financial administration, group insurance files

(f) Information storage and retrieval: library searching, text editing, indexing and abstracting

(g) Military administration: base assets, inventory control, personnel records, maintenance status reporting and control, force status, planning and war games, fire control

(h) State and local governments: vehicle license identification, driver license file searching, traffic and criminal offense records, deed searching

(i) Education: computer-aided instruction, programmed teaching, school administration

MONITORING

In these applications, the users are primarily spectators. They may be provided with a limited complement of manual controls, such as special pushbuttons, but not with a full keyboard. The information, usually in a completely preconstructed format, is displayed for use by one or more observers. In some cases the observer has no control over the information that is displayed; in other cases he can select what he wants to see from a number of choices.

An important example of this type of application is NASA launch-vehicle check-out operations. Display consoles provide specialists with information about each operating element of a launch vehicle during countdown, and aid in decisions as to the health and probability of success of the ignition and flight of the vehicle. Applications in this category include—

1. System operating monitors: data processing installations, automated systems, airline flight information, checkout systems, demonstrations
2. Paging systems
3. Security systems

COMMUNICATIONS

In this category the display unit serves as a means for holding and sometimes controlling information that is about to be or has been transmitted over some type of communications medium, either before it is transmitted or before it is accepted by the recipient. The transmitted information falls into two classes: alphanumeric messages and graphical/pictorial data. At the present time these communication roles are being filled mainly by teleprinters (for alphanumeric messages) and by facsimile systems (for graphical/pictorial data), but displays are beginning to be used. Among the applications in this category are—

1. Alphanumeric message transmission
2. Critical message validation
3. Graphical/pictorial data transmission: newspapers and magazines, criminal photographs, weather information

On the basis of the information in Table 9-1, several noteworthy general observations can be made:

1. The desired price ranges are generally lower than the cost of suitable display consoles that are currently on the market.

2. Except for the cost problem, the small alphanumeric display consoles now available are generally suitable for a large number of applications.

3. Hard-copy output, usually on a teleprinter, is desirable in most applications, though a single printer can often serve several display consoles.

4. Special features such as light-pen input, audio output, plotting capabilities, and color are needed only in a relatively few specialized applications.

10. ADVANTAGES OF ALPHANUMERIC DISPLAY DEVICES

Users and manufacturers cite several reasons for using alphanumeric display devices. The relative importance of each, however, depends on the specific characteristics and requirements of each user's application. Since each user's terminal needs are unique, the selection of display devices may be justified on one dominant feature or on overall merits.

SPEED

A display is an electronic device that is inherently faster than electromechanical competitors. Teletypewriters typically operate at 10 characters per second, while teleprinters can operate at up to 30, 60, or even 120 characters per second. For input, however, a display (and electromechanical competitors) can go only as fast as the operator types; for output it can operate up to 40,000 characters per second. When a memory is used in the display, both input to the computer and output from it can be at the same speed. Speed limitations (typically, 300 characters per second) are usually imposed on display operations when they are connected by long distance communications line to the computer. But even with these speed limitations, users are able to call for more data at one time while at the same time reducing the time lag between data output that might affect the efficiency of line usage.

HUMAN FACTORS

A display is noiseless and therefore is preferred in environments that are sensitive to disruptive sounds. This feature alone accounts for its acceptance in hospitals and law courts, to name but two examples.

FLEXIBILITY AND CONVENIENCE

A user typically has a number of unique data input and output requirements. An alphanumeric display can be used to fulfill many of these specific needs by combining input and output capabilities within one unit. In addition, unique data presentation features reduce operating complexity and facilitate operator/computer information interchange. The ability to partition display memory, for example, allows the user to display instructions or special forms to aid the operator in performing his task without having to retype permanent or semipermanent information. The data formats displayed on the screen can be changed as quickly as the computer, or the operator, can devise them. The display, therefore, is uniquely suited for nonstandard data input/output applications.

ERROR CONTROL

Immediate data display, special editing features, and the interaction between the computer and the terminal greatly simplify and improve error detection and correction. Since the data are not permanently recorded on the CRT screen, it can be changed easily. Typical operating experience indicates that 90 percent of the keyed errors are sensed by the operator and can be corrected immediately after key depression. Computer control, in many cases, can detect data input errors as they are being recorded; consequently the complexity of error detection and correction is greatly reduced, and the resulting "time lag" is minimized if not totally eliminated.

AESTHETIC CHARACTERISTICS

The compact display device incorporates the latest developments in human design engineering, making it ideally suited for today's modern office environment. Its physical appearance, its ability to eliminate various paper problems, and its prestige appeal have influenced users to select displays for front-office operations.

11. ALPHANUMERIC DISPLAY PRODUCT DESIGN CONSIDERATIONS

Several product design considerations are factors in the use of alphanumeric displays in different operating environments. These considerations affect such things as expansion capability, communication flexibility, and price.

MODULARITY

Display units are now being constructed with prewired slots for optional printed-circuit boards. Previously, the units were essentially complete packages. If additional features were required, a new model was needed or extensive factory modifications were required to expand the existing unit. Additional features or options can now be added in the field to the original unit for many displays. This design philosophy allows the user to start with a basic unit that meets his needs and then gradually add additional features as new applications develop. For example, typical modifications are increased number of maximum characters per display, added editing capability, increases in character set, added communication features and the like.

81

OPTIONAL FEATURES

Many display units offer a wide range of optional features. These features can greatly expand the capabilities of the unit. A few years ago these features usually had to be included at the time of purchase, but now they can be added at a later date. The following options are offered by many display manufacturers:

1. *Size of local storage.* This may vary from a one-character increment to increments of a multiple of the maximum number of characters that can be displayed on the screen. Several available displays can locally store several pages of characters.

2. *Total number of displayed characters.* The number of lines of characters and the number of characters per line that may be displayed on the same size screen determine not only the number of characters but also the layout of the display.

3. *Editing features.* Character replace, character insert, character delete, line insert, line delete, and the like are features that are extremely helpful in data entry and inquiry/response functions. Most displays show the "cursor symbol," or just "cursor," on the screen. It shows where the next character will be typed, either as in ordinary typewriter operations or with special operations. Many displays have special cursor-movement keys to facilitate editing. For example, four keys may be used to step the cursor left, right, up, or down.

4. *Format features.* Protected format is available on many displays. It is used to protect semifixed data on the display screen so that it cannot be unintentionally erased. Protected format is useful when filling data into standard forms. This is also referred to as "split screen." However, in its more exact connotation, split screen is another feature that allows the screen to be divided into areas so that some areas may be designated for protected format and others may remain variable.

5. *Paging or scrolling.* Paging and scrolling allow use of more memory than there are display locations on the screen. In paging, a new page or screen full of data may be called in and the data on the screen can be scrolled up or down to bring in new data, line by line, at the bottom or at the top of the screen.

6. *Other optional features.* Options include the data transmission rates, type of keyboard, associated equipment (hard-copy printer, magnetic tape cassette), limited graphics (line-drawing capability), tabulation, and different character sets.

OPERATING MODE

Display devices are designed to operate on one or more characters at a time. An unbuffered display transmits and receives one character at a time. Characters are not temporarily stored in a display memory, as has been described, but are transmitted directly to the computer one by one as the user depresses the keys. Since local memory may not be available to refresh the display, the computer or some other method must be used for memory. As previously mentioned, this memory may be a DVST or circulating delay-line storage with raster-scan display. Unbuffered devices are designed primarily to be compatible with teletypewriter operation.

A buffered display is defined as one in which a memory is used to store data in coded form for display refreshing, but also in the same form that is used for transmission to and from the computer. This form is usually an 8-bit code, with 7 bits to designate data or control characters and 1 bit for parity (error checking). The display may transmit and receive many characters, one after the other, up to the full memory capability. The memory, as mentioned previously, allows data to be edited prior to transmission. Buffered displays are available to permit the operator to select the number of characters that will be transmitted at one time—usually one character, one line, or one page. Buffered displays are usually preferred for remote multiunit installations because local editing decreases communication time, refresh is local, and many buffered units can share a single controller's communication line. Substantial savings in the cost of communications can result.

CONTROL

Alphanumeric display devices are designed to operate alone or together with several other display devices. The stand-alone units have their own controller; the multiunits share a common controller. Stand-alone units generally have the same features and capabilities as the multiunits but are cheaper when four or less displays are required. The multiunit systems essentially provide independent display operation, but, as previously mentioned, in some systems the display character capacity is decreased as more displays are added. The IBM 2260 system limits each display to 240 characters when 24 units share the controller. If 16 units are used, 480 characters can be displayed on each unit.

COMMUNICATION

Communication between the display device and the computer can be initiated by either the computer or the display operator. Computer-initiated data transmission is called polling. In this operation each display device is periodically interrogated to determine whether it requires service. Operator-initiated data transmission is a process in which each display device randomly bids for service. This is called nonpolling, interrupt, or contention operation. Different display control hardware is required for each technique. Unless the display device is designed for both polling and nonpolling, its potential market is somewhat limited. As a rule, software considerations far outweigh hardware in this area.

12. SYSTEMS USING ALPHANUMERIC DISPLAYS

Alphanumeric display devices are used in several different types of systems to perform related but essentially varied functions. In these systems the display devices operate on line to a local or remote computer or operate off line to a controller or storage device.

COMPUTER SYSTEMS

In this mode of operation, display devices are located sufficiently close (500 to 1000 feet) to the computer so that communication facilities are not required. Data are transmitted between the display and the computer by direct cable connection. By eliminating communication lines and equipment, higher data-transmission rates are more easily attained. For example, the IBM 2260 operates at up to 2460 characters per second when connected directly to a computer, but only at up to 240 characters per second when connected through a voice-grade communications line. In addition, error rates are reduced substantially.

COMMUNICATIONS SYSTEMS

Additional costs are incurred when systems require communication lines and equipment to transmit data between the computer and the display device. A wide range of communication lines and equipment is available to provide a method of operation for different data-transmission applications. Communication lines may be narrow-band lines; voice-grade telephone circuits; broad-band coaxial cable facilities; high-frequency radio transmission, or microwave transmission links. Data sets, or modems, are generally required for communications systems; for large systems with a number of remote clusters, line concentrators and transmission control units are also required. The selection of communication lines determines the data-transmission rates, and since most alphanumeric displays use voice-grade lines, a 300 character per second maximum transmission rate is typical for remote display systems.

REMOTE BATCH AND DEMAND PROCESSING SYSTEMS

In these systems the display devices are connected to a local computer that is remotely connected to the main computer. Remote batch processing reduces the volume of data communication and can substantially increase the efficiency of the main computer. The remote computer can perform a number of processing functions such as editing, reformatting, error detection, concentrating and many others that are normally done by the main computer. In addition, local storage facilities are sometimes provided so that files associated with that location can be updated and queried without interrupting the main computer. This latter technique is becoming increasingly popular in remote alphanumeric display installations.

OFF-LINE SYSTEMS

In off-line systems, the display devices are connected to a local storage system. Their function is to serve as data entry devices. The storage system may be a magnetic-tape cassette unit built into the display or provided as an optional attachment. In addition, display devices are used as terminals for stand-alone and shared key-to-storage (key-to-tape and key-to-disk) controller systems. However, the majority of key-to-storage systems do not have alphanumeric displays, but use indicators for one or more characters or employ a CRT device.

13. ASSOCIATED DISPLAY HARDWARE AND SOFTWARE

It has been stated that display devices require hardware and software to function in specific systems. In addition, optional equipment is available to expand the capabilities of alphanumeric display devices for unique applications. This section will provide a synopsis of the hardware and software that is associated with display devices.

HARDWARE

The associated hardware categories are communication equipment, printing units, and storage devices. Communication equipment is required for on-line computer operation, whereas printing units and storage devices can be used in either on-line or off-line operations.

Communications Equipment

As the name implies, communication equipment provides the linkage between the display device and the computer. This includes data sets (or modems), communication lines, and central computer communication equipment.

Modems

Data sets, or modems, are required to convert the constant-level, DC pulses generated by most data communication terminals and computers

87

into signals suitable for transmission, i.e., analogue. This signal conversion is called modulation-demodulation. Modems that permit data transmission up to 9600 bits per second on voice-grade communication lines and almost unlimited rates on broad-band lines are available from AT&T and several independent manufacturers. In addition, several display manufacturers provide modems either together with the display device or as an optional feature.

Communication Lines

The AT&T communication lines are divided into three classes: narrow-band, voice-band, and broad-band. These classes offer different data-transmission rate capabilities. Narrow-band lines provide data rates up to 300 bits per second. Voice-band-line transmission rates depend on the specific type of service. General public dial-up service provides data rates up to 2400 bits per second; leased line service provides data rates up to 9600 bits per second. Broad-band lines are basically multiples of voice-band lines; therefore, depending on the number of equivalent voice-band lines, a wide range of data rates is available. The generally available rates are 48,000, 240,000 and 1,000,000 bits per second.

Central Computer Communication Equipment

Central computer communication equipment (or the communications "front end") is located at the computer site of a system with communications and remote terminals. This front end interfaces the computer input/output channels to all communication lines going out to remote sites, whether on a dedicated basis or using the public switched network. This equipment is designed to connect to several lines at a time, and concentrates or multiplexes the data for input or output fom the computer.

Printers and Associated Devices

Teletypewriters and teleprinters have generally been used to provide hard-copy output, not only in competition with output from displays, but also as a hard-copy adjunct to displays. These devices have proved to be unsatisfactory, primarily because of their slow speeds (10 to 12.5 and 15 to 30 characters per second) and also because of their lack of automatic error-control facilities. New techniques and devices now available provide a better solution where hard copy is used with displays, usually in a ratio of one printer for six to ten displays. Among the devices being offered are the following:

1. Small desk-top printers are offered by several display manufacturers. These are controlled from the display and operate at 30 characters per second. These printers use impact or nonimpact thermal or electrostatic data recording mechanisms and are priced from $2000 to $2500. However, this type of printer is normally dedicated to one display and cannot be shared by other displays.

2. High-speed printers are stand-alone units and are designed for multiterminal installation. These printers operate at 250 to 300 characters per second, and are priced from $7000 to $10,000. They can be shared by many display devices and offer a 36-column print line.

3. Photographic devices that use Polaroid or microfilm techniques for permanent record of CRT display data are also available. However, these techniques are primarily used to record graphic rather than alphanumeric data.

4. Electrophotographic or electrostatic devices that use a CRT within the unit are also available. Anything that can be shown on the CRT can be imaged on paper, which may be standard bond or specially sensitized paper. These devices may be used along with a display to capture the data immediately. Originally they were designed to operate primarily with graphics (line drawing) displays.

5. Storage devices comprise magnetic-tape cassettes used to provide as much as 500,000 characters of local data storage for display devices. Magnetic-tape cassettes are small, compact, cartridge devices that can be used to enter and retrieve data off-line, thereby reducing the communication costs usually associated with terminal systems. These devices may be included with the display device or they may be provided as optional equipment. A wide range of features are offered, such as two-cartridge units and random access retrieval, and these afford relative advantages in specific applications. In general, the price for a magnetic-tape cassette ranges from $2500 to $4000.

SOFTWARE

The general classes of software required for on-line alphanumeric display systems include operating systems, device-control programs, and application programs.

Operating Systems

These are the organized collection of routines and procedures for operating a computer. They are included with the computer system by the computer manufacturer.

Device Control Programs

Control programs are special routines that are required to communicate with different devices. They control the flow of data between the computer and the device. These routines are provided by the computer manufacturers for their communication terminal devices; noncomputer manufacturers design or provide special hardware conversion devices to make their terminal devices compatible with these routines.

Application Programs

Application programs are special routines that process data, according to predefined steps, to arrive at a specific result. They are required in each user's environment for different applications (e.g., inventory control or order entry). These programs are usually unique for each user environment and are therefore written by the users. Some generalized application packages are available, but they usually require extensive modification to conform to a user's requirements.

14. MANUFACTURER REPORTS ON ALPHANUMERIC DISPLAY TERMINALS

To understand and apply the current technology and new developments in this field, the descriptions in this section provide detailed information on the characteristics, performance, features, and limitations of some individual, commercially available, display terminal devices.

ATLANTIC TECHNOLOGY ATC 2000 VIDEO DISPLAY

Under agreement with Atlantic Technology Corporation, the ATC 2000 video display terminal (Fig. 14-1) and related components are marketed and serviced by the MAI Equipment Corporation. Atlantic Technology Corporation currently assumes all manufacturing responsibilities and has announced its decision to produce and market an OEM version similar to the ATC 2000 under its own name at a future date. Some possible product modifications are said to include impact printing capabilities via a medium-speed line printer.

Basic Operation

The ATC video display terminal can be used in local operations, but is designed to operate remotely under a poll/address arrangement with the IBM System/360 or 370. No software modifications are necessary. All communications with the display terminal are initiated by the remote computer, and transmission of data is coordinated via a sequence of commands under program control. Manual data entry is provided via keyboard; a poll message from the computer initiates the READ operation after the addressed display has been placed in the transmit mode via a control key. One auxiliary device per single-station display or expansion unit provides printed copy of data received or transmitted by the terminal.

Fig. 14-1.   ATC 2000 Video Display Stand-Alone Terminal

Display Unit

The ATC 2000 multistation display units are available in four models: 2266, 2265, 2264, and 2263; these units have display capacities of 1920, 960, 480 and 240 characters, respectively. All models incorporate a 15-inch horizontally oriented CRT; the image area measures 8.5 x 11.0 inches. A spatial 1920-character delay-line memory within each expansion unit or single-station controller provides a one-to-one character relationship to the CRT display positions. The maximum data display can be configured in various arrangements, depending on the character capacity of the CRT;

see Table 14-1. The manufacturer states that all multistation display models can be operated interchangeably with IBM 2848/2260 control/display stations without system modifications.

Multistation Control Unit (MSCU)

The Model 2000 common controller can incorporate any combination of up to four expansion units to provide memory control interface for the display stations. One printer can be interchanged with any display unit to provide printed copy via buffered adapters. Models 4819, 4896, 4848, and 4824 expansion units can be connected to one, two, four, or eight displays, respectively. The memory capacity of each expansion unit is 1920 characters, which must be divided equally among an even number of displays. Arrangements from four 1920-character displays to thirty-two 240-character displays are possible, using one MSCU. Total buffer capacity of the Model 2000 controller is 7680 characters.

ATC Features Contrasting IBM 2260

The ATC 2000 is available in two basic configurations; both arrangements provide connection to the communications facility via a data set:

Table 14-1.   ATC 2000 Standard Display Configurations
with Horizontal CRT Orientation

DISPLAY MODEL	MAXIMUM NUMBER OF DISPLAYS	MAXIMUM DISPLAY SIZE			NOMINAL CHARACTER SIZE,* INCHES	
		LINES	CHAR/ LINE	NO. OF CHARACTERS	HEIGHT	WIDTH
2266	1	24	80	1,920	0.18	0.12
2266	1	30	64	1,920	0.22	0.15
2266	1	48	40	1,920	0.15	0.15
2265	2	12	80	960	0.18	0.12
2265	2	15	64	960	0.22	0.15
2265	2	24	40	960	0.30	0.23
2264	4	6	80	480	0.18	0.12
2264	4	12	40	480	0.33	0.23
2263	8	3	80	240	0.18	0.12
2263	8	6	40	240	0.33	0.23

* A maximum character size measuring 0.33 x 0.33 inch can be internally adjusted without distortion.

1. The single-station configuration is a pedestal-mounted unit including a 1920- or 960-character CRT display, controller, and alphanumeric keyboard housed within a single console; a desk-top version includes a controller designed to fit in a desk drawer.

2. The multistation configuration is a display complex consisting of a common control unit connected to multiple CRT keyboard/display units; all display units operate simultaneously via independent edit logic and control provided within each expansion unit.

The multistation configuration consists of the following basic components:

1. Multistation control unit (MSCU): Common controller contains communications interface and control logic; provides housing for up to four expansion units with total memory capacity of 7680 characters in modules of 1920; controls up to 32 display stations. See Table 14-2.

2. Expansion unit: Maximum of four units; four models provide connection to one, two, four, or eight displays and can be used in any combination; 1920-character capacity per unit; each unit contains its own keyboard edit logic to provide simultaneous operation of all attached display units.

3. Display station: Four models, including alphanumeric keyboards, provide maximum display capacities of 240, 480, 960, and 1920 characters; an even number of displays with the same capacity totaling 1920 characters are driven by a common expansion unit.

4. Printer (optional): A modified version of the IBM Selectric typewriter; an optional printer adapter provides connection to the ATC 2000 control unit; print operations can be initiated by the remote computer or the display operator. A single printer can be accommodated by each stand-alone display or by each expansion unit in a multistation arrangement.

Table 14-2.   ATC 2000 Expanded Multistation
Display Configurations

EXPANSION UNIT MODEL	EXPANSION UNITS PER MSCU *	DISPLAYS PER EXPANSION UNIT	MEMORY CAPACITY PER DISPLAY †	TOTAL NUMBER OF DISPLAYS PER MSCU
4819	4	1	1920	4
4896	4	2	960	8
4848	4	4	480	16
4824	4	8	240	32

* Any combination up to four identical expansion units can be used in one system.
† Total memory capacity per MSCU is 7680 bytes.

The following entries indicate features common to both single-station and multistation configurations:

1. Keyboard: Typewriter-styled, 62-key keyboard including four keys for control functions and seven keys for cursor control; 64-character alpha-numeric character set is standard and includes upper-case letters, digits, and special symbols; 96-character set, optional.

2. Cursor: A blinking, underline, nondestructive cursor is standard.

3. Character generation: The cursive stroke technique is employed.

4. CRT size: Rectangular CRT (measured diagonally) is 15 inches for all display capacities.

5. Remote edit control: The display terminal executes AUTO TAB ERASE when the remote computer responds to a transmitted message with an ACK code; causes automatic erasure of all text apart from the fixed format and repositioning of the cursor to the beginning of the first variable data field.

6. Format control: Multiple variable data fields are framed by pairs of START and END symbols entered manually when transmitting in the conversation mode or automatically when received from the remote computer; the variable data fields are part of a fixed message format; only the framed data are transmitted; when entering data into a fixed format, the cursor automatically advances from the end of a variable data field to the next START symbol.

7. Character addressing: Program positioning of the cursor by a WRITE command to a specified line and character location as a prelude to an accompanying message or an anticipated manual entry; cursor positioning responds to a three-character address sequence consisting of an address function code, line, and character address codes; this command may

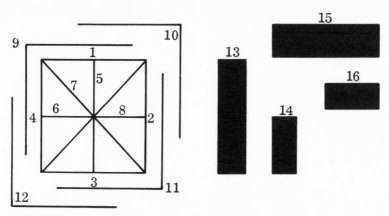

Fig. 14-2. Standard Set of Graphics Line Segments Available as an Optional Feature with the ATC 2000 Video Display Terminal

be contained several times within one message to provide spontaneous edit functions.

8. Graphic operations: Optional set of 16 line segments; access to space between lines via an expanded stroke matrix permits line symbols to be contiguous; see Figure 14-2.

Cursor

The ATC 2000 incorporates in all display models a nondestructive cursor that is automatically displayed on the CRT as a position marker to indicate the exact location to be occupied by the next character entered via keyboard or the location of an existing character to be altered via edit controls. Cursor manipulation is provided by seven keyboard control keys. The TAB key automatically positions the cursor at the beginning of the variable data fields, enabling manual insertion of a message without destroying the fixed data while in the protected text mode. The conversational mode is made possible by automatic cursor movement to the beginning of query and reply fields. Controls causing the cursor to advance from the last display position or backspace from the home position include a wraparound capability. Cursor controls are as follows:

1. NEW LINE enters a new line symbol at the cursor position (when shift key is used) and advances the cursor to the first position of the next line (will wrap around).
2. UP positions the cursor up one line; cursor occupies same location in the line (will wrap around).
3. DOWN positions the cursor down one line; cursor occupies same location in the line (will wrap around).
4. RIGHT advances the cursor one character position (will wrap around).
5. LEFT backspaces the cursor one character position (will wrap around).
6. HOME positions the cursor at the first character location of the first line.
7. TAB positions the cursor at the first character location following the next displayed START symbol; the cursor is positioned at the home location in the absence of a START symbol.

In addition to the cursor controls, the ATC 2000 incorporates a flexible set of edit functions. These edit functions are as follows:

1. ERASE positions the cursor at home position and erases the entire display.
2. TAB ERASE erases all data bracketed by START and END sym-

bols except data located to the right of, and on the same line as, a NEW LINE symbol. The operation is terminated and the cursor is positioned at the HOME location in the absence of a START symbol. The operation is also terminated at the last display position when an END symbol is not encountered following a START symbol.

3. INSERT permits data to be added to an existing text. As data is entered, the existing text is displaced to the right; the data to the right of a NEW LINE symbol is not displaced. Data displaced to the right of the last character position of a line is lost.

4. DELETE permits data to be erased from the existing text while closing the text to maintain continuity. The data to the right of a NEW LINE symbol is not displaced; neither is an END symbol nor the data to its right. Space codes are substituted for blank positions.

Table 14-3.   ATC 2000 Output to Display Characteristics

CHARACTERISTIC	DESCRIPTION
Output medium	CRT displays green characters against gray background
Character set	Digits 0–9; upper-case alphabetics; 28 punctuation and special symbols
Character size	0.18 inch high by 0.12 wide (80 char/line), or 0.22 inch high by 0.15 inch wide (64 char/line)
Character generation	Stroke
Display size	10.0 × 7.5 inches (15-inch diagonal CRT); horizontal CRT orientation
Characters per line	40, 64, 80
Lines per display	3, 6, 12, 15, 24, 30, 48
Characters per display	240, 480, 960, 1920
Buffer capacity	7680 characters per Model 2000 control unit; includes four modules of 1920 characters each
Format control	Line feed; carriage return; character addressing; cursor advance 1 space or 1 line at a time; automatic cursor wraparound from last position to first when advancing, or from first position to last when backspacing: multiple variable fields framed between START and END symbols; automatic cursor positioning within fixed format; conversational mode via split screen
Rated output speed	1200 bits/sec (120 char/sec) and 2400 bits/sec (240 char/sec) over a voice-band; 2560 char/sec with connection to System/360 channel
Effective output speed	Lower than rated speed due to exchange of control messages and header characters

Data Transmission

The ATC 2000, under local operations, can provide transmission of data serial by byte, parallel by bit at rates of up to 123.5 kilobytes per second; when operating locally with an IBM System/360 computer, data are transmitted serial by bit at 2560 characters per second. Operating remotely, data are transmitted synchronously or asynchronously in the half-duplex mode at rates up to 4800 bits per second. Remote connection to an IBM System/360 or 370 computer provides transmission rates of 1200 and 2400 bits per second. The ATC 2000 employs a modified 7-level, 10-point ASCII transmission code including character parity and START and STOP bits. See Table 14-3.

Options

The following optional features are available with the ATC 2000 video display upon order:

1. Limited graphics: Includes set of 16 various line segments with or without keyboard provisions, one set per stand-alone display or expansion unit.
2. Printer Adapter: Mechanical interface and buffer compatible with Selectric type printer or equivalent; includes a CPU-addressable, 1920-character buffer.
3. Lower case (two versions): Size change (no extra cost); true lower case (extra cost) expands character set to 92.
4. Function keys (14 keys): Enables the transmission of a one-character message to the computer; can be used for forms call-up.

BUNKER-RAMO SERIES 2200 DATA DISPLAY SYSTEM

The Bunker-Ramo Series 2200 data display system (Fig. 14-3) is designed to facilitate the rapid exchange of data between a computer and one or more remote locations under control of a stored program in a computer. A variety of cathode-ray tube display stations and nondisplay devices can be connected to a control unit, which contains the interface to the communications line. Each display or nondisplay device can be located up to 1000 cable-feet from the control unit. The nondisplay devices that can be incorporated include Teletype paper-tape readers and punches, Teletype Model 33 or 35 receive-only printers, and Teletype Model 35 keyboard send-receive units. Bunker-Ramo will supply the Teletype equipment if desired by the customer.

Bunker-Ramo has produced a number of special designs for customers: the Series 2200 system is the current standard product line. Bunker-Ramo display equipment is also known under the registered trademark TELE-REGISTER.

The Bunker-Ramo Series 2200 terminals interface an IBM System/360 or 370 computer via a BR 2238 interfacing unit, which connects directly to the IBM selector or multiplexor channel. Sofeware modifications for os and DOS BTAM and OS GPS are supplied with this interface.

The 2200 terminals can be connected to many computers over voice-band communication facilities, and direct, computer connection for local operation can be achieved through a 2235 general-purpose, high-speed computer interface.

The Bunker-Ramo Series 2200 data display system is also offered by Honeywell under the name Honeywell Series 2300 Visual Information Projection (VIP).

In a data communications environment, a Series 2200 display system can be arranged in two functionally different ways. In a nonpolling arrangement, only one control unit can be operated or one communications line, and all communications between the remote computer and the display stations are initiated by the display station operators. In a polling arrangement, up to 31 control units can be connected to one line, and all communications are initiated by the remote computer under stored program control or by special hardware. The control unit is connected to a remote computer via the public telephone network or a common-carrier-leased voice-band line, appropriate data sets, and the communications controller at the computer site.

The control unit performs a scan of associated devices periodically (nonpolling) or when a request is receiving (polling). The connected devices are tested sequentially for a pending message; if one is found, it is transmitted to the computer. Scanning of the other units is resumed only after a computer response is received or after a predetermined period of time has elapsed.

Communication between the computer and a particular control unit is performed in a half-duplex mode. In the polling arrangement, full-duplex communications facilities are used to permit simultaneous transmission from the computer to one control unit and reception from another. Communication interface features are available for transmission from 600 to 2400 bits per second. The most commonly used speeds are 1200, 1600, 1800, 2000, or 2400 bits per second.

The seven-level ASCII transmission code is employed, with an eighth bit added for character parity. Asynchronous (START/STOP) synchronization is generally employed at 1200 to 1800 bits per second; a total of

10 bits, including START and STOP bits, are transmitted for each character. Synchronous transmission is generally used at 2000 or 2400 bits per second; in this case, sync characters are transmitted prior to each message, and a total of eight bits per character is transmitted.

There are two models of the display station:

1. Model 2206/17 display station provides a removable alphanumeric keyboard with mechanical key linkages and a 12-inch rectangular cathode-ray display tube; see Figure 14-3 (left). This keyboard is for typists.

2. Model 2212 display station provides an alphanumeric keyboard arranged in two separate blocks containing numerics and alphabetics; see Figure 14-3 (right). This keyboard is for nontypists.

Either model can be used on single-station of multistation control units, or both can be intermixed. The display capacity is up to 444 (Model 2212) or up to 960 (Model 2206/17) characters. The display size is a function of the number of devices connected to the control unit. Display-only devices (no keyboard) are available; these devices are Models 2217, 2218, and 2219 display monitors.

Editing facilities available to a display station operator include movement of the cursor to the left or the right, one position at a time or repetitively, to the first position of the next line, and to the first display position. Control keys are also provided to erase one character or an entire line. The cursor is nondestructive; i.e., it does not erase the character displayed in the position the cursor occupies.

A number of special function keys provide convenient transaction code input. These keys generate unique code patterns, but the user can select the key-top markings. If the multimessage transaction feature is incorporated, only the last display station inquiry or computer response is transmitted, but previous inquiries and responses continue to be displayed. The operator can position the cursor and hence enter or alter data only in the last response. A special character code transmitted from the computer enables the operator to access any portion of the displayed data. Without the multimessage feature, all display data are transmitted each time.

The blink feature permits the computer to blink selectively all data on the screen or portions of the data at a rate of once per second.

The tab control feature allows the operator to tab to a predetermined position on the screen. The tab positions are identified by special, displayable characters included in the message.

Character and longitudinal parity checking are performed on all data received by a control unit from the remote computer; character parity bits and longitudinal check characters are generated and transferred with all data transmitted from the control unit. A "t" (Transmit mode) or an "e"

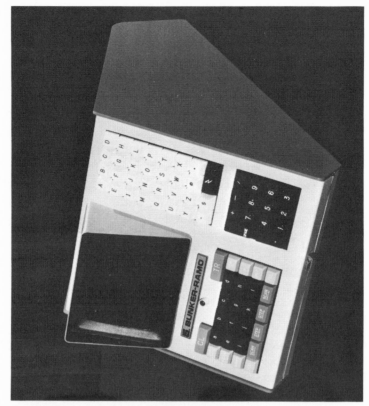

Fig. 14-3. Bunker-Ramo 2206/17 Display Station (left) and 2212 Display Station (right)

101

(Error condition) is displayed in the first displayable position to indicate the status of a display station. Detection of an error by the remote computer is indicated by failure of the control unit to receive a response within a predetermined period of time. Retransmissions must be initiated manually, but the data need not be rekeyed. For nondisplay devices, positive and negative acknowledgment messages are used to indicate successful or unsuccessful transmission; the control unit can automatically retransmit a message in response to a negative acknowledgment.

The Bunker-Ramo Series 2200 data display system can also be connected directly to a variety of computer systems via special interfaces. The 2238 is available for direct connection to the IBM System/360 computers. Other interfaces are also available. The data transfer rate, when connected directly, can be up to a maximum of 66,000 characters per second. The remainder of this section discusses the Series 2200 display system as used in a data communications environment, unless otherwise specified.

Configuration

In a data communications environment, Bunker-Ramo Series 2200 data display systems can be arranged in two functionally different ways. In a nonpolling arrangement, all communications between the computer and the display stations are initiated by the display station operators. In a polling arrangement, all communications are initiated by the computer under control of the program stored in the computer or special hardware devices.

A nonpolling arrangement consists of the following components:

1. One Model 2221, 2222, or 2223 control unit and appropriate Model 2241, 2242, 2242A, 2243, 2246, or 2246A expansion modules as needed
2. A number of associated display and nondisplay devices
3. A model 2231 communications interface and data set

A polling arrangement consists of the following components:

1. Up to 31 Model 2221, 2222, or 2223 control units and appropriate Model 2241, 2242, 2242A, 2243, 2246, or 2246A expansion modules as needed
2. A number or associated display and nondisplay devices for each control unit
3. One Model 2231 communications interface and corresponding data set for each control unit

The devices connected to each control unit can be located up to 1000 cable-feet away from the control unit. The Model 2231 communications interface permits data communications at 600 to 1600 bits per second, using an asynchronous (START/STOP) technique, and 2000 or 2400 bits per second using synchronous transmission. Two display stations can be incorporated in a Series 2200 data display system, and each includes a keyboard for manual data entry.

Control modules are available for connecting the following nondisplay devices:

1. Teletype CX paper-tape reader
2. Teletype BRPE paper-tape punch
3. Teletype Model 33 or 35 receive-only printer
4. Teletype Model 33 or 35 keyboard send-receive unit

A control module is required for each nondisplay device incorporated.

The Model 2221, 2222, or 2223 control unit contains the basic control logic for all devices connected to the control unit and contains 1032 characters of buffer storage. Four models of expansion modules are available, each of which also contains 1032 characters of storage. The buffer storage of the basic control unit and the expansion modules may be segmented to allow the connection of multiple devices. The basic Model 2222 control unit can accommodate up to 36 display stations (any model) and nondisplay devices in any combination.

As the number of devices connected to the basic control unit or to an expansion module increases, the display size or size of buffer storage allocation decreases accordingly. Table 14-4 summarizes the maximum number of devices permitted for each of the possible display formats.

Table 14-4. Bunker-Ramo 2200 Expansion
Module Allocation

NUMBER OF DEVICE PER DELAY-LINE BUFFER	NUMBER OF CHARACTERS PER DEVICE (BUFFER)		STANDARD DISPLAY FORMAT (LINES/ CHARS/RETRACE)	MAXIMUM NUMBER OF DEVICES PER CONTROL UNIT
1	1032	=	12 x 80 + 12 x 6	9
1	1032	=	24 x 37 + 24 x 6	9
2	516	=	6 x 80 + 6 x 6	18
2	516	=	12 x 37 + 12 x 6	18
4	258	=	6 x 37 + 6 x 6	36

COMPUTER COMMUNICATIONS CC-33
TELETYPE-ORIENTED DISPLAY STATION

The basic CC-33 Teletype compatible display station consists of a CRT/ keyboard and control unit that operates into computer systems using the existing Teletype hardware and software without modification. Designed for fixed-location or portable operation, the CC-33 can incorporate, with slight modification, any standard television receiver as a display device. Both alphanumeric and graphic data can be displayed. An alphanumeric keyboard provides manual data entry.

Configuration

The basic CC-33 display station configuration (Fig. 14-4) includes the following components:

1. CC-301 Model III display controller
2. CC-300 Model II TV display
3. CC-303 Model III alphanumeric keyboard

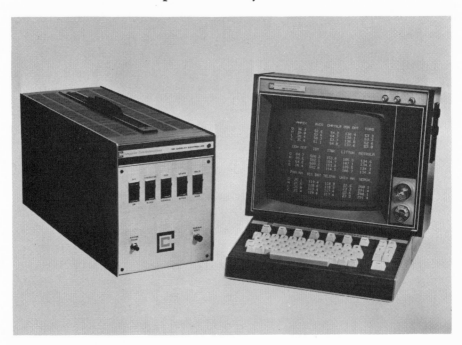

Fig. 14-4.   CC-33 Teletype-Oriented Display Station Including CC-301
Model III TV Display Controller, CC-300 Model II TV Receiver,
and CC-303 Model III Alphanumeric Keyboard

The cc-301 Model III tv display controller contains a 1024-word buffer (9 bits per word), a character/graph generator, input/output control section (for local devices), and a serial interface. The cc-300 Model II tv receiver, a 12-inch solid-state portable television receiver, is the standard display device connected to the cc-301 controller. Other models are available from cci; they differ from one another in screen size and the use of tube-type or solid-state circuitry.

Up to 16 cc-300 tv receivers can be attached to a single cc-301 controller; the same image is displayed by all receivers. In addition, any conventional monochrome television receiver can be adapted by cci to operate with the cc-301 controller; the required modification is slight.

Data can be manually entered via the cc-303 alphanumeric keyboard. Several input/output devices are available with the cc-30 communications station:

1. cc-304 light pen
2. Portable cc-305 line printer (Motorola), 300 characters per second
3. Portable cc-306 card reader, 300 cards per minute
4. cc-308 Teletypewriter adapter (connects all Teletype models)

Any combination up to seven input/output devices can be connected to a cc-301 controller when the optional input channel (option 3) and output channel (option 4) are incorporated. Additional devices, including magnetic-tape units, magnetic-disk units, paper-tape units, and others can be connected to the cc-301 controller; prices for these options are individually negotiable with cci.

Display Controller

A serial interface (option 1) is required when the cc-33 display station is connected to a communications line. The serial communications interface contained in the cc-301 controller can interface with a Bell System Series 100 or 200 data set for fixed-location operation. Alternatively, the cc-302 telephone coupler can acoustically couple the cc-301 controller to a conventional telephone set where portable operation is desired. The cc-302 coupler is compatible with the Bell System data-phone data set 103A1 or 103A2.

Display Unit

The output characteristics of the cc-300 Model II receiver are summarized in Table 14-6. Any conventional television receiver ranging from a 5-inch screen to a 23-inch screen will display the same format when connected to the cc-301 controller. When operating in the graphic mode, the display image is formed by a pattern of dots arranged in a 108 x 85 dot matrix; the viewing area on a 12-inch receiver measures 5.5 x 8 inches.

The buffer memory included in the cc-301 controller has a capacity of 1024 nine-bit words; the first 800 word locations correspond to the 800-position alphanumeric display format (960 character option available). The remaining 224 memory locations are accessible to the computer for storing and retrieving terminal identification and other information.

Each display character is formed within a 5 x 7 dot matrix. The 64-symbol character set includes upper-case alphabetics, numerics, and special symbols (including the cursor symbols). A nonstandard character set (option 2) allows the user to define a character set of up to 96 characters or symbols, employing bit configurations in columns 2 through 7 of the ASCII code chart. The display is regenerated 60 times per second.

Each character display location has an absolute memory address; the memory contents is displayed continuously and can be transmitted to the computer or output device at any time via keyboard or program control. The nondestructive cursor, displayed as a horizontal underline, indicates the location to be occupied by the next character entered into or read from the memory buffer. TV receivers varying in size from 8 inches to 27 inches (measured diagonally) are available. The maximum display format consists of 20 lines of data with 40 characters to a line; a 24-line arrangement is available as an option. The display characteristics of three typical CRT models are represented in Table 14-5.

Keyboard

The cc-303 Model III keyboard is interlocked to prevent more than one key depression at a time. A cable connection provides keyboard operations up to 150 feet from the display controller. The Model III keyboard contains 65 keys including control and cursor keys that are separated (for ease of identification) from the data entry keys. This keyboard is capable of

Table 14-5. Representative CCI Display Characteristics
of Three Standard cc-300 Screen Sizes

CRT SIZE (INCHES)	DISPLAY AREA		CHARACTER SIZE	
	ALPHANUMERIC (INCHES)	GRAPHIC (INCHES)	HEIGHT (INCHES)	WIDTH (INCHES)
8	5.5 x 4.5	5.0 x 3.25	0.125	0.094
12	8.0 x 6.5	7.25 x 4.75	0.219	0.156
18	12.0 x 10.0	11.25 x 7.00	0.313	0.219

generating a 127-character ASCII character set (except NUL). Control codes can be generated by depressing the special code key concurrently with the designated control code key. Repetitive data entry is performed by holding a key in a depressed position.

Cursor controls permit positioning the cursor (an underscore symbol) to—

1. The first character position of the first line (RESET key).
2. The first character position of the current line (RETURN key).
3. The same character position of the next line (NEW LINE key).
4. The current position on the next line (DOWN arrow).
5. The current position on the preceding line (UP arrow).
6. One space to the right (RIGHT arrow).
7. One space to the left (LEFT arrow).

When the cursor controls marked by arrows are held in a depressed position, the cursor continues to step in the specified direction and will wrap around the screen in any of the four directions. The current cursor location is contained in a cursor address register within the CC-301 controller. The cursor address can be accessed and altered by the computer.

Table 14-6 describes important output features of the CC-300 Display.

Table 14-6. CCI CC-300 Display Output Characteristics

CHARACTERISTIC	DESCRIPTION
Output medium	Cathode-ray tube; displays white characters on black background
Character set	64 characters, including upper-case alphabetics, numerics, punctuation marks, and special symbols; 96 customer-specified characters or symbols with the nonstandard character set (option 2)
Character size	0.156 inches wide and 0.187 inches high when using a 12-inch TV receiver
Display size	6.5 x 8-inch viewing area (standard 12-inch CRT); CRT sizes range from 8 inches to 27 inches (diagonal measurement)
Character generation	5 x 7 dot matrix
Characters per line	40
Lines per display	20 or 24 (option 5)
Characters per display	800 or 960 (option 5)
Buffer capacity	1024 characters
Format control	NEW LINE character; flexible cursor movement controls; fixed tab positioning
Rated output speed	Up to 110, 600, or 1200 bits/sec over public telephone network or leased voice-band or narrow-band line
Effective output speed	Limited by message length and communications facility

Optional Features

The cc-304 light pen is a narrow aperture, low-resolution photocell capable of locating a single character position (alpha mode) or any three horizontally sequential dots (graphic mode). When activated, the light pen can be used to select specific data displayed on the screen; the addresses (coordinates) of the selected data are stored for later access by the computer. After selecting the data, the operator can alert the computer by transmitting an interrupt signal.

The portable cc-305 line printer provides high-speed, nonimpact printing capabilities at 300 characters per second, which can be executed locally for off-line operations or remotely under computer program control. Any selected portion of a displayed text can be printed; the printing operation incorporates an electrothermal printing technique with a continuously moving 8.5-inch roll of paper and four separate rotating printheads. Data are printed from the buffer sequentially by character and line position in the 80-character line format made. A display-image format mode can also be employed where characters are printed only in the middle 40 page columns (positions 20 through 60), arranged identically to the displayed data configuration.

The portable cc-306 card reader reads standard 80-column punched cards photoelectrically at a rate of 300 cards per minute. The cc-306 is capable of two separate operating modes selected under computer control: the binary image mode and the Hollerith mode. In the binary image mode, each card column is interpreted as two separate 6-bit characters of data as it is read into the buffer memory. Parity is generated and bit 7 of each work is set to avoid confusion with ASCII code characters. The card reader generates EOT after five cards (800 bytes) have been read into the buffer. In the Hollerith mode, each card column is translated into its 7-bit ASCII code equivalent; parity is generated and the characters are read into consecutive buffer locations following the movement of the cursor. Data transmission is terminated when an EOT, INT, or TRANS character is read, or when data from ten cards (800 characters) have been transmitted, generating EOT. The cc-306 will function accordingly upon reading any ASCII control characters.

Data Transmission

The cc-301 Model III display controller operates in a full-duplex mode over the public telephone network or a narrow-band facility using a Bell System Series 103 or 202 data-phone data set or the cc-302 telephone coupler; equivalent data sets and telephone couplers can be used. Data are transmitted serial by bit at 110, 600, or 1200 bits per second; transmission rates are switch-selectable (option 13). The cc-301 controller accommodates serial transmission at increased rates, using higher-speed serial interfaces that are available on special request.

The cc-33 communications station employs the seven-level ASCII transmission code. An even parity bit is appended to each transmitted character.

When operating as a stand-alone display station (i.e., a single cc-301 controller and cc-300 TV receiver), an asynchronous transmission technique is employed. A total of 11 bits, including unity START and two STOP bits, seven data bits, and an even parity bit are transmitted.

Editing Facilities

Data can be altered by positioning the cursor to the desired character location and typing new data over the existing data; no expansion or contraction of data takes place. The entire screen can be erased by using the CLEAR key. The TAB key positions the cursor forward or backward to a fixed-tab STOP location at the center position of each line. After the bottom line is displayed, the cursor automatically wraps around to the first display line. Each succeeding line feed automatically erases all characters from the next line before data entry continues.

Operating Procedure

Data are entered at any location of the display by positioning the cursor to that location and keying in the data. The cursor advances one character position as each character enters. Any editing that may be necessary is performed prior to transmitting the message in the block mode. The end-of-text character is entered at the end of the message by depressing the END key. Transmission of the message follows.

The station can operate in one of two operator-selectable transmission modes: character mode or block mode. In the character mode of operation, each character entered from the keyboard is immediately transmitted. In a full-duplex system the station waits for a response from the computer and displays the returned character or message. In a half-duplex system the character is displayed locally immediately.

The computer can respond to a detected character-parity error by returning a special parity symbol, which is displayed in the current cursor position on the screen. Data can be transmitted from any input device in the system. In this mode of operation, errors can be detected and corrected on a character-by-character basis.

In the block mode, the complete message is composed prior to transmission. When the message is to be transmitted, the TRANSMIT key is depressed. The cc-301 controller functions in one of two submodes of operation when placed in the block mode. These submodes (transmit enabled and transmit disabled) are established by the computer. The controller must be placed in the transmit enabled submode to accept a message. If it is already in this mode when the TRANSMIT key is depressed, the message is immediately sent to the computer. Depressing the TRANSMIT key when the controller is in the transmit disabled submode, will lock the keyboard until the computer polls for the message.

Message Configuration

Commands received from the computer are preceded by a start-of-header (soh) character that conditions the controller to interpret the following character as a function code. Bit positions 7 through 5 of the function code select a specific input or output device (including the display unit); bit positions 4 through 1 specify one of several commands such as SELECT graphic or alphanumeric mode, LOAD or READ cursor address register, READ light pen address, HALT local input/output operations, and others. The computer can also request the status of the station, defined in a single character. When it is desired to unlock the keyboard, the computer message is terminated with an end-of-transmission (EOT) signal, which releases the keyboard to the operator.

Error Detection and Correction

Errors that occur during off-line composition are corrected by positioning the cursor under the character in error and rekeying the correct character. When transmitting a message to the computer in the character mode, the computer responds to a detected character-parity error by returning a special parity symbol, which is displayed in the position of the character received in error. The operator corrects the error by retyping the character.

Computer response to errors received in the block mode is dependent upon the controlling software. When parity errors are detected at the display station, a status bit is set and a special parity character is displayed on the screen in place of the character in error. The operator can request retransmission or can repeat the interrogation message.

COMPUTER COMMUNICATIONS CC-36 TELEVIDEO CONVERSATIONAL/BATCH STATION

The cc-36 is an integrated communications terminal designed to accommodate remote batching operations, on-line transmission and reception of data in a conversation mode, and off-line operations using local peripheral equipment. Communications with a remote computer can be provided over the public telephone network or a leased voice-band or broad-band facility. The terminal can be coupled to a standard telephone set, connected to a Bell System Series 100, 200, or 300 data set, or connected directly to the computer input/output channel.

Station controls covering input/output operations and data transmission can be initiated manually by keyboard or remotely by the computer, using the appropriate set of ASCII control codes. The CC-36 station can store and execute up to eight consecutive control code sequences, using any combination of the 17 available control codes provided in the CC-301 controller. Once initiated, the stored set of control operations is executed in the order specified without additional operator or computer intervention.

Configuration

The CC-36 televideo conversational/batch station (Fig. 14-5) is available in two basic configurations: Model I and Model II. Excluding the type of printing device used, which is the only distinguishing feature between the two models, both configurations incorporate the same basic components in an integrated console. Model I includes a nonimpact printer;

Fig. 14-5. CCI CC-36 Televideo Conversational/Batch Station Model I Including CC-305 Line Printer, CC-300 Model II TV Receiver, CC-303 Alphanumeric Keyboard, CC-306 Card Reader, and CC-301 Model II TV Display Controller

Model II includes an impact printer. The remaining components common
to both models include the following devices:

1. cc-301 Model II tv display controller
2. cc-300 Model II tv display
3. cc-303 Model III alphanumeric keyboard
4. cc-306 card reader

The cc-300 Model II tv receiver (a 12-inch, solid-state, portable television receiver), is the standard display device connected to the cc-301
controller. Other models are available from cci; they differ from one another in screen size and the use of tube-type or solid-state circuitry. Up to
16 cc-300 tv receivers can be attached to a single cc-301 controller; the
same image is displayed by all receivers. In addition, any conventional
monochrome television receiver can be adapted by cci to operate with the
cc-301 controller; the required modification is slight.

Display Controller

The cc-301 Model II tv display controller contains a 1024-word buffer
(9 bits per word), a character/graph generator, an input/output control
section (for local devices), and a serial interface. A parallel interface is
also included to provide direct connection to a computer via a channel
adapter (computer interface). In this configuration, data can be transferred at rates up to 500,000 characters per second.

A serial interface (option 1) is required when the cc-36 station is connected to a communications line. The serial communications interface can
also operate using data sets or over direct connection at rates up to 50,000
bits per second.

Up to 32 remote cc-36 stations, each operating over a separate line, can
be connected to a single computer input/output channel via the cc-72
communications multiplexor located at the computer site. A cc-72 line
adapter, contained in the cc-72 cabinet, is required for every two communications lines. A channel adapter is required to match the cc-72 multiplexor to the computer input/output channel. The channel adapters are
designed to provide a direct parallel connection between the computer and
a cc-36 station; an optional serial interface is required when the channel
adapter is to be connected to a remote cc-36.

A family of channel adapters is available to meet the interface requirements of some of the major computer manufacturers. The channel adapters
presently available from cci are listed below.

1. cc-7011 connects to storage access channel of an ibm 1130
   computer.

2. cc-7012 connects to selector or multiplexor channels of an ibm System/360 or 370 computer.

3. cc-7013 connects to data channel of a cdc 3000 Series computer.

4. cc-7014 connects to sds Sigma Series computer.

5. cc-7015 connects to input/output bus of a dec pdp-8, Linc-8, or pdp-12 computer.

The cc-72 remote master controller enables the computer to address up to 32 cc-301 controllers and related devices, all operating over the same line. Each cc-301 controller can be located up to 5000 cable-feet from the master controller. A cc-721 line adapter, contained in the master control cabinet, is required for every two cc-301 controllers.

Display Unit

Any conventional television receiver ranging from a 5-inch screen to a 23-inch screen will display the same format when connected to the cc-301 controller. When operating in the graphic mode, the display image is formed by a pattern of dots arranged in a 108 x 85 dot matrix; the viewing area on a 12-inch receiver measures 5.5 x 8 inches.

The buffer memory included in the cc-301 controller has a capacity of 1024 nine-bit words; the first 800 word locations correspond to the 800-position alphanumeric display format (960-character option available). The remaining 224 memory locations are accessible to the computer for storing and retrieving terminal identification and other information.

Each display character is formed within a 5 x 7 dot matrix. The 69-symbol character set includes upper-case alphabetics, numerics, and special symbols (including the cursor symbol). The display is regenerated 60 times per second. Each character display location has an absolute memory address; the memory contents is displayed continuously and can be transmitted to the computer or output device at any time via keyboard or program control. The nondestructive cursor, displayed as a horizontal underline, indicates the location to be occupied by the next character entered into or read from the memory buffer. TV receivers varying in size from 8 inches to 27 inches (measured diagonally) are available. The maximum display format consists of 20 lines of data with 40 characters to a line; a 24-line arrangement is available as an option. The display formats of three cci crt models are presented in Table 14-5.

Keyboard

The cc-303 Model III keyboard operates electromechanically and is interlocked to prevent more than one key depression at a time. A cable connection provides keyboard operations up to 150 feet from the display controller. The Model III keyboard contains 65 keys, including control and cursor keys that are separated (for ease of identification) from the data entry keys. This keyboard is capable of generating a 127-character ASCII character set (except NUL). Control functions can be generated by depressing only the control function key. Control codes other than those specified by the control function keys can be generated by depressing the control key concurrently with the designated control code key. Repetitive data entry is performed by holding a key in a depressed position.

Cursor controls permit positioning the cursor (an underscore symbol) to—

1. The first character position of the first line (RESET key).
2. The first character position of the current line (RETURN key).
3. The same character position of the next line (NEW LINE key).
4. The current position on the next line (DOWN arrow).
5. The current position on the preceding line (UP arrow).
6. One space to the right (RIGHT arrow).
7. One space to the LEFT (left arrow).

When the cursor controls marked by arrows are held in a depressed position, the cursor continues to step in the specified direction and will wrap around the screen in any of the four directions. The current cursor location is contained in a cursor address register within the CC-301 controller. The cursor address can be accessed and altered by the computer.

Line Printer

The basic CC-36 terminal provides high-speed printing devices to produce printed copy of any selected portion of a displayed text initiated locally via keyboard or by remote program control. This system also facilitates on-line computer-to-print and off-line key-to-print operations. Two basic terminal configurations are available, incorporating different printing devices.

The CC-36 Model I includes the CC-305 line printer for nonimpact printing capability at 300 characters per second. The printing operation employs an electrothermal printing technique with a continuously moving 8.5-inch roll of paper and four separate rotating printheads. Data are printed from the buffer sequentially by character and line position in the 80-character line format mode. A display image format mode can also be employed where characters are printed only in the middle 40-page columns (positions 20 through 60), arranged identically to the displayed data configuration.

The CC-36 Model II includes an impact line printer with a 132-character buffer. Printing is executed via rotating drum and a shuttle type of print mechanism at 300 lines per minute. Up to 80 characters per line can be printed, using a standard 64-character set. Single spacing provides 6 to 8 lines per inch. Data are printed from the buffer sequentially by character and line position.

Card Reader

The cc-306 card reader reads standard 80-column punched cards photo-electrically at a rate of 300 cards per minute. The cc-306 is capable of two separate operating modes selected under computer control: the binary image mode and the Hollerith mode. In the binary image mode, each card column is interpreted as two separate 6-bit characters of data as it is read into the buffer memory. Parity is generated and bit 7 of each word is set to avoid confusion with ASCII code characters. The card reader generates EOT after five cards (800 bytes) have been read into the buffer. In the Hollerith mode, each card column is translated into its 7-bit ASCII code equivalent; parity is generated and the characters are read into consecutive buffer locations following the movement of the cursor. Data transmission is terminated when an EOT, INT, or TRANS character is read, or when data from ten cards (800 characters) have been transmitted, generating EOT. The cc-306 will function accordingly upon reading any ASCII control characters.

Data Transmission

The cc-301 display controller operates in a half-duplex mode over the public telephone network at up to 2000 bits per second or over a leased voice-band line at up to 2400 bits per second. The cc-301 can also operate in a half-duplex mode over broad-band facilities at up to 50,000 bits per second, using a Bell System Series 300 data set or its equivalent.

The cc-36 station employs the seven-level ASCII transmission code. An even parity bit is appended to each transmitted character.

When operating as a stand-alone display station (i.e., as a single cc-301 controller and cc-300 TV receiver), an asynchronous transmission technique is employed. A total of 10 bits including unity START and STOP bits, seven data bits, and an even parity bit are transmitted.

When the cc-72 remote master multiplexor is employed in a multistation environment, a synchronous transmission technique is used. Each character totals eight bits, including an even parity bit. A SYN character precedes each transmission.

Editing Facilities

Data can be altered by positioning the cursor to the desired character-location and typing new data over the existing data; no expansion or contraction of data takes place. The entire screen can be erased by using the CLEAR key. When it is desired to retain fixed data, as in a fixed format, a NEW LINE symbol is used at the end of each entry. The NEW LINE symbol causes the cursor to skip all succeeding characters in the line and move to the beginning of the next line. The TAB key positions the cursor forward or backward to a fixed-tab STOP location at the center position of each line.

Operating Procedure

Data are entered at any location of the display by positioning the cursor to that location and keying in the data or reading cards. The cursor advances one character position as each character enters. Any editing that may be necessary is performed prior to transmitting the message. The end-of-text character is entered at the end of the message by depressing the END key; transmission of the message follows. The complete message is composed on the display or read in from cards prior to transmission. When the message is to be transmitted, the TRANSMIT key is depressed, or the transmit function is provided by the stored control sequence. The cc-301 controller functions in one of two submodes of operation when placed in the block mode. These submodes (transmit enabled and transmit disabled), are established by the computer. The controller must be placed in the transmit enabled submode to accept a message. If it is already in this mode when the TRANSMIT key is depressed, the message is immediately sent to the computer.

When operating with the cc-72 remote master controller, depressing the TRANSMIT key sets a status indicator within the master controller. The computer can sample the status indicators and selectively initiate transmission from a waiting display terminal. The master controller can also alert the computer to a waiting message by sending an interrupt signal when a status indicator is set.

Message Configuration

The message transmitted from the cc-36 station includes a start-of-text (STX) character, the message, and an end-of-text (EXT) character. A message is transmitted in sequence, beginning at the cursor position and ending with the ETX character. Messages received from the computer can completely override any local operations. Commands received from the computer are preceded by a start-of-header (SOH) character, which conditions the controller to interpret the following character as a function code. Bit positions 7 through 5 of the function code select a specific input or output device (including the display unit); bit positions 4 through 1 specify one of several commands, such as, SELECT graphic or alphanumeric mode, LOAD or READ cursor address register, READ light pen address, HALT local input-output operations, and others. The computer can also request the status of the station, defined in a single character. When it is desired to unlock the keyboard, the computer message is terminated with an end-of-transmission (EOT) signal, which releases the keyboard to the operator.

When the cc-72 remote master controller is included, computer messages are prefixed by an SOH and a single address character; the address character specifies which of the cc-301 controllers is to receive the message.

Error Detection and Correction

Errors that occur during off-line composition are corrected by positioning the cursor under the character in error and rekeying the correct character. When transmitting a message to the computer in the character mode, the computer responds to a detected character-parity error by returning a special parity symbol, which is displayed in the position of the character received in error. The operator corrects the error by retyping the character.

Computer response to errors received in the block mode is dependent upon the controlling software. When parity errors are detected at the display station, a status bit is set and a special parity character is displayed on the screen in place of the character in error. The operator can request retransmission or can repeat the interrogation message.

CDC 200 USER TERMINAL

The Control Data 200 user terminal (Fig. 14-6) is a visual communications terminal designed to facilitate rapid access and exchange of alphanumeric data between a Control Data Series 3000, 6000, or 7000 computer and one or more remote single-station terminals under control of a stored computer program. While it functions best with a Control Data computer, this display station can operate efficiently in any commercial-oriented computer system; communications software packages or required program modifications are not a standard provision with the 200 user terminal.

Basic Operation

The 200 user terminal is designed to operate in a poll/address environment; all communications between the remote computer and the display station are initiated by the computer. Messages transmitted in either direction must be acknowledged by the recipient. The basic terminal can be expanded to provide both conversational and batch-processing capabilities through the addition of a card reader and printer; off-line key-to-print and card-to-print operations can be executed by the terminal operator. The 200 user terminal is available only in single-station terminal arrangements, which can be multidropped in several locations via voice-band communications facilities.

Fig. 14-6.   CDC 200 User Terminal Including Model 222-1 Line Printer and Model 224-2 Card Reader

Display Unit

The 217-2 remote entry/display station (Fig. 14-7) is a single-station CRT/keyboard unit connected to a display controller to complete the basic 200 user terminal configuration. The display incorporates a 14-inch (diagonal) rectangular CRT oriented horizontally to present a viewing area 6 inches high by 8 inches wide. A 64-symbol alphanumeric character set including upper-case alphabetics, numerics, punctuation, and special symbols can be generated via keyboard or computer program; each displayed character is constructed within a 5 x 7 dot matrix. A total character capacity of 1000 or 1040 eight-bit word positions in the controller's delay-line memory provides maximum display formats of 20 fifty-character lines or 13 eighty-character lines, respectively. A chain of markers (underlines of character positions) facilitates keyboard data entry; the leftmost symbol in the chain, called the entry marker (cursor), indicates the position of the next entered character to be displayed. Table 14-7 summarizes the CDC 217-2 entry-marker control functions.

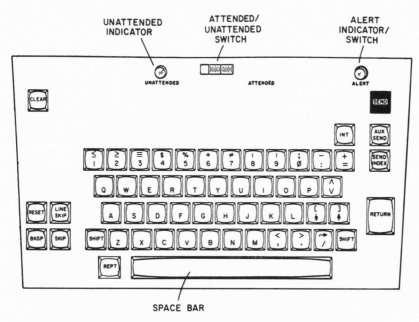

Fig. 14-7.   CDC 217-2 Entry/Display Station Keyboard

Data Transmission

The 200 user terminal operates synchronously in the half-duplex mode over a leased voice-band line at 300 characters per second (2400 bits per second) or over the public telephone network at 250 characters per second (2000 bits per second). A seven-level transmission is employed; each transmitted character includes seven data bits plus parity. One of two transmission codes (modified external BCD or modified internal BCD) can be switch-selected at time of installation. A 128-character code set includes 64 characters to initiate control functions. A precedence code (ESCAPE) is required to designate each control code.

Configuration

The basic 200 user terminal (Fig. 14-8) consists of an entry/display station fixed upon a cabinet-mounted equipment controller. Optional input/output devices incorporated into the basic terminal arrangement can be configured according to one of the following combinations:

1. Card reader 224-2 and line printer 222-1 or 222-2
2. Card reader 224-2 and typewriter printer 218-1
3. Card reader 224-2
4. Line printer 222-1 or 222-2
5. Typewriter printer 218-1

A configurator including standard components and optional features of the cdc 200 is provided in Figure 14-8.

Table 14-7. CDC 217-2 Display Entry Marker
(Cursor) Controls

KEY	CONTROL FUNCTION
Space	Stores a space code in the entry-marker position of memory; advances entry marker one position
Return	Stores a carriage return code in the entry-marker position; advances the entry marker to the first display position of the next line
Skip	Advances the entry marker one position; data are not affected
Slew	Causes repeated advance during key depression
Clear	Erases all data from memory and crt screen; the entry marker is repositioned to the home display location (upper-left corner)
Backspace	Return the entry marker one position to the left; data are not affected
Reset	Positions the entry marker to the home display location (upper-left corner)
Line skip	Advances the entry marker to the first display position of the next line; data are not affected

DELTA DATA SYSTEMS DELTA 1 VIDEO DISPLAY TERMINAL

Delta Data Systems Corporation states that the Delta 1 video display terminal (Fig. 14-9) can be interchanged on a plug-to-plug compatibility basis with the ibm 2260/2848 or 2265/2845 display systems under local or remote operating conditions. No software modifications are required. There is a high degree of similarity to the ibm system in relation to configuration, message sequence, and transmission characteristics.

Basic Operation

The Delta 1 video display is designed primarily to facilitate rapid access and exchange of alphanumeric data with an ibm System/360 or 370 computer in a local environment or remotely via a 2701 data adapter unit over a voice-band communications facility. Features including hardware con-

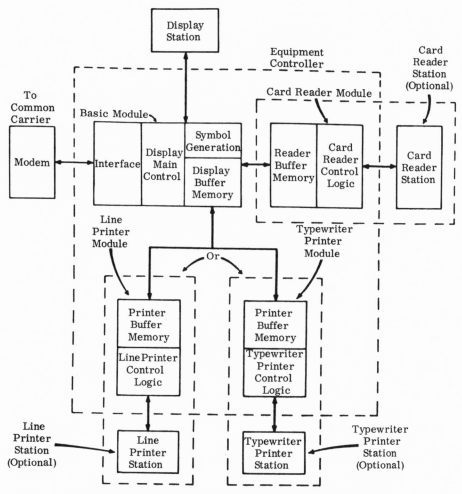

Fig. 14-8. CDC 200 User Terminal Configurations
Including Optional Features

nection and software packages are available to accommodate operations with various other types of computers. All communications are initiated by the remote computer in a polling arrangement so that coordination of transmitted data is maintained via command sequences under program control. One auxiliary device per controller can be incorporated to provide printed copy.

Five READ commands are provided for transmission of data from the display station to the remote computer:

1. *Transmit message* transmits data located between the existing cursor position and the end-of-message symbol (♠); in the conversation mode the cursor is automatically returned to the first character position following the previous EOM symbol before the transmission sequence is executed.

Fig. 14-9.   Delta 1 Video Display Terminal

2. *Transmit display* repositions the cursor to the first display location and initiates transmission of the entire display memory contents; concluding the transmission, the cursor is returned to the starting location.

3. *Transmit line* transmits data located between the existing cursor position and the end of the line; cursor advances to the first position of the next line.

4. *Transmit Y address counter* transmits the address contained in the Y address counter; this is the address of the current cursor location and includes all character positions on the same line; the line address can range from zero to 23.

5. *Transmit X address counter* transmits the address contained in the X address counter; this address is the current character position of the cursor on a line; the command is usually preceded by a Y address to designate the current line location of the cursor; the character address can range from zero to 39.

Three WRITE commands are provided for transmission of data from the remote computer to the display station:

1. *Enter addressed display:* Received data is displayed beginning at

the current cursor position; a line feed/carriage return operation is automatically executed when more than 40 characters are entered to a line.

2. *Enter addressed line:* Received data are displayed beginning at the initial position on the line designated by the first character (Y address) following STX in the message; initiates an automatic line feed/carriage return operation.

3. *Enter addressed position:* Received data are displayed, beginning at the line position designated by the first character (X address) following STX in the message; initiates an automatic line feed/carriage return operation.

All entry commands that advance to cursor include wraparound (i.e., uninterrupted writing from the last display location to the home position).

Editing Facilities

The Delta 1 incorporates an extensive set of edit functions that can be executed in conjunction with cursor manipulation via keyboard or remote program control. Cursor controls include—

1. LEFT: Cursor backspaces one position to the left; cursor returns (wraps around) to the last character position on a line when initially located on first position of that line.

2. RIGHT: Cursor advances one position to the right; cursor returns (wraps around) to the first position on a line when initially located on the last position of that line.

3. UP: Positions the cursor up one line; cursor occupies same position in the line.

4. DOWN: Positions the cursor down one line; cursor occupies same position in the line; wraps around from the last line to the first line.

5. RETURN: Cursor advances to the first position of the following line (line feed/carriage return).

6. HOME: Cursor is repositioned to the initial display position of the first line.

7. BACKSPACE: Cursor returns one position to the left; cursor returns (wraps around) to the last character position of the same line if enabled when initially located on first position of a line.

8. TAB: Cursor advances to the first position of the next variable data field when in the fixed format mode.

NEW LINE: Displays a NEW LINE symbol (◢) to define the end of a line of data to be transmitted or the end of a variable data field in the fixed format mode.

Edit controls include—

1. *Insert* permits data characters to be added to an existing text; cursor defines the initial entry location of data to be inserted after shifting the locations initially occupied; the remaining text that follows the inserted data is advanced one position to accommodate each added character.

2 *Insert line* permits a line of data to be added to an existing text; cursor defines the initial entry location of the line to be inserted after shifting the line initially occupied; text located below the inserted data is dropped one line to accommodate each added line.

3. *Delete* permits data characters to be erased from an existing text, which is then closed to maintain continuity; cursor defines the point of deletion; the remaining text following the deleted data is backspaced one position for each character erased.

4. *Delete line* permits a line of data to be erased from an existing text, which is then closed; cursor defines the initial character position of the line to be deleted; text located below the deleted data is moved up one line for each line erased.

5. *Clear message* erases all data between the cursor and the end-of-message (EOM) symbol by substituting space characters; cursor is relocated to the position immediately following the EOM symbol.

6. *Clear display* erases all displayed data by substituting space characters; cursor is returned to the starting location as defined by the first deleted character position.

7. *Clear line* erases all data between the cursor and the end of the line containing the cursor by substituting space characters; cursor is returned to its initial position on the line.

8. *Set blink* initiates blinking of data inserted at the location occupied by the cursor; cursor is advanced one position.

9. *Clear blink* terminates blinking at the character position occupied by the cursor; cursor is advanced one position.

Delta 1 Features Contrasted with IBM 2265 Display Station

Remote Read Operations

This feature provides commands instructing the display to transmit text beginning at an addressed character position or an addressed line, to transmit selected text framed between the cursor and the end of the line or an EOM symbol, and to transmit the entire display.

Remote Write Operations

This provides commands initiating display of a received message, beginning of a specified line, or character address as well as the home position; cursor positioning includes wraparound.

Remote Cursor Control

This control provides exceptionally flexible cursor manipulation via program control, as well as manual operation. It enables the remote computer to position the cursor at any fixed location on the display by supplying an absolute address to the terminal. All cursor control functions can be executed anywhere within the transmitted text for optimum format capability.

Remote Edit Control

Remote edit provides functions to alter or modify the displayed text. It includes provision for insertion or deletion of text at addressed locations as specified in the command. It also provides for erasure of data framed by the cursor and the end of a line or an EOM symbol, or the entire display.

Selective Blink (Optional)

This allows alternate display/nondisplay of any character or groups of characters designated by the cursor location under keyboard or program control. Reset facilities also selectively terminate the blink. This feature can be utilized for both fixed and variable data when operating in the fixed format mode.

Graphic Mode (Optional)

The graphic mode provides graphic facilities to generate straight and curved vectors under program control. The display screen is divided into 8192 points, each corresponding to an addressable character position in the refresh memory.

Refresh Memory

Refresh memory incorporates a 1024-byte magnetic-core storage. Six bits provide character storage. The remaining two bits can be used to store blink and format data.

Character Generation

This feature incorporates a read-only memory to provide permanent storage for each of the 64 standard display characters. It generates a 5 x 7 dot matrix to display each character.

Keyboard

This unit includes a conventional typewriter-styled keyboard with provisions for manual data entry, edit control, display control, and selection of modes of operation. It generates upper-case alphabetics, numerics, and 24 special symbols. Up to ten special controls for additional input/output devices are optionally available.

Display

The display unit incorporates a 12-inch (measured diagonally) cathode-ray tube (CRT) mounted in a desk-top housing, standard. The maximum display format consists of 960 characters, arranged on 24 lines with 40 characters per line. Additional standard or larger-sized display monitors connected to the same control unit are available as options to provide duplicate displays at different locations.

Teletype Compatible Serial Controller (Optional)

This unit provides remote communications at standard teletype speeds of 110 bits per second, using a full-duplex facility. One of two modes of operation can be employed:

1. Normal mode: When operating in this mode, data entered via keyboard is immediately displayed and is transmitted by block directly to the remote computer. Incoming data are displayed as received. The transmitted data are contained within cursor and EOM symbols when in the conversation mode, and within variable data fields when in the fixed format mode. The entire display is transmitted when neither of these modes is selected.

2. Echoplex mode: When operating in the Echoplex mode, data entered via keyboard is transmitted directly to the remote computer as each character is keyed in. Each character entered or an error symbol (CAN), if received incorrectly, is returned for display.

Options

The Delta 1 options include—
1. A light pen
2. Selective blink feature

3. Additional display monitors
4. Color displays
5. Provisions for printed copy
6. A communications interface
7. A 96-character set that provides either lower-case alphabetics, line-drawing characters, or graphic symbols. (Use of the additional 32 characters for any one of these features excludes the selective blink capability.)

IBM 2260 DISPLAY STATION

The IBM display station (Fig. 14-10) is designed to facilitate rapid access to data stored in an IBM System/360 or 370 computer, under the control of a stored program in the computer. The 2260 displays data on the face of a cathode-ray tube and may include a keyboard for data entry by the operator.

Multiple 2260 display stations can be controlled by a 2848 display control. The 2848 control may be connected directly to a multiplexor or selector channel of an IBM System/360 (Model 30, 44, 44, 50, 65, 67, or 75) or

Fig. 14-10. IBM 2260 Display Station

System/370 computer, or it may be connected remotely via a common-carrier-leased voice-band line, appropriate data sets, and a 2701 data adapter unit incorporating an IBM terminal adapter Type III. Each 2260 display station may be located at up to 2000 cable-feet from the 2848 control. The various configuration possibilities using the 2848 control are presented in Table 14-8.

The data transmission rate between a directly connected 2260 station and the computer is 2560 characters per second. When the 2260 is connected remotely, the data transmission rate is 120 or 240 characters per second (1200 or 2400 bits per second, respectively).

The functional operation of the 2260 when connected to a System/360 or 370 computer is similar to its operation when connected remotely.

Table 14-8. IBM 2848 Display Control Configuration
Possibilities

COMPONENTS	2848 DISPLAY CONTROL		
	MODEL 1	MODEL 2	MODEL 3
Basic 2848 display control; maximum number of:			
Display adapters	2	1	1
2260 display stations	4	2	2
1053 printers	0	0	1 *
3857 Expansion panel †; maximum number of:			
Display adapters	6	4	3
2260 display stations	12	8	6
1053 printers	0	0	0
3858 Expansion panel †; maximum number of:			
Display adapters	4	3	—
2260 display stations	8	6	—
1053 printers	1 *	1 *	—
Fully expanded configuration; maximum number of:			
Display adapters	12	8	4
2260 display stations	24	16	8
1053 printers	1	1	1
Display size:			
Number of lines per display	6	12	12
Number of characters per line	40	40	80
Total number of characters per display	240	480	960

* Requires special printer adapter.

† Either or both expansion panels can be included in a Model 1 or 2 2848 display control configuration.

Basic Operation

The 2260 display stations and associated 2848 display control operate in a half-duplex mode. All communication between the display complex and the remote computer is initiated by the computer. Displayed data are received from the remote computer or are keyed into the 2260 by the operator. When data are to be entered, the operator keys in the data and depresses the ENTER key. Then the displayed data will be transmitted to the computer the next time the computer requests a transfer.

Except when an error is detected in a command sequence, all data messages are acknowledged, to indicate correct or incorrect reception by both the 2848 control and the remote computer.

The seven-level ASCII transmission code is employed, with an eighth bit added for character parity. A total of ten bits are transmitted for each character, including START and STOP bits. The remote System/360 computer automatically converts the seven-level code into an eight-level code by adding a bit (see Table 14-9). These converted codes do not correspond to the internal EBCDIC code of the System/360 or 370 computer (see Table 14-10). If extended internal computation or output at the computer site is desired, data received from a 2260 display station will need to be converted to the internal code by the stored program in the System/360 computer.

Display Complex

A display complex consists of the following components:
1. One 2848 display control, Model 1, 2, or 3
2. 2260 display stations, up to 24, 16, or 8 depending on which model of the 2848 is incorporated
3. One 1053 Model 4 printer (optional)

The maximum number of display stations and the maximum display size for each model of the 2848 display control are shown in Table 14-11.

The 2848 display control provides the basic control logic and buffer storage for all units and a character generator for converting the 7-bit ASCII data codes into a 35-bit video display code. Display adapters contain delay-line buffers for each display station; these buffers store video display codes and continuously regenerate the display. Characters and symbols are displayed by a 5 x 7 dot matrix; each bit of the video display code corresponds to one dot-matrix position. One display adapter is required for each pair of display stations. A separate adapter is required for connecting the 1053 printer.

Table 14-9. IBM 2260 Display Station ASCII Data
Transmission Codes (Note 6)

Bits						Col 0	Col 1	Col 2	Col 3	Col 4	Col 5	Col 6	Col 7
b7 →						0	0	0	0	1	1	1	1
b6 →						0	0	1	1	0	0	1	1
bx →						0	0	0	0	1	1	1	1
b5 →						0	1	0	1	0	1	0	1
	b4	b3	b2	b1	Col→ Row↓	0	1	2	3	4	5	6	7
	0	0	0	0	0	Note 1 / Note 2		SP	0		P	@	P
	0	0	0	1	1	SOH			1	A	Q	A	Q
	0	0	1	0	2	STX			2	B	R	B	R
	0	0	1	1	3	ETX		!	3	C	S	C	S
	0	1	0	0	4	EOT		$	4	D	T	D	T
	0	1	0	1	5		NAK	%	5	E	U	E .	U
	0	1	1	0	6	ACK		&	6	F	V	⊦	V
	0	1	1	1	7			'	7	G	W	G	W
	1	0	0	0	8		CAN	(	8	H	X	H	X
	1	0	0	1	9			)	9	I	Y	I	Y
	1	0	1	0	10	LF		*	.	J	Z	J	Z
	1	0	1	1	11			+	;	K	Note 4	K	Note 5
	1	1	0	0	12	Note 3		,	<	L		L	¬
	1	1	0	1	13			-	:	M		M	
	1	1	1	0	14			.	>	N		N		
	1	1	1	1	15			/	?	O	-	O	.

NOTES:

1. Displayed on 2260's as the EOM (—) symbol. Prints on the 1053 Model 1 printer as the exclamation mark (!).

Displayed on 2260's as the CHECK (|) symbol. Prints on the 1053 Model 1 printer as the quote symbol (").

3. Displayed on 2260's as the NEW LINE (◣) symbol. Causes a carriage return and line feed on the 1053 Model 1 printer.

4. Displayed on 2260's as the START MI (▶) symbol. Prints on the 1053 Model 1 printer as a cent sign (¢).

5. The codes represented by the characters within the dotted outline are the ASCII-8 codes for the lower-case alphabetic characters. These codes are converted to upper case by the 2848 and displayed as upper-case characters. If retrieved by a read operation, the codes will be in the upper-case bit configuration.

6. The eight-bit codes shown in this table are the codes as they appear in the core memory of the remote computer. The ASCII transmission code is obtained by deleting bit X. This conversion is performed by the 2701 data adapter unit prior to transmitting data to a 2260 display station and after receiving data from a 2260. See Table 14-10 for the data codes used when a 2260 is connected directly to a System/360 or 370 input/output channel.

7. Graphic representations are undefined for the bit patterns outside the heavily outlined portions of the chart. These bit patterns are referred to as undefined graphic bit patterns. If an undefined graphic bit pattern is sent from channel to the device, the graphic that will be displayed or printed by the device is not specified.

8. IBM reserves the right to change at any time the graphic displayed or printed by this device for an undefined graphic bit pattern.

Table 14-10. IBM 2260 EBCDIC Data Codes
for Local Operation (6)

Bits 0,1	00				01				10				11			
Bits 2,3	00	01	10	11	00	01	10	11	00	01	10	11	00	01	10	11
Bits 4,5,6,7																
0000					SP	&	-					Note 5				0
0001							/		A	J	/		A	J		1
0010									B	K	S		B	K	S	2
0011		Note 1							C	L	T		C	L	T	3
0100									D	M	U		D	M	U	4
0101		NL							E	N	V		E	N	V	5
0110									F	O	W		F	O	W	6
0111									G	P	X		G	P	X	7
1000					Note 2	Note 3			H	Q	Y		H	Q	Y	8
1001									I	R	Z		I	R	Z	9
1010					¢	!		:								
1011					.	$	,	#								
1100					<	*	%	@								
1101					(	)	_	'								
1110					+	;	>	=								
1111					|	¬	?		Note 4							

NOTES:

1. Displayed on 2260's as the NEW LINE (▲) symbol. Causes carriage return and line feed on the 1053 Model 1 printer.

2. Displayed on 2260's as the START MI (▶) symbol. Prints on the 1053 Model 1 printer as a cent sign (¢).

3. Displayed on 2260's as the EOM (━) symbol. Prints on the 1053 Model 1 printer as an exclamation mark (!).

4. Displayed on 2260's as the CHECK (❘) symbol. Prints on the 1053 Model 1 printer as a quote (") symbol.

5. The codes represented by the characters within the dotted outline are the EBCDIC codes for the lower-case alphabetic characters. These codes are converted to upper case by the 2848 and displayed as upper-case characters. If retrieved by a READ operation, the codes will be in the upper-case bit configuration.

6. The data codes in this table are used when the 2260 is connected directly to a System/360 or 370 computer input/output channel (via a 2848 Control). These codes correspond to the internal code of the System/360 or 370 computers. Bit 7 of the EBCDIC code is the low-order bit and corresponds to bit 1 of the ASCII code.

7. Graphic representations are undefined for the bit patterns outside the heavily outlined portions of the outlined portions of the chart. These bit patterns are referred to as undefined graphic bit patterns. If an undefined graphic bit pattern is sent from channel to the device, the graphic that will be displayed or printed by the device is not specified.

8. IBM reserves the right to change at any time the graphic displayed or printed by the device for an undefined graphic bit pattern.

Table 14-11. IBM 2260 Display Configurations

2848 DISPLAY CONTROL	MAXIMUM NUMBER OF 2260 DISPLAY STATIONS	MAXIMUM SIZE OF DISPLAY		
		LINES	CHAR/LINE	CHARACTERS
Model 1	24	6	40	240
Model 2	16	12	40	480
Model 3	8	12	80	960

The display station consists of a 12-inch-diameter cathode-ray tube with a display field 4 inches high by 9 inches wide. A numeric or alphanumeric keyboard can be incorporated in each 2260 display station, or the station can be used without a keyboard for display purposes only. Figure 14-10 shows the 2260 display station with alphanumeric keyboard.

The 1053 Model 4 printer is a modified version of the IBM Selectric typewriter and is similar to the printers used in IBM 1050 data communications systems. All display stations connected to one 2848 display control share the one 1053 printer.

The printer adapter contains a buffer for storing data to be printed. This permits a printing operation to proceed simultaneously with operations by the display station. A print operation can be initiated by the remote

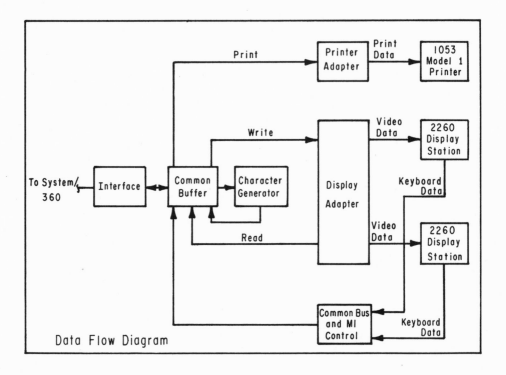

Data Flow Diagram

computer; a display station operator can also cause the station display to be printed.

Commands

The IBM 2260 display station, in combination with a 2848 display control, is capable of responding to eight commands transmitted by the remote computer.

There are four READ commands for transmitting data from the display station to the computer:

1. Specific poll to 2260 station: Initiates transfer of data displayed by a specific station to the computer, provided the START symbol is displayed and the ENTER key has been depressed.

2. Specific poll to printer: Initiates transmission of printer status to computer (e.g., busy, ready, not ready).

3. General poll: Initiates transfer of data to computer from all stations that have the START symbol displayed and in which the ENTER key has been depressed. Messages are transferred sequentially and are accompanied by the address of the corresponding display station.

4. Read addressed full display station buffer: Initiates unconditional transfer to the computer of the entire buffer for the addressed station.

Selection portions of the display can be transmitted in response to a specific or general poll; see the section "Editing Facilities" below.

There are four WRITE commands for transferring data to a display station or printer:

1. Write addressed display station: Conditions the 2848 control and the addressed station for reception and display of the the associated message.

2. Erase/write addressed display station: Causes the display of the addressed station to be erased and the cursor to be positioned at the first displayable position.

3. Write printer: Conditions the 2848 control and the 1053 printer for reception and printing of the associated message. A positive indication of status is returned if the printer is busy or not ready.

4. Write display station line address: Same as "write addressed display station" except that the display is started on the indicated line instead of the first line. The line-addressing feature is required in the 2848 display control for the use of this command.

Editing Facilities

The 2260 display station makes limited editing facilities available to the operator. The standard cursor (destructive) can be moved one position at a time, either forward or backward; each position occupied by this cursor is erased. The optional nondestructive cursor can be moved forward or backward and also up or down one line at a time. This cursor does not erase the contents of each position it occupies. Either cursor wraps around (i.e., moves from the first display position to the last when backspaced or from the last display position to the first when advanced). The entire display can be erased by the operator at any time. Either cursor can be advanced to be first position of the next line by depressing the NEW LINE key. This operation also causes the NEW LINE symbol to be displayed in the cursor position of the previous lines.

When transmitting in response to a specific poll or general poll command, data located between the NEW LINE symbol and the end of that line is not transferred. When receiving, a NEW LINE code in the text data causes the display to jump to the beginning of the next line; data between the NEW LINE symbol and the end of the line is not erased. This "split-screen" capability allows fixed information such as table or entry headings to be displayed continuously without the need for retransmitting them each time.

Error Checking and Correction

Character and longitudinal parity checking is performed on all data received by the 2848 control from the remote computer; character parity bits and longitudinal check characters are generated and transferred with all data transmitted from the 2848 control. If the remote computer returns a negative acknowledgment, indicating that an error has been detected at the computer site, the 2848 control automatically retransmits the message. The 2848 control also checks the parity and validity of each command sequence received from the computer. If errors are detected, the 2848 does not make a response of any kind.

Programming Support

IBM states that the software support for the 2701 data adapter unit is being extended to cover 2260 display stations as remote terminals under BTAM and QTAM for the operating System/360 and under BTAM for the disk operating system.

Configuration

A network of 2260 display stations is composed of
1. One 2848 display control, Model 1, 2, or 3

2. Multiple 2260 display stations, each with no keyboard, numeric keyboard (Table 14-12), or an alphanumeric keyboard

3. One 1053 Model 4 printer if desired

Table 14-8 shows the maximum number of display units that can be connected to each model of the 2848 control, and the features required. The display size also varies for each model of the 2848 control; these variations are also shown in Table 14-11.

Each station may be located up to 2,000 feet from the 2848 display control. The 2848 control and 2260 display station network can communicate over a common-carrier-leased voice-band line with an IBM System/360 (Model 30, 40, 44, 50, 65, 67, or 75) or System/370 computer system incorporating an IBM 2701 data adapter unit. The transmission speed is 1200 or 2400 bits per second, depending on the data set adapter selected. Once installed, the transmission speed is fixed; i.e., the operator cannot select between the two speeds. The 2848 control can also be connected directly to a control unit position of an input/output channel of an IBM System/360 (Model 30, 40, 44, 50, 65, 67 or 75) or System/370 computer system.

Table 14-12. IBM 2260 Numeric Keyboard Character Set*

NO SHIFT	SHIFT
1	$
2	@
3	%
4	,
5	.
6	/
7	—
8	+
9	¤
0	#
Sp	Advance

* Control characters are the same as for the alphanumeric keyboard; see Table 14-9.

In addition to the capability to connect a 1053 printer, two other optional features are available: line addressing and nondestructive cursor. To incorporate the line addressing capability, only one line addressing feature is required, regardless of the number of display stations. To incorporate the nondestructive cursor, one nondestructive cursor feature is required in the 2848 control, and one nondestructive cursor adapter is required for each display adapter. All display stations connected to the same 2848 display control must use the same type of cursor.

Message Configuration

Communication between the remote computer and a 2260 display station or 1053 printer is initiated when the computer transmits a four-character addressing sequence to the 2848 display control. This sequence consists of the following characters: EOT (poll or read) or SOH (write), 2848 address, device address, and command character. The two general types of commands are POLL (or READ) and WRITE.

When a POLL command addressed to a display station is received, the appropriate 2260 station responds with a text message consisting of the following characters: STX, 2260 address text, ETX, and LRC (longitudinal redundancy check). If a parity error is detected in the buffer when transmitting, the CAN character will be inserted just before the ETX character. If the computer receives the message without detecting an error, an ACK character is transmitted. If an error is detected, the NAK character is transmitted and the 2848 control automatically retransmits the message.

After the message has been correctly received and the acknowledgment transmitted, the computer can transmit one or more messages to the display station. Each message from the computer consists of the following characters: STX, text, ETC, and LRC. Each message is acknowledged with an ACK or NAK character. If the command is a general POLL, the other display stations connected to the 2848 control are tested following the completion of the transmission from the first station. If the computer directs a message to one of the stations during the execution of a general POLL operation, the operation must be reinitiated following the transmission of text from the computer, to ensure that all stations are polled.

If the command is a WRITE command, the 2848 responds with an ACK character if it receives the command correctly and a NAK if not. The computer then transmits one or more messages to the addressed station in the same format as above. Each message is acknowledged with an ACK or NAK by the 2848. If the command is a line address WRITE, the line address is inserted following the STX character in the computer text message. The 2848 control will make no response if it detects a parity error or an invalid command or address in the addressing sequence.

A one-character response of EOT or SOH from the 2848 control is transmitted to indicate the following: a negative response to a POLL command, end of transmission to a READ command, data lost condition to a WRITE command, buffer overflow, or printer busy when addressed. The EOT character normally terminates communication.

The text may contain up to 240, 480, or 960 characters, depending on which model of the 2848 control is being used; see Table 14-8. Except for data following a NEW LINE symbol, all displayed characters and symbols are included in the text, excluding the nondestructive cursor; see Table 14-9. The displayed data between a NEW LINE symbol and the end of the line is not transmitted when a 2260 is polled, and will not be overwritten or erased during a WRITE operation.

Operating Procedure

A message to be transmitted from a 2260 display station is composed by positioning the cursor at the desired starting position, depressing the SHIFT key and START key (which enters the START MI symbol in the cursor position), and keying the data. Controls are provided to space forward or backward one position at a time and to move the cursor to the beginning of the next line. The optional nondestructive cursor can be moved up or down one line at a time. The cursor identifies the next display position to be entered. When the standard destructive cursor is moved to a position already containing a display character, that position is erased. The nondestructive cursor can be moved freely without erasing data.

To transmit a message, the SHIFT key and ENTER key are depressed; this action locks the keyboard and puts the display station in a WAIT condition. When the station is polled by the remote computer, the data stored in the buffer will be transmitted to the computer. A successful transmission causes the START MI symbol to be erased and the keyboard unlocked. If a transmission error is detected at the remote computer, an automatic re-transmission can be requested. For certain types of errors, other correction techniques may be used, as controlled by the stored program in the remote computer.

IBM 2265 DISPLAY STATION

The IBM 2265 display station (Fig. 14-11) is designed to facilitate rapid access to data stored in an IBM System/360 or 370 computer, under control of a stored program in the computer. The 2265 displays data on the face of a cathode-ray tube and may include a keyboard for data entry by the operator.

The 2845 control can be connected remotely to a multiplexor or selector channel of an IBM System/360 (Model 25, 30, 40, 44, 50, 65, 67, 75) or System /370 computer via a common-carrier-leased voice-band line, appropriate data sets, and a 2701 data adapter unit incorporating an IBM terminal adapter Type III. The 2265 display station may be located up to 50 cable-feet from the 2845 control. When the 2265/2845 is connected remotely, the data transmission rate is 120 or 240 characters per second (1200 or 2400 bits per second, respectively). The 2265/2845 station can operate in a multi-station environment. Up to sixteen 2265/2845 stations can be connected to a single communications line.

Basic Operation

The 2265 display station and associated 2845 display control operate in a half-duplex mode. All communication between the display complex and the remote computer is initiated by the computer. Displayed data are received from the remote computer or are keyed into the 2265 by the operator. When data are to be entered, the operator keys in the data and depresses the ENTER key. The displayed data will be transmitted to the computer the next time the computer requests a transfer.

Fig. 14-11.   IBM 2265 Display Station

Except when an error is detected in a command sequence, all data messages are acknowledged, to indicate correct or incorrect reception by both the 2845 control and the remote computer.

The seven-level ASCII transmission code is employed, with an eighth bit added for character parity. A total of ten bits are transmitted for each character, including START and STOP bits. The remote System/360 computer automatically converts the seven-level code into an eight-level code by adding a bit; see Table 14-13. These converted codes do not correspond to the internal EBCDIC code of a System/360 or 370 computer. If extended internal computation or output at the computer site is desired, data received from a 2265 display station will need to be converted to the internal code by the stored program in the System/360 or 370 computer.

Display Complex

A display complex consists of the following components:
1. One 2845 display control, Model 1
2. One 2265 display station, Model 1
3. One 1053 Model 4 printer (optional)

The 2845 display control contains the basic control logic, buffer storage, character generator, and communications interface for the 2265 display station. The stroke technique is employed to generate the display characters. A data set adapter is required to interface the 2845 control with a data set. Two data set adapters are available for operation at 1200 and 2400 bits per second. An interval clock is provided for 1200 bit per second operation; an external clocking signal is required for the higher-speed operation.

The display station consists of a 14-inch cathode-ray tube and an optional alphanumeric keyboard that can be directly attached to the display unit or located up to 5 feet away. One of two display formats can be specified: 15 rows with 64 characters per row, or 12 rows with 80 characters per row. A total of 960 characters can be displayed using either format.

The 1053 Model 4 printer is a modified version of the IBM Selectric typewriter and is similar to the printers used in IBM 1050 data communications systems. Only one 1053 Model 4 printer can be connected to a 2845 display control via an optional 1053 adapter. The buffered adapter accepts computer messages of up to 240 characters or data entered via the 2265. A print operation can be initiated by the remote computer; a display station operator can also cause the station display to be printed.

Commands

The IBM 2265 display station, in combination with a 2845 display con-

Table 14-13. IBM 2265 Display Station ASCII Data Transmission Code (6)

Bits (B4 B3 B2 B1)	Col/Row	0	1	2	3	4	5	6	7
0 0 0 0	0	Note 1 / Note 2		SP	0		P	@	P
0 0 0 1	1	SOH			1	A	Q	A	Q
0 0 1 0	2	STX			2	B	R	B	R
0 0 1 1	3	ETX		#	3	C	S	C	S
0 1 0 0	4	EOT		$	4	D	T	D	T
0 1 0 1	5		NAK	%	5	E	U	E	U
0 1 1 0	6	ACK		&	6	F	V	F	V
0 1 1 1	7			'	7	G	W	G	W
1 0 0 0	8		CAN	(	8	H	X	H	X
1 0 0 1	9			)	9	I	Y	I	Y
1 0 1 0	10	LF		*	:	J	Z	J	Z
1 0 1 1	11			+	;	K		K	Note 5
1 1 0 0	12	Note 3		,	<	L	Note 4	L	¬
1 1 0 1	13			–	=	M		M	
1 1 1 0	14			.	>	N		N	|
1 1 1 1	15			/	?	O	–	O	

NOTES:

1. Displayed and printed as the EOM (▬) symbol.
2. Displayed and printed as the CHECK (❙) symbol.
3. Displayed on 2265's as the NEW LINE (◢) symbol. Causes a carriage return and line feed on the 1053 Model 4 printer.
4. Displayed and printed as the SOM (▶) symbol.
5. The codes represented by the characters within the dotted outline are the ASCII-8 codes for the lower-case alphabetic characters. These codes are converted to upper case by the 2845 and displayed as upper-case characters. If retrieved by a READ operation, the codes will be in the upper-case bit configuration.
6. The eight-bit codes shown in this table are the codes as they appear in the core memory of the remote IBM System/360 or 370 computer. The ASCII transmission code is obtained by deleting bit X. This conversion is performed by the 2701 data adapter unit prior to transmitting data to a 2265 display station and after receiving data from 2265.
7. Graphic representations are undefined for the bit patterns outside the heavily outlined portions of the chart. These bit patterns are referred to as undefined graphic bit patterns. If an undefined graphic bit pattern is sent from channel to the device, the graphic that will be displayed or printed by the device is not specified.
8. IBM reserves the right to change at any time the graphic displayed or printed by this device for an undefined graphic bit pattern.

trol, is capable of responding to eight commands transmitted by the remote computer.

There are four READ commands for transmitting data from the display station to the computer:

1. Specific poll to 2265 station: Initiates transfer of data displayed by a specific station to the computer, provided the SOM symbol is displayed and the ENTER key has been depressed.

2. Specific poll to printer: Initiates transmission of printer status to computer (e.g., busy, ready, not ready).

3. General poll: Initiates transfer of printer status and/or displayed data to computer from the addressed 2845 display control. The message from a 2265 station is transferred if the SOM symbol is displayed and the ENTER key has been depressed. Messages are accompanied by the address of the corresponding display station.

4. Read addressed full display station buffer: Initiates unconditional transfer to the computer of the entire buffer for the addressed station.

Selected portions of the display can be transmitted in response to a specific or general POLL; see the section "Editing Facilities" below.

There are four WRITE commands for transferring data to a display station or printer:

1. Write addressed display station: Conditions the 2845 control and the addressed station for reception and display of the associated message.

2. Erase/write addressed display station: Causes the display of the addressed station to be erased and the cursor to be positioned at the first displayable position.

3. Write printer: Conditions the 2845 control and the 1053 printer for reception and printing of the associated message. A positive indication of status is returned if the printer is ready and not busy.

4. Write display line address: Same as "write addressed display station" except that the display is started on the indicated line instead of on the first line. The line-addressing feature is required in the 2845 display control for the use of this command.

Editing Facilities

The 2265 display station provides a flexible set of edit functions incorporating a high degree of cursor mobility. A nondestructive cursor is standard; a destructive cursor may be specified at no additional cost.

Cursor controls include:

1. ADVANCE advances cursor one character position. The destructive cursor causes a blank to be stored in the cursor position.

2. BACKSPACE backspaces cursor one character position. If cursor occupies first character position on line, it is moved to the last character position of the previous line.

3. SPACE/ERASE advances the cursor one character position, erasing the position occupied by the cursor. A blank is stored in the cursor position when the destructive cursor is used.

4. DOWN positions the cursor down one line; cursor occupies same location in line. The cursor wraps around (i.e., moves from the last line to the first line).

5. UP positions the cursor up one line; cursor occupies same location in line. The cursor wraps around (i.e., moves from the first line to the last line).

The cursor is moved at a rate of nine characters per second when the Advance or Backspace keys are held down. The destructive cursor erases each character location occupied by the cursor. Either cursor can be advanced to the first position of the next line by depressing the NEW LINE key. This operation also causes the NEW LINE symbol to be displayed in the position occupied by the cursor prior to initiating the NEW LINE function. The cursor moves to the first position of the first line when the cursor occupies a position on the last line prior to the NEW LINE function (wrap around).

When transmitting in response to a specific POLL or general POLL command, data located between the NEW LINE symbol and the end of that line are not transferred. When receiving, a NEW LINE code in the text data causes the display to jump to the beginning of the next line; data between the NEW LINE symbol and the end of the line are not erased. This split-screen capability allows fixed information such as table or entry headings to be continuously displayed without the need for retransmitting them each time.

The line-addressing feature permits the cursor, under program control, to be positioned to the first character position of any line.

Other edit functions include—

1. ERASE DISPLAY erases entire display, relocating cursor to the first displayable character location.
2. ERASE TO END OF LINE erases entire line beginning with the character location following the cursor: the cursor is not moved.
3. ERASE TO END OF SCREEN erases all data following the cursor to the last displayable character location.

Error Checking and Correction

Character and longitudinal parity checking is performed on all data received by the 2845 control from the remote computer; character parity bits and longitudinal check characters are generated and transferred with all data transmitted from the 2845 control. If the remote computer returns a negative acknowledgment, indicating that an error has been detected at the computer site, the 2845 control automatically retransmits the message. The 2845 control also checks the parity and validity of each command sequence received from the computer. If errors are detected, the 2845 does not make a response of any kind.

Programming Support

IBM states that the software support for the 2701 data adapter unit is extended to cover 2265 display stations as remote terminals under BTAM and QTAM for the operating System/360 and under BTAM for the disk operating system.

Configuration

The 2265 display station includes—

1. One 2845 display control, Model 1
2. One 2265 display station, Model 1
3. One 1053 Model 4 printer if desired

Up to sixteen 2265/2845 stations may be connected to the same communications line (multistation operation). The 2265 Display may be located up to 50 feet from the 2845 display control.

The 2845 control and 2265 display station network can communicate over a common-carrier-leased voice-band line with an IBM System/360 (Model 25, 30, 40, 44, 50, 65, 67, 75, or 85) or System/370 computer system incorporating an IBM 2701 data adapter unit. The transmission speed is 1200 or 2400 bits per second, depending on the data set adapter selected. Once installed, the transmission speed is fixed; i.e., the operator cannot select between the two speeds.

In addition to the capability to connect a 1053 printer, two other optional features are available: line addressing and destructive cursor.

Message Configuration

Communication between the remote computer and a 2265 display station or 1053 printer is initiated when the computer transmits a four-character addressing sequence to the 2845 display control. This sequence consists of the following characters: EOT (poll or read) or SOH (write), control address, device address, and command character. The command character specifies one of the eight commands.

When a POLL command addressed to a display station is received, the appropriate 2265 station responds with a text message consisting of the following characters: STX, station address, text, ETX, and LRC (longitudinal redundancy check). If a parity error is detected in the buffer when transmitting, the CAN character is inserted just prior to the ETX character. If the computer receives the message without detecting an error, an ACK character is transmitted to the 2265. If an error is detected, the NAK character is transmitted and the 2845 control automatically retransmits the message.

After the message has been correctly received and the acknowledgment transmitted, the computer can transmit one or more messages to the display station. Each message from the computer consists of the following characters: STX, text, ETX, and LRC. Each message is acknowledged with an ACK or NAK character.

If the command is a general POLL, printer status is first interrogated (if 1053 adapter is installed) to determine that the printer is waiting for a computer message and is not busy (ready status). A positive response to printer status is provided by the 2845 control, which responds: STX, printer address, ETX, and LRC. The required response to this sequence is STX, text, ETX, and LRC. After accepting the printer message, the 2845 responds with ACK. Another message may be received by the printer or the operation is terminated by SOH or EOT. The general POLL must be reinitiated after a printer operation to interrogate the 2265 display status; or, if a negative response to printer status was transmitted by the 2845, the 2265 display status is interrogated.

If the command is a WRITE command, the 2845 responds with an ACK character if it receives the command correctly and a NAK if not. The computer then transmits one or more messages to the addressed station in the same format as above. Each message is acknowledged with an ACK or NAK by the 2845. If the command is a line address WRITE, the line address is inserted following the STX character in the computer text message. The 2845 control will make no response if it detects a parity error or an invalid command or address in the addressing sequence.

A one-character response of EOT or NAK from the 2845 control is transmitted to indicate: a negative response to a POLL command, end of transmission to a READ command, data lost condition to a WRITE command, buffer overflow, or printer busy when addressed. The EOT character normally terminates communication.

The text may contain up to 960 characters. Except for data following a NEW LINE symbol, all displayed characters and symbols are included in the text, excluding the cursor. The displayed data between a NEW LINE symbol and the end of the line is not transmitted when a 2265 is polled and will not be overwritten or erased during a WRITE operation.

Operating Procedure

A message to be transmitted from a 2265 display station is composed by positioning the cursor at the desired starting position, depressing the SHIFT key and START key (which enters the SOH symbol in the cursor position), and keying the data, using NEW LINE symbols where applicable. Controls are provided to space forward or backward, move up or down a line at a time, and return the cursor to the beginning of the next line. The cursor identifies the next display position to be entered. When the optional destructive cursor is moved to a position already containing a display character, that position is erased. The standard nondestructive cursor can be moved freely without erasing data.

To transmit a message, the ENTER key is depressed; this action locks the keyboard and puts the display station in a wait condition. When the station is polled by the remote computer, the data stored in the buffer will be transmitted to the computer. A successful transmission causes the SOH symbol to be erased and the keyboard unlocked. If a transmission error is detected at the remote computer, an automatic retransmission may be requested. For certain types of errors, other correction techniques may be used, as controlled by the stored program in the remote computer.

RCA 8752-100 VIDEO DATA DISPLAY SYSTEM

The RCA 8752-100 video data terminal (Fig. 14-12) is a visual communications terminal designed to permit rapid exchange of data between an RCA 2, 3, 6 or 7 or an RCA Spectra 70 (Model 35, 45, 46, 55, 60) or 61 computer and a remote operator. The basic terminal is designed to operate as a single station in a polling or nonpolling environment. Multistation operation in a polling environment is obtained as a feature. An adapter is also available for connecting a teletypewriter if hard copy is desired.

Configuration

The 8752-100 video data terminal contains a cathode-ray tube (CRT) display, a separate keyboard, a 1280-character magnetostrictive delay-line buffer, character generation, and control logic.

The 8755-100 video data switch allows multiple 8752-100 terminals at one location to share one communications line in a nonpolling environment. The video data switch can accommodate up to eight 8752-100 terminals. In this configuration the switch scans each of the 8752-100 terminals until it finds one in the transmit mode. The scanning is then interrupted and that terminal is connected to the line. A timer in the data switch monitors the time required for the computer to respond. The terminal is disconnected and the scanning continues when the timed interval has elapsed or a response is received from the processor. The timer may be manually set for an interval of 15 or 30 seconds, or it may be locked out. Each 8752-100 terminal can accommodate a teletype Model 33 or 35 receive-only teletypewriter when the printer adapter feature is incorporated.

Fig. 14-12.   RCA 8752-100 Video Data Terminal

Transmission Characteristics

The 8752-100 video data terminal operates asynchronously in half-duplex mode over the public telephone network or a leased voice-band line at up to 120 characters per second (1200 bits per second). The Bell System 202C data-phone data set (for use on leased voice-band lines) or 202D, or the RCA 6711 data set (for use over the public telephone network), is compatible with the 8752-100 terminal. The transmission code used by the 8752-100 terminal is a modified seven-level ASCII code with an even parity bit, a START bit, and a STOP bit added. A total of ten bits are transmitted per character. The low-order bit of each character is transmitted first.

Display Unit

The display portion of the 8752-100 video data terminal is a 12-inch rectangular CRT with a 5.6-inch high by 8-inch wide viewing area. Characteristics of the display unit are shown in Table 14-14. The monoscope technique is used to generate each character of a 64-symbol character set consisting of upper-case alphabetics, numerics, punctuation marks, and special symbols.

Table 14-14. RCA 8752-100 Display Characteristics

CHARACTERISTIC	DESCRIPTION
Output medium	Cathode-ray tube; displays white characters against black background
Character set	64 characters, including upper-case alphabetics, numerics, punctuation marks, and special symbols
Character size	Nominally 0.10 inch wide and 0.14 inch high
Display size	8 inches wide by 5.6 inches high
Characters per line	54, 80, or 81
Lines per display	14 or 20
Characters per display	1080 or 1134 characters
Buffer capacity	1280 characters
Format control	Return characters, data insert function or data format feature; split-screen capability; flexible cursor movement controls
Rated output speed	Up to 120 char/sec (1200 bps)
Effective output speed	Limited by message length and communications facility

Keyboard

The keyboard included with the 8752-100 video data terminal contains 62 keys, including cursor editing, and control keys arranged in conventional typewriter style. The keyboard is not permanently attached to the display unit and may be positioned up to 20 cable-feet from the display.

Cursor controls allow the operator to position the cursor (an underscore) to—

1. The first character position of the next line (or to the first character position of the first line when the cursor is positioned on the last line).

2. The next position to the right (which can be the first position of the next line or the first position of the first line).

3. The adjacent position to the left (this function is terminated when the first position of the line is reached).

Editing Facilities

Editing facilities available for the 8752-100 video data terminal include data insert, which allows data to be inserted in a line of text; existing data is displaced to the right with each character inserted. Data displacement propagates from line to line, except that control characters are not displaced beyond the end of the line. This function is deleted when the data format feature is installed.

The data format feature provides for receiving display format messages. These messages are displayed with reduced brightness. After receipt of a format message, the cursor is positioned to the beginning of the first data field. As data are entered from the keyboard, the cursor is advanced to the next position until the end of the data field is reached. At this point the cursor is positioned to the beginning of the next data field and data entry continues until the last data field is completed. When data entry is completed and the transmit control is depressed, only the data that have been entered in the data fields within the format are transmitted.

Other editing facilities include screen erase, which erases the entire contents of the buffer memory and positions the cursor to the beginning of the display area; line erase, which erases the character in the cursor position and all following characters on that line; character erase, which erases the character in the cursor position; and format data erase, which erases the data entered from the keyboard in conjunction with the data format feature.

Erase functions are controlled by the master erase key and require simultaneous depression of two keys. The line erase function will erase only nonformat data when the data format feature is incorporated.

Operating Procedure

Message composition is performed when the terminal is in the WRITE mode. Data can be entered at any location on the display by positioning the cursor and keying the data. The cursor advances one character position for each character entered and returns to the beginning of the next line when the end of a line is reached. The RETURN function erases the characters to the right of the cursor in the current line when the RETURN key is depressed, and unconditionally returns the cursor to the beginning of the next line.

After the message is composed and the end-of-text (ETX) character is entered, the message can be visually verified; if in error, the message can be altered by means of the editing controls in conjunction with the cursor controls. If the message is correct, the communications link is established and the transmit mode is applicable. The message is transmitted, but the contents of the display memory remain unchanged. Following the transmission of ETX, the terminal is automatically switched to the RECEIVE mode, and the cursor returns to the start of the message. If a computer response is not received within a reasonable period of time, the operator can switch to the WRITE mode and retransmit the message.

The received computer message is preceded by start-of-text (STX) and is displayed, beginning at the first character position of the first line. Existing data (the inquiry) are overwritten by the message. The balance of the screen is erased, the terminal is automatically switched to the WRITE mode, and the cursor is returned to the beginning of the screen when ETX is received. Further input from the communications line is inhibited, and the displayed computer message remains on the screen until erased.

The transmit and receive modes are modified when the message segment address (MSA) function is used. With MSA, each message transmitted begins at the cursor position and ends with ETX. The cursor advances with each character transmitted, as in the normal Transmit mode, but the cursor does not return to the start of the message; it remains at the location following the ETX character. A received computer message is displayed, starting at that cursor location. With the MSA function, both inquiry and response messages can be displayed simultaneously and can be separated by the use of LINE RETURN, NULL, or SPACE characters at the beginning of the computer-response message.

Message Configuration

The message configuration for the 8752-100 video data terminal includes a start-of-text (STX) character (automatically inserted), the text, and an end-of-text (ETX) character. When the station selection feature is used, the terminal is under the control of the computer. The terminal is polled by a transmit start code (TSC), a two-character sequence including EOT and a customer-assigned terminal address character. (Up to 26 address codes can be specified.) The received EOT character places all terminals on the multistation line in the SELECT mode. The addressed terminal responds to a TSC with a text message or a no-text message (identified by an EOT), or the terminal does not respond. The remote computer must be programmed to handle a no-response condition.

Multistation Operation

The station selection feature allows up to twenty-six 8752-100 video data terminals, each incorporating this feature, to communicate in a multi-station arrangement over a single leased line with a remote computer. All communications are initiated by the computer by polling or addressing the terminals.

Error Detection and Correction

Character parity is checked on all data received by the 8752-100 terminal; a parity bit is generated and transferred with each character transmitted from the terminal. If a parity error is detected by the terminal, that character is displayed as a brightened area. The terminal does not generate or recognize and acknowledgment messages for automatic retransmission.

Software

RCA provides four software packages for implementing communications-oriented programs: primary communications oriented system (PCOS), multichannel communications system (MCS), DOS/basic communications (CIA), and TSOS/CAM (time sharing). PCOS provides an independent, though limited, operating environment. It permits concurrent operation of a single user's communication program with up to six data-transcription programs. MCS operates under the tape/disk operating system (TDOS) and provides extensive data-communications support. Although message-switching applications can be accommodated, MCS is primarily intended for use in either remote batch-processing or inquiry/response data-communications applications. Provisions are made to accommodate the RCA 8752-100 video data terminal in both the PCOS and the MCS environment.

RAYTHEON DIDS-400 DIGITAL INFORMATION DISPLAY SYSTEM

The Raytheon DIDS-400 (Fig. 14-13) is a visual communications terminal designed to facilitate rapid and efficient exchange of data between a computer and one or more remote stations under control of a program stored in the computer. The DIDS-400 can operate in a polling or nonpolling environment and in a single-station or multistation arrangement.

Fig. 14-13. Raytheon DIDS-400 Display Console

Configuration

Two models of the display console are available: Models 401 and 402. Both models possess the same display characteristics and keyboard layout.

Model 401 is designed for operation in a polling or nonpolling (query-response) environment and is connected to either the compact Model 425, the standard Model 425, or the Model 450 control unit. Teletype Model 33 or 35 receive-only teleprinters can be combined with a Model 401 display when hard copy is desired. The Model 441 printer adapter provides buffering and control for one teletype teleprinter and is used to interface the teleprinter to the 425 or 450 control unit. As an option, a printer may be connected to a display for printout directly from the display buffer.

The compact Model 425 control unit permits connection of any combination of up to twelve 441 printer adapters and 401 display consoles; the attached devices are selectively interfaced with a single voice-band via a data set. The Model 425 and the programmable Model 450 can control up to a maximum of 64 positions.

The Model 402 display is essentially designed for single-station operation, although a multiunit station can be achieved via the Model 426 multiplex switch unit. The switch unit can accommodate any combination of up to eight Model 402 displays and Model 442 printer adapters; the attached devices are interfaced with a single voice-band via a data set. Each 442 adapter accommodates one teletype Model 33 or 35 receive-only teleprinter.

Table 14-15. Raytheon DIDS-400 ASCII Transmission Code

b_1			0	1	0	1	0	1	0	1	
b_2			0	0	1	1	0	0	1	1	
b_3			0	0	0	0	1	1	1	1	
b_7	b_6	b_5	b_4								
0	0	0	0	NULL	SOH	STX	ETX	EOT				CONTROL CHARACTERS
0	0	0	1	TAB		LINE RESET		FRAME RESET	CR			
0	0	1	0					ERASE		SYN	ETB	
0	0	1	1									
0	1	0	0	.	!	≡	✕	$	%	&	'	
0	1	0	1	(	)	*	+	,	−	.	/	
0	1	1	0	Ø	1	2	3	4	5	6	7	
0	1	1	1	8	9	:	;	<	=	>	?	DISPLAYED CHARACTERS
1	0	0	0	@	A	B	C	D	E	F	G	
1	0	0	1	H	I	J	K	L	M	N	O	
1	0	1	0	P	Q	R	S	T	U	V	W	
1	0	1	1	X	Y	Z	[	⊞	Δ		⊠	

(1) Model 402 display terminal control characters include STX, ETX, EOT, and CR only.

(2) Model 425 control unit tab control option uses the "[" and " " codes for nondisplayable control characters.

(3) Symbol identification:
   ≡ Cursor character (inverted "L" optional)
   ✕ End of message character
   △ Carriage return character
   ⊠ Parity error character

Transmission Characteristics

The Model 425 control unit is hardwired and operates synchonously, in a half-duplex mode, over the public telephone network at 2000 bits per second or over leased voice-band line at 2400 bits per second. The 425 is compatible with the Bell System 201A data-phone data set for connection to the public telephone network, or with the 201B for connection to a leased voice-band line.

The Model 450 control unit is a general-purpose, programmable, terminal interchange and operates in a full-duplex mode over one or more leased voice-band lines. It is compatible with the Bell System 201B data set.

The Model 402 display console or Model 426 multiplex switch operates asynchronously, in a half-duplex mode, over the public telephone network or a leased voice-band line at up to 1200 bits per second. The 402 and 426 are compatible with the Bell System 202C data-phone data set for connection to the public telephone network, or with the data set 202D for connection to a leased voice-band line. Operation at 2400 bits per second synchronously is an option.

Table 14-16. Raytheon DIDS-400 Display Characteristics

CHARACTERISTIC	DESCRIPTION
Output medium	12- or 14-inch rectangular cathode-ray tube; displays green characters against black background
Character set	64 characters, including upper-case alphabetics, numerics, punctuation marks, and special symbols
Character size	Nominally 0.15 inch wide and 0.15 to 0.20 inch high (adjustable)
Display size	8.5 inches wide by 6.5 inches high
Characters per line	40, 44, 65, or 80
Lines per display	12, 13, 16, or 23 lines
Characters per display	480-1, 472
Buffer capacity	480-1, 472
Format control	Horizontal tab characters (opt); insert and delete functions; split-screen capability; flexible cursor movement controls; protected field capability (opt)
Rated output speed	Up to 100,000 char/sec with direct connection; Model 402 display operates at 120 or 250 char/sec over voice-band line; Models 425 and 450 control units operate at 250 or 300 char/sec over voice-band line
Effective output speed	Limited by message length and communications facility

The transmission code used with the 425 and 450 control units is a modified seven-level ASCII, plus one parity bit (odd or even) per character. The 402 terminal also employs a seven-level ASCII, plus an even parity bit per character; for operation at 1200 bits per second, a total of ten bits are transmitted for each character, including one START and one STOP bit. See Table 14-15.

For compatibility with the polling and transmission procedures of IBM System/360 or 370, display consoles and control units can be furnished that operate synchronously in ten-bit ASCII code with the required acknowledgments.

Display Unit

The characteristics of the DIDS-400 display unit, which are the same for both consoles, are shown in Table 14-16. The monoscope technique is used to generate each character of a 64-character set, which consists of upper-case alphabetics, numerics, and special symbols. The characters are regenerated 60 times per second. The keyboard included with the Model 401 or 402 display console contains 60 keys, including control, cursor, and editing keys, arranged in conventional typewriter style. Console controls provide for positioning the cursor to—

1. The first character position of the top line.
2. The first character position of the preceding line.
3. The first character position of the following line.
4. The next TAB STOP position (optional).
5. One space to the right.
6. One space to the left.

A cycle key depressed simultaneously with a character or function key causes repetitive action at a rate of 6 times per second if depressed part way and 15 times per second if fully depressed.

Editing Facilities

The editing controls included with the Model 401 or 402 display console provide for inserting a character into or deleting a character from a line of text. The edited line of text expands or contracts to compensate for the inserted or deleted characters. When a character is deleted from a line of text, a blank space occurs to the right of the text; when a character is inserted in a full line of text, the last character position to the right is lost. The line of text or the message to the right of the cursor may be erased. The cycle feature may be used in conjunction with an edit function.

A special masking control option, available with the Model 401 console only, permits restricted areas to be established within the display; data entry from the keyboard is prevented in these areas. The restricted portion is bracketed by MASK and TAB characters, which are entered by a computer message. The TAB character can be entered from the keyboard for use in simple tabulation and can be erased via the keyboard unless preceded by a MASK character.

Operating Procedures

Data can be entered at any location on the display by positioning the cursor to the location and then entering the data. The cursor is advanced one character position as each character is entered. Editing is performed prior to message transmission. The end-of-message (EOM) key, which is depressed at the end of the message, causes a special symbol to be displayed at the end of the composed message. The EOM key also causes the cursor to be repositioned to the top-left corner of the screen and the transmit function to become operative. All data between the cursor and EOM symbol, except for restricted areas bracketed by MASK and TAB symbols (401 option) are transmitted. Partial-screen transmission is possible by positioning the cursor to the starting location of the message before the transmit key is depressed. The keyboard is locked out during the transmit cycle until a computer response is received or until the operator manually releases the keyboard. Display consoles compatible with IBM System/360 or 370 are provided with a key for entering the START MI character.

Message Configuration

The message configuration for the Model 425 control unit includes a start-of-header (SOH) character, one or more address characters that identify a specific control unit or display console, the text, and an end-of-transmission block (ETB) character. Transmission is synchronized by sync characters preceding each message. An odd or even parity character or a cyclic check character is optional.

The message configuration for the Model 402 display terminal includes a start-of-text (STX) character, a display address, text, and an end-of-text (ETX) character. An end-of-transmission (EOT) character can be substituted for the ETX character.

Error Detection and Correction

Errors that occur during off-line composition can be corrected by positioning the cursor over the character in error and rekeying the correct character. A detected transmission error occurring during a computer message causes a special symbol to be displayed in place of that character. Automatic retransmission request upon detection of a transmission error is optional.

If a transmission error occurs when the start-of-message (SOM) character or the address character is received, the message is not displayed and the operator must repeat the query. If the EOM character is not received by the display, the display remains on line and the message is displayed. The receive mode is terminated in this case by depressing the SHIFT and CLEAR keys.

Multistation Operation

Polling options are available for the Model 425 control unit and the Model 402 display terminal. The 425 control unit with the polling option responds to four separate commands: transmit message from a specific display, transmit mesage from all displays associated with one control unit, transmit message from the first display ready to transmit, and receive computer message addressed to a specified display.

The polling option available with the Model 402 terminal permits polling an individual display, polling all displays common to a specific multiplex switch unit, or both. A broadcast address option, also available for the 402 terminal, allows all display devices to receive the same computer message.

The Model 450 programmable control unit can be programmed for any communications protocol desired and can in turn poll Model 402 display consoles on its tributary circuits as well as control up to 64 Model 401 consoles in a local mode.

Line Selection Keys

The DIDS-401 display console is available in a data-select version that includes 20 line-selection keys and a badge reader for Hollerith-coded identification cards. The controller for this data-select console can control up to 64 display consoles and is designed for a local high-speed interface to a computer. The line-selection keys allow the user to identify to the computer the line on the display he is interested in, and the computer can be programmed to respond with a second appropriate display. In this manner a sequence of screens can be called up, each one defining more closely the data or record desired until it is produced; or a similar sequence of screens can specify the details of an entry or an order to be processed by the computer.

Options

Other options include keys for entering function codes or more than one character per key and interfaces for printers other than teletype. Raytheon states that the cost of these options is negotiated individually.

SANDERS 620 STAND-ALONE DATA DISPLAY SYSTEM

The Sanders 620 stand-alone data display system (Fig. 14-14) is designed to facilitate rapid exchange of data between a computer and a remote station under control of a stored program in the computer. The 620 is a self-contained unit and includes a keyboard, input/output module, and memory module. A Teletype Model 33 or 35 receive-only teleprinter or

Fig. 14-14.   Sanders 620 Stand-Alone Data Display System with
Horizontal Screen Orientation

Univac 8541-02 can be connected to the 620 via an optional hard-copy interface. The transmission rate is governed by the specific communications interface and can range from 110 bits per second to 2400 bits per second.

There are two communications interfaces available for the 620: asynchronous and synchronous. The asynchronous interface provides selectable transmission rates of 110, 1000, 1200, 1800, 2000, and 2400 bits per second; the synchronous interface provides selectable transmission rates of 2000 and 2400 bits per second.

The seven-level ASCII transmission code is employed, with an eighth bit added for character parity. When the asynchronous communications interface is used, one START bit and one or two STOP bits are added to each character transmitted, resulting in a 10- or 11-bit character. Character length is eight bits with the synchronous communications interface.

The Model 6220 display unit contains a 780-character memory module, composed of magnetostrictive delay lines, in addition to editing logic, character generation circuits, control logic, a communications interface, and keyboard. It provides a 9.5-inch by 7.5-inch image area. Normally, the long side of the cathode-ray tube (CRT) is mounted horizontally. The CRT can be mounted vertically if desired. The image area is arranged in 32 lines of 64 or 84 (optional) characters per line when horizontal orientation is specified, and 40 lines of 52 characters per line with vertical orientation. A maximum of 768 characters can be simultaneously displayed on the screen, but they can be displayed in any of the more than 2000 display locations. Various control and format characters also occupy positions in the buffer and therefore reduce the number of data characters that can be displayed. The stroke technique is employed to generate the displayed characters.

The display unit provides controls for adjusting focus, brightness, page size, page centering, and character size.

The Model 6240 keyboard unit may be attached directly to the display unit or may be connected remotely at a distance of up to 10 cable-feet. The keyboard has 51 keys arranged in conventional typewriter style plus an array of 16 special function keys located at the right of the keyboard. Of the 16 special function keys, 11 provide discrete control functions and the 5 remaining keys are adaptable to a variety of customer uses. Depressing a key causes the generation of a unique ASCII character or control code.

Editing Facilities

Four operating modes are available for the 620: type, format type (optional), conversation (optional), and hard copy (optional). Functional keys associated with these operating modes include—

1. FORMAT TYPE initiates data entry mode; permits data to be entered into the buffer memory replacing any previous text.

2. TYPE initiates format mode; permits data to be entered into the buffer memory only in areas (variable fields) specified by a previously stored display format.

3. CONVERSATION TYPE initiates conversation mode; permits data to be entered into the buffer memory following the last line of displayed data.

4. CLEAR erases all data stored in memory (format type or conversation modes); erases only data contained in variable fields specified by stored format (type mode).

5. SEND transmits the entire displayed page (format type mode); transmits data contained in variable fields or data bracketed by left and right delta symbols (type mode); transmits last displayed line (conversational mode).

The hard-copy mode can be entered from the format type, type, or conversational mode to specify transferring all data stored in the memory or only data contained in variable fields (type mode). Data are transferred to the attached printer unit when the COPY key is depressed or if a COPY code is contained in an incoming data message.

Cursor Controls

Six control keys provide a high degree of cursor mobility by directing the cursor to any one of five positions. When used with the format type mode (requires format option), four of the cursor control keys place control characters (formatters) in the buffer memory. The formatters are used to structure the data entered in the format type mode, and can be erased only by typing over in the format type mode. Cursor controls include—

1. HORIZONTAL TAB (optional) establishes four character spaces between segments of the displayed text for each HORIZONTAL TAB formatter stored.

2. VERTICAL TAB (optional) establishes four line spaces following the last displayed line of text for each VERTICAL TAB formatter stored.

3. CARRIAGE RETURN establishes a single space between displayed lines, with the cursor positioned at the initial character location for each key depression or each CARRIAGE RETURN formatter stored.

4. FRONTSPACE/BACKSPACE establishes a single character space forward or backward for each key depression or FRONTSPACE/BACK-SPACE formatter stored.

5. RESET returns the cursor to the display position of the initial char-

acter stored in memory; when used with type mode, the cursor is returned to the initial character position of the first variable field. Reset formatters are stored in memory.

6. SHIFT provides control for dual-operation keys, including the cursor control keys described above.

7. CYCLE LEFT/RIGHT steps the cursor forward or backward at a 30-step-per-second rate for duration of key depression. The backward limiting position is the initial character location in memory or inital character location of the first variable field; the forward limiting position is the last character location in memory or final character location of the last variable field. Cursor will not wrap around when in format type mode.

A repeat key causes repetition of any operation associated with a simultaneously depressed key as long as both keys are depressed.

The Sanders 620 data display system can also interface the 731 display communications buffer for operation in an IBM System/360 or 370 environment.

Configuration

The 620 data display system includes—

1. Model 6220 display unit
2. Model 6240 keyboard
3. Optional Model 6250 hard-copy adapter
4. Model 6201 or 6202 input/output module

Up to 16 Model 620 display terminals can be connected to the same communications line via a Model 716 serial distributor. One keyboard unit can be connected to each display unit. The keyboard unit may be attached to the display unit or located 10 feet away from it.

SANDERS 720 DATA DISPLAY SYSTEM

The Sanders 720 data display System (Fig. 14-15) is designed to facilitate rapid exchange of data between a computer and one or more remote stations under control of a stored program in the computer. Multiple cathode-ray tube (CRT) display units may be connected to a control unit, which contains the interface for the communications line. The control unit may also be connected directly to a computer. Each display unit may be located up to 1000 cable-feet from the control unit. Several types of nondisplay devices, including teletype paper-tape readers and punches and teletype Models 33 or 35 receive-only printers, may also be incorporated through the use of special adapters.

Fig. 14-15.   Sanders 720 Data Display System with
Vertical Screen Orientation

The data transmission rate between a directly connected 720 station and the computer averages about 47,500 characters per second. When the 720 is connected remotely, the transmission rate is governed by the specific communications interface and may range from 110 bits per second to 9600 bits per second.

Two communications interfaces are available for the 720: asynchronous and synchronous. The asynchronous interface provides transmission rates of 110, 1000, 1200, 1800, 2000, 2400, 3600, 4800, 7200, and 9600 bits per second. The synchronous interface provides transmission rates of 2000, 2400, 3600, 4800, 7200, and 9600 bits per second.

The seven-level ASC II transmission code is employed, with an eighth bit added for character parity. When the asynchronous communications interface is used, one START bit and one or two STOP bits are added to each character transmitted, resulting in a 10- or 11-bit character. Character length is eight bits, with the synchronous communications interface; 2 to 6 sync characters are transmitted prior to data characters.

The Model 701 control unit may contain up to three 1024-character memory modules composed of magnetostrictive delay lines. Each memory module provides buffering for one, two, or four display units; the same number of display units must be attached to each memory module. The 1024 character locations contained in a memory module are divided equally among the number of attached display units. In addition to the memory modules, the control unit contains the communications interface, editing logic, character generation circuits, multiplexing logic, and control logic.

The basic Model 716 serial distributor can accommodate up to four control units and is used to interface the control units to a single leased line. The serial distributor operates in the full-duplex mode, which permits concurrent polling of one control unit while transmitting from another. Up to 16 control units can be accommodated by the Serial distributor with the addition of up to 3 Model 7180 expansion units; each expansion unit accommodates four control units.

The Model 708 display unit provides a 7.5 x 9.5-inch image area. Normally, the long side of the cathode-ray tube (CRT) is mounted vertically so that the displayed information appears in a conventional page format. The CRT can be mounted horizontally if desired. The image area is arranged in 40 lines of 52 characters per line when the vertical orientation is specified, or in 32 lines of 64 or 84 (optional) characters per line with the horizontal orientation. A maximum of 256, 512, or 1024 characters can be displayed on the screen, but they can be displayed in any of the more than 2000 display locations. Various control and format characters occupy positions in the buffer and therefore reduce the number of data characters that can be displayed. The stroke technique is employed to generate the displayed characters.

Each display unit provides controls for adjusting focus, brightness, page size, page centering, character size, and character tilt. The character tilt control varies the displayed character from a vertical position to a slanted (italic) position.

The Model 722 or 7240 keyboard unit may be attached to a display unit or may be connected remotely at a distance of up to 10 cable-feet. The keyboard has 51 keys arranged in either conventional typewriter (722) or keypunch (7240) style plus an array of 16 special function keys located at the right of the keyboard. Of the 16 special function keys, 11 provide discrete control functions; the 5 remaining keys are adaptable to a variety of custom uses. Depressing a key causes the generation of a unique ASCII character or control code.

Editing Facilities

The 720 data display system incorporates a very flexible set of edit functions. Editing operations are divided into two categories: data entry (operator) mode operations and format (programmer) mode operations. Data entry operations are controlled by a group of four keys and enable the operator to enter, manipulate, or erase data within a preset format. Format mode operations are controlled by a group of seven keys and enable a programmer or supervisor to enter, manipulate, or erase the data formats used to structure data entered in the data entry mode:

Data entry mode functional keys include—

1. TYPE permits data to be entered into the buffer memory, replacing any previous text.
2. INSERT permits data to be added to an existing text. As data are entered, the existing text is automatically spread to accommodate the added text.
3. DELETE permits data to be erased from the existing text while closing the text to maintain continuity.
4. SEND BLOCK transmits a block of text; a block is defined as the text that is bracketed by two HOME characters.

Format mode functional keys include—

1. FORMAT TYPE permits format data to be entered into the buffer memory.
2. FORMAT INSERT permits format data to be added to the existing format.
3. FORMAT DELETE permits format data to be erased from the existing format.
4. MOVE CURSOR permits the cursor to be positioned at any location on the viewing screen.
5. CLEAR erases all data stored in the buffer memory segment associated with the display unit.
6. SEND PAGE transmits the entire displayed page.
7. RESET CURSOR returns the cursor to the display position of the initial character stored in the buffer memory (home position).

The Sanders Model 737 Photopen® cursor controller is used with one

Model 708 display unit. This device contains a light-sensing element and outputs a signal in sychronization with the appearance of a character on the screen within the field of view (one character) of the Photopen. An outlining circle of light, projected by the light pen, identifies the field of view. The amplified output from the Photopen is used to reposition the cursor to the Photopen's present location when the cursor button on the Photopen is depressed. The SEND BLOCK button on the Photopen initiates transmission of the block of text identified by the cursor.

Cursor Controls

Six control keys provide a high degree of cursor mobility by directing the cursor to any one of eight positions. When used with the format type or format insert functions, four of the cursor control keys place control characters (formatters) in the buffer memory. The formatters are used to structure the data entered in the data entry mode, and can be erased only with the format delete function. The formatters include—

1. HORIZONTAL TAB/BACK TAB establishes four character spaces between segments of the displayed text for each HORIZONTAL TAB character stored.
2. VERTICAL TAB establishes four line spaces following the last displayed line of text for each VERTICAL TAB character stored.
3. CARRIAGE RETURN/BACK RETURN establishes a single space between displayed lines with the cursor positioned at the initial character location.
4. HOME establishes the initial position for a block of text; the HOME or starting position for the first block of text is always the upper-left margin. (A block of text is the text included between two HOME characters.) The SEND BLOCK key transmits the block of text that contains the cursor.
5. FRONTSPACE/BACKSPACE establishes a single character space forward or backward.
6. SHIFT provides control for dual-operation keys, including the cursor control keys described above.

Other Controls

A REPEAT key causes repetition of any operation associated with a simultaneously depressed key as long as both keys are depressed. Specific characters can be made to blink by entering a START BLINK (SB) control character before entering the characters to be blinked. A clear blink (CB) control character is entered when blinking is to be discontinued. The SB and CB control characters are located on the shifted positions of the VERTICAL TAB and HOME keys.

731 Display Communications Buffer

The 731 display communications buffer is specifically designed to interface a 720 data display system with an IBM System/360 or 370 and is capable of operating in a local or remote mode. In the local mode, data are transferred between the 720 system and the System/360 or 370 computer in parallel-by-bit fashion at 47,500 characters per second. Up to 96 display units may be directly connected to a single System/360 multiplexor or selector channel. In the remote mode, data are transferred synchronously, in serial-by-bit fashoin, at 2000, 2400, 3600, 4800, 7200, or 9600 bits per second. Up to 16 half-duplex lines can be connected to a 731 buffer.

Configuration

A 720 data display system includes—

1. Model 701 control unit
2. Up to 12 Model 708 display units
3. Up to 12 Model 722 or 7240 keyboard units (one per display unit)
4. Optional Model 737 Photopen cursor controllers (one per display unit)
5. Optional Model 706 hard-copy adapter (one per control unit)
6. Optional Model 718 or 719 paper-tape reader/punch adapter (one per control unit)

Up to four Model 701 control units and their associated components may be connected to the same communications line via a Model 716 serial distributor. Up to three Model 7180 expansion units may be incorporated to expand the basic interface capability of four control units to a maximum of 20 increments of 4.

A 701 control unit may contain up to three memory modules. Each memory module may service one, two, or four 708 display units. The same number of display units must be connected to each memory module.

ULTRONIC SYSTEMS VIDEOMASTER 7000 DISPLAY TERMINAL

Configuration

The basic Ultronic Systems VM-7000 is a stand-alone desk-top video terminal (Fig. 14-16) that consists of three separate units:

1. One 12-inch diagonal CRT display monitor
2. One alphanumeric keyboard (see Figure 14-17)
3. One control unit

The display monitor and keyboard are detachable, and each connects to the control unit via its own 10-foot cable. One control unit is required to service each keyboard/display terminal. As many VM-7000 terminals as are required in a practical system can be multidropped on one communications line when operating under IBM System/360 or 370 control. The control unit of each terminal requires a separate data set to interface the line, except where two or more terminals are collocated. The need for a separate data set interfacing each terminal to the line, in a given multistation arrangement, can be eliminated through the use of an optional direct- or remote-connected serial distributor (depending on the proximity

Fig. 14-16.   Ultronic Systems VM-7000 Display Terminal Including Control Unit (left) and Keyboard and Display Monitor (right)

to the computer). Figure 14-18 illustrates a typical multidrop arrangement of multiple vm-7000 terminal components.

Ultronic Systems provides two equivalent data set models from their data pump product line, both of which meet EIA Standard RS232B specifications and have the following transmission characteristics:

1. Series 1200 data pump: Half-duplex (200 ± 25 or 20 ± 2-millisecond turnaround) or full-duplex mode; serial format; asynchronous data rates up to 1200 bits per second; operation over public switched-network or four-wire Type 3002 leased line (with C1 conditioning); external clocking via vm-7000.

2. Series 2400 data pump: Full-duplex mode; serial format; synchronous data rate at 2400 bits per second; operation over four-wire Type 3002 leased line (with C2 conditioning); internal clocking.

When the optional hard-copy feature is required, up to four vm-7000 terminals can be connected to a single printer via a printer-distributor unit. Without the distributor, each display must be connected to a separate printer. In addition to the 960-character memory employed to refresh data on the display monitor, each vm-7000 control unit incorporates a separate 960-character memory to serve as buffer storage for one auxiliary printer.

Fig. 14-17. Ultronic Systems VM-7000 Alphanumeric Keyboard

Optional Features

The basic vm-7000 configuration may be modified to include the following optional equipment features as required:

1. Printer: Nonimpact, thermal printing mechanism provides single-copy output of data received from remote computer or associated display(s); operates at 30 characters per second on 80-column print line.

2. Serial distributor: Allows more than one vm-7000 display terminal (or ibm 2848 display controller) to interface a single 1200 or 2400 bit per second modem; the need for a modem is eliminated entirely if the multiple vm-7000's are physically located within the prescribed cable distances from the ibm 2701 Type III data adapter unit. The serial distributor can provide interfaces for up to four vm-7000's (or ibm 2848's) or can reserve one interface as an input to an additional serial distributor. Five serial distributors can be cascaded in this manner, providing interfaces for a maximum of 16 vm-7000's or ibm 2848's (or a combination therof) to a single modem, remote or directly to an ibm 2701 Type III dau. The serial distributor is a transparent device; it does not alter the command structure be-

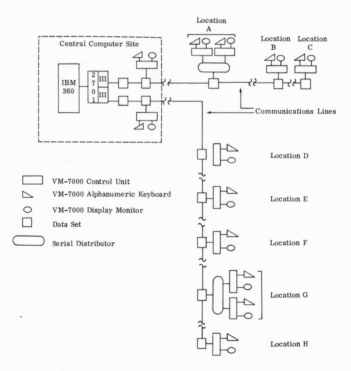

Fig. 14-18.   Ultronic Systems VM-7000 Multidrop Configuration

tween the central computer and the terminals and does not affect the vm-7000's compatibility with the ibm System/360 or 370.

Compatibility

VM-7000 terminals can be arranged to operate with or replace ibm 2265/2845 display stations in an identical configuration without hardware

Table 14-17. Ultronic Systems
vm-7000 ascii Code Set

B7				0	0	0	0	1	1	1	1
	B6			0	0	1	1	0	0	1	1
		B5		0	1	0	1	0	1	0	1
B4	B3	B2	B1	0	1	2	3	4	5	6	7
0	0	0	0			SP	0		P	A_T	
0	0	0	1	SOH		Note 1	1	A	Q		
0	0	1	0	STX		Note 2	2	B	R		
0	0	1	1	ETX		#	3	C	S		
0	1	0	0	EOT		$	4	D	T		
0	1	0	1		NAK	%	5	E	U		
0	1	1	0	ACK		&	6	F	V		
0	1	1	1			'	7	G	W		
1	0	0	0		CAN	(	8	H	X		
1	0	0	1			)	9	I	Y		
1	0	1	0	Note 3 LF		*	:	J	Z		
1	0	1	1			+	;	K			
1	1	0	0			,	<	L			¬
1	1	0	1			-	=	M	Note 4		
1	1	1	0			.	>	N			|
1	1	1	1			/	?	O	—		

NOTES:　1. Displayed on VM-7000 as an EOM (▬) symbol.
　　　　2. Displayed on VM-7000 as a CHECK (▯) symbol.
　　　　3. Displayed on VM-7000 as a New Line (◢) symbol.
　　　　4. Displayed on VM-7000 as a SOM (▶) symbol.

or software modifications to the existing system. This compatibility allows the vm-7000 to communicate with the ibm System/360 (Models 30, 40, 44, 50, 65, 67, or 75) or System/370 when interfaced through a Model 2701 data adapter unit, Type III. The application program for the vm-7000 can be implemented through ibm-supplied btam or qtam programming-systems support packages, which operate under ibm System/360 operating system (os) or ibm System/360 disk operating system (dos).

All hardware and software design considerations relative to the ibm System/360 also apply to configurations structured around any version of the System/370 announced to date, provided an ibm 2701 dau is incorporated as the front end.

Message Configuration

The vm-7000 uses 71 of the 128 possible seven-level ascii code characters in data exchanges with the remote computer; see Table 14-17. When equipped with an optional printer, the vm-7000 can execute the eight separate commands described in Table 14-18, operating in a polled environment. Execution of each command is controlled and monitored by exchanges of a single ascii communication control character or by a sequence of characters that contains one or more control characters.

Table 14-18. Ultronic Systems vm-7000
Polling Command Functions

POLLING COMMAND	ADDRESSING SEQUENCE/RESPONSE		CONTROL FUNCTION
	COMPUTER	TERMINAL	
Specific POLL	EOT Cntl Addr Dev Addr POLL Cmnd[1]*		Interrogates addressed vm-7000 to determine availability of message entered for transfer to computer; tests for depression of transmit (TR) key and display of start-of-message (SOM) symbol
		STX vm-7000 Addr Text CAN[2] ETX LRC[3]	Indicates TR depressed, SOM displayed; pending message transmitted to computer; same response, without text, if SOM not displayed

Table 14-18. (contd.)

POLLING COMMAND	ADDRESSING SEQUENCE/RESPONSE		CONTROL FUNCTION
	COMPUTER	TERMINAL	
		EOT	Negative response indicates no message pending from display Indicates TR not depressed
	STX EOT or ACK[1]		Positive response disables vm-7000 transmit condition and restores keyboard
	EOT or SOH		Negative response does not disable vm-7000 transmit condition or restore keyboard
		EOT	Concludes operation
	STX, Text ETX LRC[1,4]		Computer message transmitted for display
READ addressed full vm-7000 buffer	EOT Cntl Addr Dev Addr READ Cmnd[1]		Causes all character data displayed at addressed vm-7000 to be transmitted to computer
		STX vm-7000 Addr Text CAN[2] ETX LRC[3,5,6]	Reads out and transmit all buffer data to computer regardless of TR key status
	STX Text ETX LRC[1,4]		Transmits computer message for display
WRITE addressed vm-7000	SOH Cntl Addr Dev Addr WRITE Cmnd[1]		Requests addressed vm-7000 to acknowledge readiness for computer message

* Numbers in parentheses refer to notes at end of table.

Table 14-18. (contd.)

| POLLING COMMAND | ADDRESSING SEQUENCE/RESPONSE | | CONTROL FUNCTION |
	COMPUTER	TERMINAL	
		ACK[5,6]	Indicates readiness to receive computer message
	STX Text ETX LRC[1,4]		Transmits computer message for display beginning at cursor location; over-writes existing displayed data
ERASE/ WRITE addressed vm-7000	SOH Cntl Addr Dev Addr ERASE Cmnd[1]		Causes erasure of addressed vm-7000 screen; relocates cursor to home position
		ACK[5,6]	Indicates screen erased, cursor in upper-left position ready to receive text
	STX Text EXT LRC[1,4]		Transmits computer message for display beginning at upper-left screen position
WRITE vm-7000 line address	SOH Cntl Addr Dev Addr WRITE Cmnd[1]		Requests addressed vm-7000 to acknowledge readiness for computer message beginning at display line to be specified
		ACK[5,6]	Indicates readiness to receive text
	STX Line Addr Text ETX LRC[1,4]		Transmits computer message for display beginning at first position of line specified
Specific POLL printer	EOT or SOH Cntl Addr Dev Addr POLL Cmnd[1]		Determines availability of printer to receive computer message

Table 14-18. (contd.)

| POLLING COMMAND | ADDRESSING SEQUENCE/RESPONSE | | CONTROL FUNCTION |
	COMPUTER	TERMINAL	
		NAK[7]	Indicates printer not ready
		EOT[7]	Indicates printer busy
		STX Prntr Addr ETX LRC[3]	Indicates printer ready to receive computer message; resets printer request
	SOR or EOT		Concludes operation
	STX Text ETX LRC[1,4,8]		Transmits computer message for printing

General
POLL
VM-7000
	EOT or
	  SOH
	Cntl Addr
	Dev Addr
	  (FF)
	POLL
	  Cmnd[1]
			Determines availability of printer to receive computer message
			
			Determines availability of pending display message entered for transfer to computer

		EOT	Negative response indicates printer request not set and no display message pending
		STX Prntr Addr ETX LRC[3]	Indicates printer not busy, request is set and ready to receive computer message
		STX Dsply Addr Text ETX LRC[3]	Indicates TR depressed, SOM displayed; pending message transmitted to computer; same response, without text, if SOM not displayed

173

Table 14-18. (contd.)

POLLING COMMAND	ADDRESSING SEQUENCE/RESPONSE		CONTROL FUNCTION
	COMPUTER	TERMINAL	
	SOH or EOT[9]		Negative response does not disable VM-7000 transmit condition or restore keyboard
	STX EOT[9] or ACK[1]		Positive response disables VM-7000 transmit condition and restores keyboard
		EOT	Concludes operation
	STX Text ETX LRC[1,4,8,9]		Transmits computer message for display or printing
WRITE Printer	EOT or SOH Cntl Addr Dev Addr WRITE Cmnd[1]		Determines availability of printer to receive computer message
		NAK[7]	Printer not ready
		EOT[7]	Printer busy
		ACK	Printer ready to receive computer message; resets printer request
	SOH or EOT		Concludes operation
	STX Text ETX LRC[1,4,8]		Transmits computer message for printing

174

The addressing sequence of each computer POLL command comprises four separate bytes (seven-bit ASCII characters), which can be recognized by the VM-7000 terminal:

1. First byte: Contains one of two control characters (SOH or EOT), which place VM-7000 in control mode.

2. Second byte: Contains a numeric character designating one of various possible VM-7000 control unit addresses.

3. Third byte: Contains one of three device addresses for directing the interrogation to a display station, printer (optional), or to both (general POLL).

4. Fourth byte: Contains one of a maximum eight (up to five without printer option) possible commands that specifies the polling operation to be executed, see Table 14-18.

NOTES:

1. No response from terminal to this computer message may indicate address recognition failure, invalid command, invalid address, address sequence party error, or defective communications facilities.

2. CAN is inserted in terminal message if buffer parity error is detected during transmission to computer.

3. NAK response from computer to this terminal message indicates request for retransmission.

4. ACK response from terminal acknowledges receipt of this computer message without error; NAK response indicates character (VRC) or block (LRC) parity error detected upon receipt of this computer message.

5. STX EOT returned from computer indicates positive response to this terminal message and restores keyboard.

6. SOH or EOT returned from computer indicates negative response to this terminal message and does not restore keyboard.

7. NAK or EOT terminal response to computer poll sets printer request.

8. EOT terminal response to this computer message indicates printer buffer is in overflow condition.

9. This computer response requires general POLL to be issued again in order to receive additional pending terminal messages.

UNIVAC UNISCOPE 100 DISPLAY TERMINAL

The Univac Uniscope 100 Display (Fig. 14-19) is a visual communications terminal that facilitates rapid and efficient exchange of alphanumeric data between a computer and one or more remote stations under control of a stored computer program.

Basic Operation

The Uniscope 100 is a low-cost, alphanumeric display designed for a broad range of applications that require direct operator interaction with a

Fig. 14-19. Univac Uniscope 100 Display Terminal Including
Alphanumeric and Numeric Entry Keyboards

centralized computer system. Owing to its modular construction, this terminal can operate as either a data entry or display device. It may be located at the central computer site and connected via a direct channel interface, or at a remote site and connected over telephone lines via a data set interface. Up to 31 terminals may use a single communications line or may be connected to a computer input/output channel by using a multiplexor.

The Uniscope 100 is designed to operate in a polling environment; all transmissions between the computer and the terminal are initiated by the computer. Messages (in either direction) must be acknowledged by the recipient.

Terminals may be configured singly or multiplexed in clusters, or these two methods may be combined on a single communications line (voice-grade, high-speed, or channel). Each terminal contains its own memory and control logic; the multiplexor serves only to direct messages to the proper terminal in its cluster.

Every singly configured terminal or multiplexed cluster operates in half-duplex mode, but when a line is shared by several units or clusters, operation is in full-duplex mode. Provisions are included in the control logic of the terminals to allow the computer to interrupt transmission to one display controller in order to permit polling and initiation of data transmission from another terminal (or cluster) connected to the same communications line.

A keyboard unit provides all operator controls and keys required to operate the CRT and initiate data transmission. The keyboard may be removed from the display and connected with an optional cable up to 20 feet in length. There are three keyboard divisions:

1. Editing and cursor control keys
2. Basic typewriter keyboard
3. Numeric entry keyboard

All keyboard options include the editing and cursor control keys and may include both or either of the other keyboards.

Visual output is strictly alphanumeric in a viewing area 10 inches wide by 5 inches high. Data are arranged into one of four optional formats:

1. Six lines of 80 characters each
2. Twelve lines of 80 characters each
3. Sixteen lines of 32 characters each
4. Sixteen lines of 64 characters each

Character generators are available for either 64 or 96 distinct characters. The latter permits display of the full ASCII character set, including upper- and lower-case alphabetics.

A selective data blink feature enables blinking of any combination of characters. This feature uses two control characters: one to activate and one to deactivate blinking of a character or set of contiguous characters. Hard copy from the display is available via an optional interface to an incremental printer.

Split-screen operation enables operator designation and rapid changing of an active screen area without affecting the remainder of the display. During split-screen operation, only the active screen area is used for message exchange between the display and computer.

Controlled text scrolling is available on a full-screen basis and within split-screen operation. It is implemented by program use of the LINE IN-SERT and LINE DELETE edit functions.

Display Unit

The Uniscope 100 incorporates the same display tube as the Uniscope 300. It is a 13-inch diagonal cathode-ray tube mounted with the long dimension horizontal. Screen-viewing area is 10 inches by 5 inches, arranged in a variety of formats, permitting a maximum of 1024 characters to be displayed. The tube phosphor is type P31, with both color elements green, and a flicker-free refresh rate of 60 times per second. Tube brightness is manually variable.

Visual output is provided in the form of alphanumeric characters on the cathode-ray tube. Characters appear white against a dark background, normally 0.113 inch wide by 0.150 inch high, in lines of up to 64 characters; or 0.091 inch wide by 0.135 inch high, in lines of 80 characters. Options provide for a 64- or 96-character set. The latter character set contains the full ascii code, including lower-case alphabetics.

Each display is freestanding and contains all components required for its own operation. The addition of a basic multiplexor permits up to eight terminals to interface with a single communications line. Multiplexor options permit additional terminals (in increments of 4) to be added; up to two such expansions are possible, for a total of 16 terminals. Cascading two terminal multiplexors accommodates 31 terminals on a single communications line. Every Uniscope 100 contains a computer core memory with a sufficient number of seven-bit characters to meet the requirements of the particular format option selected.

Displayed data can be printed via a communication output printer (cop) using the auxiliary interface option. The auxiliary interface is a general-purpose, parallel channel that permits a receive-only printer to interface the display memory. The cop is housed in a separate cabinet and prints up to 30 characters per second with 132 print positions. Displayed data can be printed by computer instruction or by the operator.

Operator input is accomplished through a keyboard, shown in Figure 14-20, which includes keys for editing and cursor control and optionally alphanumeric and/or numeric entry of data. Keyboard labeling for the typewriter keyboard varies according to the character set selected (64 or 96 characters). When the numeric keyboard is included, a redundant space key is povided so that the controls normally used with a numeric keyboard (space, tab, and carriage return) are available immediately adjacent to it. The feel of the keyboard is comparable to that of an electric typewriter and permits input at a rate of at least 80 words per minute without loss of data. The keyboard may be removed from the display and connected with an optional cable up to 20 feet in length.

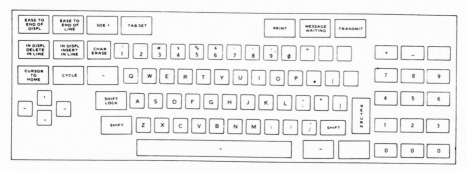

Fig. 14-20.   Univac Uniscope 100 Keyboard Layout

The Uniscope 100 includes a blinking capability that enables blinking of selected characters or character strings. Blinking is accomplished by bracketing the character or characters to be blinked with two unique, non-displayable characters (blink on and blink off). Selective data blinking can be activated as part of a computer message only, not by direct keyboard input. When the cursor is associated with a displayable character, both will automatically be blinked.

A split-screen capability is included and allows use of portions of the screen for active message interchange without disturbing the remainder of the display. During split-screen operation, the active area of the screen is that area between the cursor position and the previous start-of-field symbol. The operator can freely position the cursor to change dynamically the active screen area, and can split the screen into as many different areas as are necessary and useful. This split-screen feature allows the computer and the operator to exchange messages without requiring transmission of the entire contents of the display each time.

Data Transmission

Data can be transmitted over the public telephone network, leased common-carrier voice-band lines, or directly over a channel. The standard transmission mode for each terminal is half-duplex, but when two or more terminals share a communications line, full-duplex communication is realized. Transmission is serial by bit with the high-order bit of each character transmitted first. The transmission code is standard seven-level ASCII code plus character parity, as shown in Table 14-19.

Table 14-19. Univac Uniscope 100 ASCII Code

					96-Character Set							
						64-Character Set						
Bit Positions b7 → b6 → b5 →					$^0{}_0{}_0$	$^0{}_0{}_1$	$^0{}_1{}_0$	$^0{}_1{}_1$	$^1{}_0{}_0$	$^1{}_0{}_1$	$^1{}_1{}_0$	$^1{}_1{}_1$
b4	b3	b2	b1	col → row ↓	0	1	2	3	4	5	6	7
0	0	0	0	0	NUL	DLE	SP	Ø	@	P	`	P
0	0	0	1	1	SOH	DCI	!	1	A	Q	a	q
0	0	1	0	2	STX	DC2	"	2	B	R	b	r
0	0	1	1	3	ETX	DC3	#	3	C	S	c	s
0	1	0	0	4	EOT	DC4	$	4	D	T	d	t
0	1	0	1	5	ENQ	NAK		5	E	U	e	u
0	1	!	0	6	ACK	SYN	&	6	F	V	f	v
0	1	1	1	7	·BEL	ETB	'	7	G	W	g	w
1	0	0	0	8	BS	CAN	(	8	H	X	h	x
1	0	0	1	9	HT	EM	)	9	I	Y	i	y
1	0	1	0	10	LF	SUB	*	:	J	Z	j	z
1	0	1	1	11	VT	ESC	+	;	K	[	k	{
1	1	0	0	12	FF	FS	,	<	L	\	1	¦
1	1	0	1	13	CR	GS	–	=	M	]	m	}
1	1	1	0	14	SO	RS	.	>	N	∧	n	~
1	1	1	1	15	SI	US	/	?	O	_	o	∥

The following data transmission features are standard on all communication interfaces:

1. Interleaved message transmission: During the time the computer is transmitting a long output message to one display, the display logic enables the computer to insert polling messages to other displays. This permits improved performance in systems involving substantial computer output volume.

2. Segmented message: This feature allows the computer to address any point on the screen and send a message of any length up to the end of the screen. This permits changing individual characters, words, or blocks of data without disturbing the rest of the screen.

3. Parity: Character and message parity are used in all communications interface options in transmission and reception. The Uniscope 100 checks parity on received data and provides an appropriate acknowledgment that conforms to ASCII standards. Parity is also generated by the Uniscope 100 for transmitted data.

4. Status poll: The computer can issue a status poll to a display and receive an indication of whether data are available for a normal poll. This allows the computer to continue to poll at times when it is not ready to accept data.

Editing Facilities

A flexible set of edit functions is incorporated. Any one of seven editing functions can be executed via a set of five keys. Two of the editing functions are performed by depressing the shift key in conjunction with an edit key.

Edit keys include the shift key plus the following keys:

1. CHARACTER ERASE erases the character in the cursor position and replaces it with a space.
2. ERASE TO END OF LINE causes space character (blanks) to be entered in each character position beginning at the cursor location and continuing to the end of the line.
3. ERASE TO END OF DISPLAY replaces all characters from the cursor position to the end of the display with spaces.
4. INSERT permits entry of data into an existing text by displacing all characters one space to the right of, and including, the cursor position; the last character on the line is discarded. When the SHIFT

key is used in conjunction with the INSERT key, all characters from the cursor position to the end of the display are displaced one position to the right and the last character of the display is discarded.

5. DELETE allows data to be erased from the existing text while closing the text to maintain continuity. All characters to the right of the cursor are displaced one space to the left. When the SHIFT key is used in conjunction with the DELETE key, all characters from the cursor to the end of the display (upper-left corner) are displaced one space to the left.

Two significant operations, each initiated by a computer message, allow a specific line of text to be added or deleted; each such message may contain a new line of text. When the computer message specifies a LINE INSERT function, all lines below and including that containing the cursor are moved down one line; the bottom line is erased. The cursor line is left blank or a new line of text is inserted. A line may be deleted by a computer message that positions the cursor to the start of the line and then specifies an ERASE TO END OF LINE function. A special CYCLE key operates with all others except the ERASE, DELETE, INSERT, SHIFT LOCK, PRINT, MESSAGE WAITING, TRANSMIT, and CURSOR TO HOME keys. When simultaneously depressed with another key, the CYCLE key causes the second key function to be repeated at a rate of approximately 10 Hertz.

Cursor

The cursor is a unique character that is constantly displayed on the CRT and marks the position that will be occupied by the next character entered via the keyboard. It also marks the last character of text when data are transmitted to the computer. When the cursor is positioned over a displayable character, both blink at a preset rate between four and ten times per second. The cursor advances one position for each character entered from the keyboard and can be moved by the cursor controls.

Eight control keys provide a large degree of cursor manipulation. When used with the edit keys, the cursor locates data to be inserted in text, deleted from text, and erased from text. Cursor control keys include—

1. SCAN FORWARD moves the cursor one position to the right; if this key is held down, the cursor moves at a rate of 10 positions per second.

2. SCAN BACK positions the cursor one position to the left; if this key is held down, the cursor moves at a rate of 10 positions per second.

3. SCAN UP positions the cursor up one line; if this key is held down, the cursor moves at a rate of 10 lines per second.

4. SCAN DOWN positions the cursor down one line; if this key is held down, the cursor moves at a rate of 10 positions per second.
5. CURSOR TO HOME moves the cursor to the first character position on the display.
6. RETURN moves the cursor to the first character position of the next line.
7. SPACE moves the cursor one position to the right.
8. TAB moves the cursor one position to the right of a TAB STOP character. The TAB STOP character is not displayed but remains stored in the buffers; the cursor stops at the end of the display if a TAB STOP character is not detected. TAB STOPS may be inserted by the central computer or directly from the keyboard.

The following key, provided on the typewriter keyboard only, may also be used for editing functions: BACK SPACE moves the cursor one position to the left.

Line insert and line delete editing functions provide a rapid, simple method of obtaining scrolling for an operator through large amounts of data. Line insert and line delete functions are computer designated, causing the last or first lines of the active display area to be deleted from the screen, automatically moving the remaining lines down or up on the screen, and allowing a new line to be placed at the top or bottom of the displayed text. These functions can be used in conjunction with split-screen operation so that the active screen area is from the line in which the cursor appears to the previous start-of-field (SOF) symbol or the top of the screen. Use the keyboard with appropriate programming can allow the operator to roll up or down one line for each operation of a predefined key or to activate an automatic scrolling up or down at a preselected roll rate.

Error Detection and Correction

Character and longitudinal parity are generated with each message transmitted and are checked for every message received. If no transmission errors are detected in a received message, a positive acknowledgment indication is included in the next message to the computer from that control unit response to the computer's poll. The acknowledgment can be returned in a NO TRAFFIC message, which indicates there is no more data to transmit.

If an error is detected, the affected display station will not accept any more data and the partial message remains on the display screen until a retransmission is received (sent automatically in reply to a computer request).

Options

Univac Uniscope 100 display terminals are designed to satisfy a wide variety of interface requirements. Terminals can be operated singly or can be multiplexed over the public telephone networks or leased common-carrier lines, or operated via a channel interface directly to a computer. Optionally, the modem may be incorporated into the terminal itself.

The following interface options are available with the Uniscope 100:

1. Direct interface: Permits communications via direct wire connection to a CTMC or DCS for synchronous operation without a modem at 2400, 4800, or 9600 bits per second.

2. Synchronous interface: Provides a synchronous serial interface to a modem conforming with RS232 interface standards (Bell System 201A, 201B, or equivalent data sets); also provides terminal multiplexor capabilities when interfaced with a synchronous modem.

3. Asynchronous interface: Provides an asynchronous serial interface to a modem conforming with RS232 standards (Bell System 103A/F at 300 bits per second, or 202 C/D at 1200, 1600, or 1800 bits per second); also provides serial asynchronous operations for a terminal multiplexor at 300, 1200, 1600, or 1800 bits per second, interfaced with an asynchronous modem.

4. Compatible interface synchronous: Permits ASCII communications to an IBM computer with a 2701 and SDA II, or a 2703 and Synchronous Base 1; provides interface to either a modem or the Uniscope 100 terminal multiplexor.

5. Computer interface asynchronous: Permits ASCII communications to an IBM computer with a 2701 and terminal adapter Type III; provides interface to either a modem or the Uniscope 100 terminal multiplexor.

6. Auxiliary interface: Provides a general-purpose parallel channel that permits the communications output printer to interface the display memory.

The following terminal multiplexor options are also available:

1. Multiplexor expansion: Expands the capacity of the multiplexor to a total of 16 display positions in increments of 4 (maximum of two expansions per multiplexor); cascading two multiplexors accommodates 31 displays.

2. Synch/async interface: Provides communications interface to either a modem or terminal multiplexor; synchronous with Bell System 201A, 201B, or equivalent data sets; asynchronous with Bell System 103 A/F, 202 C/D, or equivalent data sets; includes EIA RS232 interface.

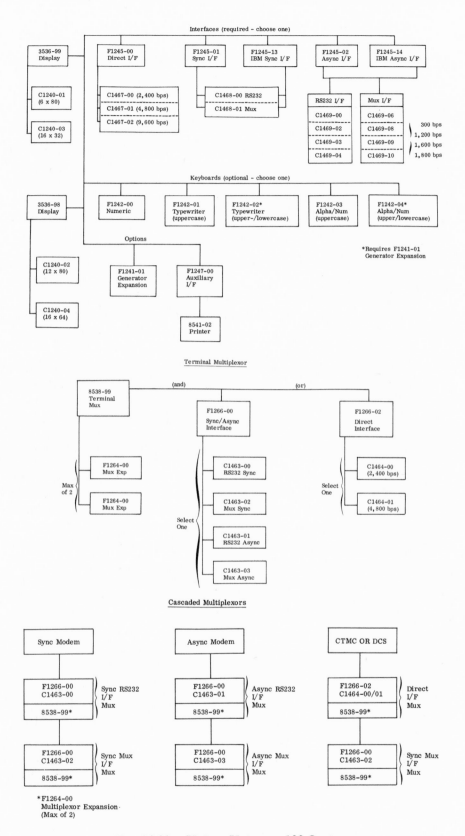

Fig. 14-21. Univac Uniscope 100 Options

185

3. Direct interface: Provides synchronous interface for direct connection ot a CTMC or DCS without modems at 2400 or 4800 bits per second.

A configurator illustrating the choice of options available with the Uniscope 100 is provided in Figure 14-21.

Configuration

Considering the wide variety of Uniscope 100 screen, format, character set, keyboard, and interface options, a terminal can be readily adapted for a particular application.

In an operating environment, there are three basic types of configurations, shown in Figure 14-22:

1. Single-station operation over a direct channel or communications lines to the computer

2. Multistation operation, with up to 31 terminals multiplexed over a direct channel or communications lines to the computer

3. Mixed single-station and multistation clusters sharing the same communications lines to the computer.

The basic multiplexor permits connection of up to eight Uniscope 100 terminals to one data channel. An expansion feature permits up to eight more terminals on the same channel. A maximum of two expansion features may be added to provide a total of 16 terminals; cascading two multiplexors accommodates 31 terminals on one channel. Cable is available in 5-foot increments to a maximum of 5000 feet from either the DCS or CTMC to the display terminal of the modem to the display terminal. Cable distance between the modem and the display or multiplexor is limited to a maximum of 50 feet.

Each Uniscope 100 terminal operates in half-duplex mode. However, operation over any of he multistation communications configurations is effectively full-duplex. The polling logic ensures that only one terminal at a time will transmit over a single communications line.

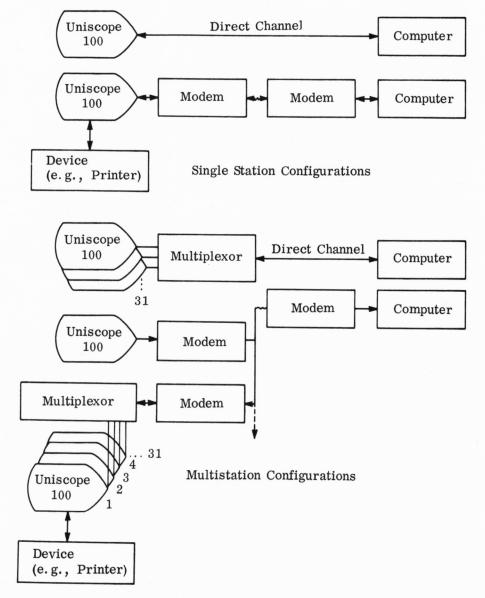

Fig. 14-22. Univac Uniscope 100 Configurations

APPENDIX: MANUFACTURERS DIRECTORY

Adage, Inc., 1079 Commonwealth Ave., Boston, Mass. 02215

Alphacom, Inc.* (formerly Alphameric Data Corp.), Princeton-Hightstown Rd., Cranbury, N.J. 08512

American Data Systems, 8851 Mason St., Canoga Park, Calif. 91306

Ann Arbor Terminals, 918 Green St., Ann Arbor, Mich. 48104

Applied Digital Data Systems, Inc., 89 Marcus Blvd., Hauppauge, N.Y. 11787

Atlantic Technology Corp., Somers Pt. Shopping Center, Somers Pt., N.J. 08244

Beehive Medical Electronics, Inc., 1473 S. Sixth, W. Salt Lake City, Utah 84104

Bendix Corp., East Joppa Rd., Baltimore, Md. 20204

Bunker-Ramo Corp., Business and Industry Div., 35 Nutmeg Drive, Trumbull, Conn. 06609

Bunker-Ramo Corp., Electronics Div., Westlake Village, Calif. 91360

Burroughs Corp., 6071 Second Ave., Detroit, Mich. 48232

Centronics Data Computer Corp., 1 Wall St., Hudson, N.H. 03051

Compucord, Inc., 225 Crescent St., Waltham, Mass. 02154

Computek, Inc., 143 Albany St., Cambridge, Mass. 02139

Computer Communications, Inc., 533 W. Slauson Ave., Culver City, Calif. 90230

Computer Consoles, Inc., 317 Main St., E. Rochester, N.Y. 14445

* Out of business.

Computer Displays, Inc. (*see* Adage, Inc.)

Computer-Optics, Inc., 295 Madison Ave., New York, N.Y. 10017

Computer Terminal Corp., 9725 Data Point Dr., San Antonio, Tex. 78229

Computer Terminals of Minnesota, Inc., 4815 W. 77th St., Minneapolis, Minn. 55435

Conrac Corp., 600 N. Rimsdale Ave., Covina, Calif. 91722

Control Data Corp., 8100 34th Ave. S., Minneapolis, Minn. 55440

Control Data Corp., MDM Communications Div., 3519 W. Warner Ave., Santa Ana, Calif. 92704

Corning Data Systems, 3900 Electronics Dr., Raleigh, N.C. 27602

Courier Terminal Systems, Inc., 2202 E. University Dr., Phoenix, Ariz. 85034

Data 100 Corp., 7450 France Ave. S., Minneapolis, Minn. 55435

Data Access Systems, Inc., 503 Rt. 10, Mt. 19, Dover, N.J. 07801

Delta Data Systems Corp., Woodhaven Industrial Pk., Cornwells Heights, Pa. 19020

A. B. Dick Co., 5700 W. Touhy Ave., Chicago, Ill. 60648

Digital Equipment Corp., 146 Main St., Maynard, Mass. 01754

Digital Scientific Corp., 11661 Sorrento Valley Rd., San Diego, Calif. 92121

Ferranti-Electric, Inc., East Bethpage Rd., Plainview, N.Y. 11803

Foto-Mem, Inc., Strathmore Rd., Natick, Mass. 01760

Four-Phase Systems, 10420 N. Tantau Ave., Cupertino, Calif. 95014

General Electric Co., Telecommunications Products, Mountain View Rd., Lynchburg, Va. 24502

Harris-Intertype Corp., P.O. Box 37, Melbourne, Fla. 32901

Hazeltine Corp., Industrial Products Div., Little Neck, N.Y. 11362

Hendrix Electronics, Inc., Grenier Industrial Vil., Londonderry, N.H. 03053

Honeywell, Old Connecticut Path, Framingham, Mass. 01701

Honeywell, EDP Div., 60 Walnut St., Wellesley Hills, Mass. 02181

Honeywell, Information Systems, P.O. Box 12313, 4000 N.W. 39th St., Oklahoma City, Okla. 73112

Honeywell, Information Systems, 13430 N. Black Canyon Hwy., Phoenix, Ariz. 85020

Hypertech, 7343 W. Wilson Ave., Harwood Heights, Ill. 60656

IBM Corp., Data Processing Div., 112 East Post Rd., White Plains, N.Y. 10602

Imlac Corp., 296 Newton St., Waltham, Mass. 02154

Incoterm Corp., (formerly International Computer Terminals, Inc.), Hayes Memorial Dr., Marlborough, Mass. 01752

Infoton, Inc., Second Ave., Burlington, Mass. 01803

Interactive Terminals Corp. (subsidiary of Bendix Corp.), 197 Albany St., Cambridge, Mass. 02139

ITT Corp., 187 East Union Ave., E. Rutherford, N.J. 07073

Logitron, Inc. (*see* Interactive Terminals)

MAI Equipment Corp., 300 E. 44th St., New York, N.Y. 10017

Mark Computer Systems, Inc., One Patterson Place, Garden City, N.Y. 11530

NCR Co., Main and K St., Dayton, Ohio 45409

Philco-Ford Corp., 1002 Gemini Ave., Houston, Tex. 77058

Photophysics Data Systems, 1255 Terra Bella Ave., Mountain View, Calif. 94040

Raytheon Co., 1415 Boston-Providence Tpke., Norwood, Mass. 02062

RCA, Information Systems Div., Camden, N.J. 08101

Sanders Associates, Inc., Daniel Webster Hwy. S., Nashua, N.H. 03060

Science Associates, Box 38128, Dallas, Tex. 75218

Spiras Systems, Inc., 332 Second Ave., Waltham, Mass. 02154

Stromberg DatagraphiX, Inc., P.O. Box 2449, San Diego, Calif. 92112

Sugarman Laboratories, 295 Northern Blvd., Great Neck, N.Y. 11020

Sycor, Inc., 100 Phoenix Dr., Ann Arbor, Mich. 48104

SYS Computer Corp., 17-25 DiCarolis Ct., Hackensack, N.J. 07601

TEC, Inc., 6700 S. Washington Ave., Eden Prairie, Minn. 55343

Tektronix, Inc., P.O. Box 500, Beaverton, Ore. 97005

Teletype Corp., 5555 Touhy Ave., Skokie, Ill. 60676

Terminal Communications, Inc., P.O. Box 9363, Raleigh, N.C. 27603

Texas Scientific Corp., 3600 Yoakum, Houston Tex. 77006

Time-Sharing Terminals, Inc., 2351 Shady Grove Rd., Rockville, Md. 20850

Ultronic Systems Corp., Mount Laurel Industrial Pk., Moorestown, N.J. 08057

Univac Data Processing Div., Sperry Rand Corp., P.O. Box 8100, Phila., Pa. 19101

Viatron Computer Systems Corp., Rt. 62, Bedford, Mass. 01730

Video Systems Corp., 7300 N. Crescent Blvd., Pennsauken, N.J. 08110

Wyle Computer Products, 128 Maryland St., El Segundo, Calif. 90245

Xerox Data Systems, 701 S. Aviation Blvd., El Segundo, Calif. 90245

Xerox Data Systems, 5300 W. Century Blvd., Los Angeles, Calif. 90045

GLOSSARY

ASCII (American Standard Code for Information Interchange). A seven-bit code adopted as an American National Standard in order to facilitate the interchange of data among various types of data processing and data communications equipment.

Audio Response Unit. *See* Voice-Response Unit. A unit of signaling speed, equal to the number of discrete conditions or signal events per second. *Note*: In the case of a train of binary signals, and therefore in most data communications applications, one baud equals one bit per second.

Carrier, Communications Common. A company that furnished communication services to the general public and which is regulated by appropriate local, state, or federal agencies; term usually refers to telecommunication companies.

Cathode-Ray Tube (CRT). An electron tube with a phosphor-covered face that emits light when energized by its electron beam.

Character Generator. Hardware that will generate a finite set of characters onto a display surface.

Code. A set of unambiguous rules that specifies the exact manner in which data are to be represented by the characters of a character set.

Communications Link. The physical means of connecting one location to another for the purpose of transmitting information between them (e.g., a telegraph, telephone, radio, or microwave circuit).

Contrast. The relationship of the brightest to the darkest portions of a display image.

Conversational Mode. A mode of operation that implies a dialogue between a computer and its user, in which the computer program examines the input supplied by the user and formulates questions or comments that are directed back to the user.

CRT Displays. Displays that utilize cathode-ray tubes as the viewing element. (*See also* Raster Scan; Storage Tube; and Directed Beam.)

Cursor. A movable marker, visible on a CRT display and used to indicate the position at which the next operation (e.g., insertion, replacement, or erasure of a character) is to take place.

Data. Any representation of a fact or idea in a form capable of being communicated or manipulated by some process. The representation may be more suitable for interpretation either by human operators (e.g., printed text) or by equipment (e.g., punched cards or electric signals). *Note:* Information, a closely related term, is the meaning that humans assign to data by means of the known conventions used in its representation.

Data Set. A device furnished by a common carrier that provides the appropriate interface between a communications link and a data processing machine or system. *See also* Modem.

Data Transcription. Conversion of data from one medium to another without alteration of its information content. *Note:* The conversion may be performed by a manual keystroke operation, by a computer system, or by a specialized converter, and may or may not involve changes in the format of the data.

Directed Beam. The CRT method of tracing the elements of a display image in any sequence given by the computer program, where the beam motion is analogous to pen movements. This contrasts with the raster-scan method, which requires the display elements to be sorted in the order of their appearance (usually top to bottom, left to right).

Display Background. That portion of a display image that cannot be altered by the user. This is sometimes called the static portion of the display.

Display Buffer. A storage device or memory area that holds data required to generate a display image. This could include a portion of computer memory, direct access storage, or a special-purpose storage device.

Display Console. A hardware complex that consists of a display device plus one or more computer input devices. The types of input devices commonly employed are alphanumeric keyboards, function keys, and light pens.

Display Device. A device capable of presenting information on a viewing surface or image area that uses display elements such as points, line segments, and/or alphanumeric characters to construct the display. This term usually refers to a CRT, but also may be applied to such devices as plotters, microfilm recorders, and page printers.

Display Elements. The basic hardware-generated functions such as points, line segments, and characters used to construct a display image.

Display Foreground. The collection of display elements, entities, and/or groups of a display image that are subject to change by the program or by the use in interactive mode.

Display Image. The collection of display elements that are visually represented together on the viewing surface of a display device.

Duplex. Refers to method of bidirectional transmission of data. *See also* Full Duplex; Half-duplex.

EBCDIC (Extended Binary Coded Decimal Interchange Code). An eight-bit code that represents an extension of a six-bit BCD code, which was widely used in computers of the first and second generations. *Note:* EBCDIC can represent upto 256 distinct characters. It is the principal code used in many of the current computers.

Edit. To modify the form or format of data. Editing may involve the rearrangement of data, the addition of data (e.g., insertion of dollar signs and decimal points), the deletion of data (e.g., suppression of leading zeros), code translation, and the control of layouts for printing (i.e., provision of headings and page numbers).

External Storage. A storage device or medium that is not permanently linked to a computer but can hold data in a form acceptable to it. External storage may or may not be made accessible to a computer as the operator chooses (e.g., magnetic tape, punched cards, punched tape).

Flicker. A blinking or pulsation of a display image on a CRT. Flicker occurs when the refresh rate is so low that regeneration becomes noticeable.

Flying Spot Scanner. A system that encodes a picture by raster scanning and recording the brightness at each addressable point.

Format. The predetermined arrangement of data (e.g., characters, items, and lines), usually on a form or in a file.

Full Duplex. Pertaining to the simultaneous, independent transmission of data in both directions over a communications link; synonymous with duplex. *See also* Half-duplex.

Half-duplex. Pertaining to the alternate, independent transmission of data in both directions—but in only one direction at a time—over a communications link.

Function Key. A pushbutton or switch that may be pressed to send an identifiable signal to the display control program.

Graphics. The art of image generation and manipulation. Graphics usually applies to computer-generated displays that contain lines and points.

Hard Copy. A permanent page-printed record of a display image.

Hardware. Physical equipment such as mechanical, magnetic, electrical, and electronic devices.

Information Retrieval. The methods, procedures, and equipment for recovering specific information from stored data, especially from collections of documents or other graphic records.

Inquiry Station. An input/output device that permits a human operator to interrogate a computer system and receive prompt replies in a convenient form.

Intensity Level. One of the discrete levels of brightness of the light emitted by a CRT, usually under program control.

Interactive Mode. A method of operation that allows on-line man-machine communications. Commonly used to enter data and to direct the course of a program.

Internal Storage. A storage device that is permanently linked to a computer and directly controlled by it (e.g., high-speed core storage).

Joystick. A three-dimensional positioning device for manipulating the cursor or other display images. X and Y coordinate tracking signals are generated by similar movements of the upright shaft while rotation of the shaft generates the Z axis signals.

Light Pen. A stylus that detects, within a limited area, light generated on a CRT. It can provide an interrupt that may be interpreted by the display control program to determine either positional or display-element identifying information.

Linearity. A measurement of the straightness of a plotted line segment.

Machine Readable. Pertaining to data represented in a form that can be used by a data processing machine (e.g., by a card reader, magnetic-type unit, or optical character reader).

Medium. Any agency or means for representing data; usually a material on which data are recorded. *Note:* Among the most widely used media are punched cards, punched tape, magnetic tape, and printed forms.

Menu. A list of options on a display that allows an operator to select his next action by indicating one or more choices with an input device.

Message Switching. A technique for controlling the traffic within a data communications network. It involves the reception of messages from various sources at a switching center, the storage of each message until the proper outgoing communications link is available, and the ultimate retransmission of each message to its destination or destinations.

Modem. A modulator-demodulator or data set that provides the appropriate interface between a data processing machine and a communications line.

It converts machine-generated binary pulses to analog signals and vice-versa for transmission and reception of digital data between remote stations.

Multiplex. To transmit two or more messages over a single channel or other transmissions facility. This can be accomplished either by splitting the channel's frequency band into two or more narrower bands (frequency-division multiplexing) or by interleaving the bits, characters, or words that make up the various messages (time-division multiplexing).

Noise. (1) Random variations of one or more characteristics of any entity such as voltage, current, or data. (2) Loosely, any disturbance that tends to interfere with normal operation of a device or system.

Phosphor. The chemical coating on the inside face of a CRT which emits visible light when energized by an electron beam.

Random Access. Pertaining to a storage device in which the access time is not significantly affected by the location of the data to be accessed. Thus, any item of data that is stored on-line can be accessed within a relatively short time (usually less than 1 second).

Raster Scan. A technique for generating or recording an image with an intensity controlled, line-by-line sweep across the entire display surface. *Note:* This technique is used to generate a picture on a TV set and to digitize an image with a flying-spot scanner.

Real Time. (1) Pertaining to the actual time during which a physical process takes place. (2) Pertaining to a mode of operation in which the instants of occurrence of certain events in the system must satisfy restrictions determined by the occurrence of events in some other independent system. For example, real-time operation is essential in computers associated with process control systems, message-switching systems, and reservation systems.

Refresh Rate. The rate at which a display is regenerated.

Regeneration. The process of repeatedly displaying an image on a CRT display device. Since the image is retained by the phosphor for only a short period of time, the image must be regenerated in order to remain visible.

Resolution. The smallest distance between two display elements that can be visually detected as two distinct elements.

Scrolling. The continuous vertical or horizontal movement of the display image. As new data are moved onto the display surface at one edge, the old data are moved off at the opposite edge.

Serial Access. Pertaining to a storage device in which there is a sequential relationship between the access times to successive locations, as in the case of magnetic tape.

Signal. An event or phenomenon that conveys data from one point to another.

It can be initiated and controlled at the source and recognized at one or more destinations (e.g., an electric impulse).

Simplex. Pertaining to a communications link that is capable of transmitting data in only one direction.

Software. The collection of programs and routines associated with a computer (such as assemblers, compilers, utility routines, and operating systems) that facilitate the programming and operation of the computer.

Storage. The retention of data for subsequent reference. A device into which data can be inserted and retained, and from which data can be obtained at a later time. *Note:* Various types of storage are used in current computer systems (e.g., core storage, disk storage, drum storage, read-only storage).

Storage Tube. A CRT that retains an image for an extended period of time without regeneration.

Telecommunications. The transmission of signals over long distances, such as by radio or telegraph.

Terminal. A point or device in a system or communications network at which data can either enter or leave.

Time Sharing. (1) The use of a given device by a number of other devices, programs, or human users, one at a time and in rapid succession. (2) A technique or system for furnishing computing services to multiple users simultaneously while providing rapid response to each of the users. *Note:* Time-sharing computer systems usually employ multiprogramming and/or multiprocessing techniques, and they are often capable of serving users at remote locations via a data communications network.

Trackball. An X and Y coordinate positioning device for manipulating the cursor or other display images. X and Y axis tracking signals are generated via similar movements of the device.

Voice-Response Unit. A device that accepts digitally coded input (usually from a computer) and converts it into machine-generated, human-voice messages that can be transmitted over telephone lines. Usually, the human-voice messages are replies to digital inquiries entered via pushbutton telephones. Same as "audio response unit" (ARU).

INDEX